Graph Algorithms

Graph Algorithms

Guest Editor

Jesper Jansson

MDPI

Basel • Beijing • Wuhan • Barcelona • Belgrade • Novi Sad • Cluj • Manchester

Guest Editor
Jesper Jansson
Department of
Communications and
Computer Engineering,
Graduate School of
Informatics
Kyoto University
Kyoto
Japan

Editorial Office
MDPI AG
Grosspeteranlage 5
4052 Basel, Switzerland

This is a reprint of the Special Issue, published open access by the journal *Algorithms* (ISSN 1999-4893), freely accessible at: https://www.mdpi.com/si/algorithms/graph_algorithms.

For citation purposes, cite each article independently as indicated on the article page online and as indicated below:

Lastname, A.A.; Lastname, B.B. Article Title. *Journal Name* **Year**, *Volume Number*, Page Range.

ISBN 978-3-7258-4509-5 (Hbk)
ISBN 978-3-7258-4510-1 (PDF)
https://doi.org/10.3390/books978-3-7258-4510-1

Contents

Algorithms **2013**, *6*, 457-458; doi:10.3390/a6030457

OPEN ACCESS

algorithms

ISSN 1999-4893

www.mdpi.com/journal/algorithms

Editorial

Editorial: Special Issue on Graph Algorithms

Jesper Jansson

Laboratory of Mathematical Bioinformatics, Bioinformatics Center, Institute for Chemical Research, Kyoto University, Gokasho, Uji, Kyoto 611-0011, Japan; E-Mail: jj@kuicr.kyoto-u.ac.jp

Received: 9 August 2013; in revised form: 9 August 2013 / Accepted: 9 August 2013 / Published: 12 August 2013

Abstract: This special issue of *Algorithms* is devoted to the design and analysis of algorithms for solving combinatorial problems of a theoretical or practical nature involving graphs, with a focus on computational complexity

Keywords: graph algorithms; computational complexity; fixed-parameter tractability; exact algorithms; approximation algorithms; heuristics; computational studies

1. Introduction

Because of their simplicity and generality, graphs have been used for a long time in many different areas of science and engineering, *e.g.*, to describe how objects such as the atoms of a molecule are connected, or to express various types of constraints such as precedence constraints in a complex manufacturing process. More recently, graphs have found new applications in emerging research fields like social network analysis, the design of robust computer network topologies, frequency allocation in wireless networks, and bioinformatics (*i.e.*, to represent metabolic pathways, protein–protein interactions, evolutionary relationships, or other kinds of structured biological information). The amount of data in such applications can be enormous, and therefore, the resulting graphs may be huge, which motivates further development of fast and space-efficient algorithms in the near future for solving various (old and new) graph problems exactly or approximately.

2. Special Issue

A special issue of *Algorithms* was proposed in order to stimulate new and original research on graph algorithms. In response to the call for papers, researchers from all over the world submitted a total of fifteen articles, covering a wide range of related topics. All submissions were evaluated by experts;

based on their anonymous reviews, nine of the articles were then selected for inclusion in the special issue. After several rounds of revision, the final versions were published in [1–9].

Acknowledgements

As Guest Editor of this Special Issue, I would like to thank all of the contributing authors for submitting their work to *Algorithms*; the reviewers for their valuable and detailed comments that helped us select the best articles; and the publishers, Editor-in-Chief Professor Kazuo Iwama, and Assistant Editors Ms. Chelly Cheng, Ms. Wanda Gruetter, Ms. Maple Lv, and Ms. Phoenix Zhao for their support and assistance.

References and Notes

1. Prosser, P. Exact Algorithms for Maximum Clique: A Computational Study. *Algorithms* **2012**, *5*, 545–587.
2. Toda, T. Extracting Co-Occurrence Relations from ZDDs. *Algorithms* **2012**, *5*, 654–667.
3. Bonizzoni, P.; Dondi, R.; Pirola, Y. Maximum Disjoint Paths on Edge-Colored Graphs: Approximability and Tractability. *Algorithms* **2013**, *6*, 1–11.
4. Marzban, M.; Gu, Q.-P. Computational Study on a PTAS for Planar Dominating Set Problem. *Algorithms* **2013**, *6*, 43–59.
5. Uehara, R. Tractabilities and Intractabilities on Geometric Intersection Graphs. *Algorithms* **2013**, *6*, 60–83.
6. Isaacs, J.T.; Hespanha, J.P. Dubins Traveling Salesman Problem with Neighborhoods: A Graph-Based Approach. *Algorithms* **2013**, *6*, 84–99.
7. Takes, F.W.; Kosters, W.A. Computing the Eccentricity Distribution of Large Graphs. *Algorithms* **2013**, *6*, 100–118.
8. Akutsu, T.; Tamura, T. A Polynomial-Time Algorithm for Computing the Maximum Common Connected Edge Subgraph of Outerplanar Graphs of Bounded Degree. *Algorithms* **2013**, *6*, 119–135.
9. Tazehkand, J.S.; Hashemi, S.N.; Poormohammadi, H. New Heuristics for Rooted Triplet Consistency. *Algorithms* **2013**, *6*, 396–406.

Algorithms **2012**, *5*, 545-587; doi:10.3390/a5040545

OPEN ACCESS

algorithms

ISSN 1999-4893

www.mdpi.com/journal/algorithms

Article

Exact Algorithms for Maximum Clique: A Computational Study

Patrick Prosser

Computing Science, University of Glasgow, Glasgow G12 8QQ, UK;
E-Mail: Patrick.Prosser@glasgow.ac.uk; Tel.: +44-141-330 4934; Fax: +44-141-330-4934

Received: 11 September 2012; in revised form: 29 October 2012 / Accepted: 29 October 2012 / Published: 19 November 2012

Abstract: We investigate a number of recently reported exact algorithms for the maximum clique problem. The program code is presented and analyzed to show how small changes in implementation can have a drastic effect on performance. The computational study demonstrates how problem features and hardware platforms influence algorithm behaviour. The effect of vertex ordering is investigated. One of the algorithms (MCS) is broken into its constituent parts and we discover that one of these parts frequently degrades performance. It is shown that the standard procedure used for rescaling published results (*i.e.*, adjusting run times based on the calibration of a standard program over a set of benchmarks) is unsafe and can lead to incorrect conclusions being drawn from empirical data.

Keywords: maximum clique; exact algorithms; empirical study

---

1. Introduction

The purpose of this paper is to investigate a number of recently reported exact algorithms for the maximum clique problem. The actual program code used is presented and critiqued. The computational study aims to show how implementation details, problem features and hardware platforms influence algorithmic behaviour.

1.1. The Maximum Clique Problem (MCP)

A simple undirected graph G is a pair (V, E) where V is a set of vertices and E a set of edges, where vertex u is adjacent to vertex v if and only if $\{u, v\}$ is in E. A *clique* is a set of vertices $C \subseteq V$ such that every pair of vertices in C is adjacent in G. Clique is one of the six basic NP-complete problems given in [1]. It is posed as a decision problem [GT19]: Given a simple undirected graph $G = (V, E)$ and a positive integer $k \leq |V|$ does G contain a clique of size k or more? The optimization problems is then to find the *maximum clique*, where $\omega(G)$ is the size of a maximum clique.

A colouring of the graph is an upper bound on the size of the maximum clique. When colouring a graph any pair of adjacent vertices are given different colours. We do not use colours but use integers to label the vertices. The minimum number of different colours required is then the *chromatic number* of the graph $\chi(G)$, and $\omega(G) \leq \chi(G)$. Finding the chromatic number is NP-complete.

1.2. Exact Algorithms for MCP

We can address the decision and optimization problems with an exact algorithm, such as a backtracking search [2–14]. Backtracking search incrementally constructs the set C (initially empty) by choosing a *candidate vertex* from the *candidate set* P (initially all of the vertices in V) and then adding it to C. Having chosen a vertex the candidate set is then updated, removing vertices that cannot participate in the evolving clique. If the candidate set is empty then C is maximal (if it is a maximum we save it) and we then backtrack. Otherwise P is not empty and we continue our search, selecting from P and adding to C.

There are other scenarios where we can cut off search, *i.e.*, if what is in P is insufficient to unseat the *champion* (the largest clique found so far) search can be abandoned. That is, an upper bound can be computed. Graph colouring can be used to compute an upper bound during search, *i.e.*, if the candidate set can be coloured with k colours then it can contain a clique no larger than k [4,5,11–14]. There are also heuristics that can be used when selecting the candidate vertex, different styles of search, different algorithms to colour the graph and different orders in which to do this.

1.3. Structure of the Paper

In the next section, we present in Java the following algorithms: Fahle's Algorithm 1 [4], Tomita's MCQ [12], MCR [15] and MCS [13] and San Segundo's BBMC [11]. By using Java and its inheritance mechanism, algorithms are presented as modifications of previous algorithms. Three vertex orderings are then presented. Starting with the basic algorithm MC we show how minor coding details can significantly impact on performance. Section 3 presents a chronological review of exact algorithms, starting at 1990. Section 4 is the computational study. The study investigates MCS, determines where its speed advantage comes from, and measures the benefits resulting from the bit encoding of BBMC and the effectiveness of three vertex orderings. New benchmark problems are then investigated. Finally, an established technique for calibrating and scaling results is put to the test and is shown to be unsafe. We then conclude.

2. The Algorithms: MC, MCQ, MCR, MCS and BBMC

We start by presenting the simplest algorithm [4] which I will call MC. This sets the scene. It is presented as a Java class, as are all the algorithms, with instance variables and methods. Each algorithm is first described textually and then the actual implementation is given in Java. Sometimes a program trace is given to better expose the workings of the algorithm. It is possible to read this section skipping the Java descriptions, however the Java code makes it explicit how one algorithm differs from another and shows the details that can severely affect the performance of the algorithm.

MC is essentially a *straw man*: It is elegant but too simple to be of any practical worth. Nevertheless, it has some interesting features. MCQ [12] is then presented as an extension to MC, our first algorithm that uses a tight integration of search algorithm, search order and upper bound cut off. Our implementation of MCQ allows three different vertex orderings to be used, and one of these corresponds to MCR [15]. The presentation of MCQ is somewhat laborious but this pays off when we present two variants of MCS [13] (MCSa and MCSb) as minor changes to MCQ. BBMC [11] is presented as an extension of MCQ, but is essentially MCSa with sets implemented using bit strings. Figure 1 shows the hierarchical structure for the algorithms presented. In the code presented, we endeavour to use the same procedure names as in the original publications.

Figure 1. The hierarchy of algorithms.

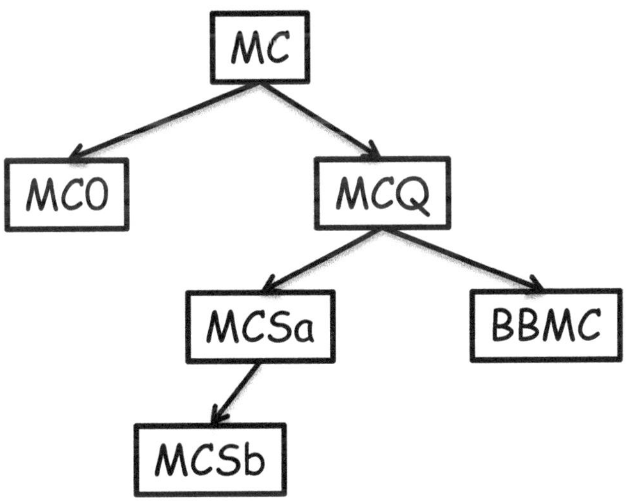

2.1. MC

MC is similar to Algorithm 1 in [4]. Fahle's Algorithm 1 uses two sets: C the growing clique (initially empty) and P the candidate set (initially all vertices in the graph). C is *maximal* when P is empty and if $|C|$ is a *maximum* it is saved, *i.e.*, C becomes the champion. If $|C| + |P|$ is too small to unseat the champion search can be terminated. Otherwise the search iterates over the vertices in P in turn selecting a vertex v, creating a new growing clique C' where $C' = C \cup \{v\}$ and a new candidate set P' as the set of vertices in P that are adjacent to v (*i.e.*, $P' = P \cap neighbours(v)$), and recursing. We will call this MC.

Listing 1. The basic clique solver.

```
import java.util.*;

public class MC {
    int[] degree;    // degree of vertices
    int[][] A;       // 0/1 adjacency matrix
    int n;           // n vertices
    long nodes;      // number of decisions
    long timeLimit;  // milliseconds
    long cpuTime;    // milliseconds
    int maxSize;     // size of max clique
    int style;       // used to flavor algorithm
    int[] solution;  // as it says

    MC (int n,int[][]A,int[] degree) {
        this.n = n;
        this.A = A;
        this.degree = degree;
        nodes = maxSize = 0;
        cpuTime = timeLimit = -1;
        style = 1;
        solution = new int[n];
    }

    void search(){
        cpuTime              = System.currentTimeMillis();
        nodes                = 0;
        ArrayList<Integer> C = new ArrayList<Integer>();
        ArrayList<Integer> P = new ArrayList<Integer>(n);
        for (int i=0;i<n;i++) P.add(i);
        expand(C,P);
    }

    void expand(ArrayList<Integer> C, ArrayList<Integer> P){
        if (timeLimit > 0 && System.currentTimeMillis() - cpuTime >= timeLimit) return;
        nodes++;
        for (int i=P.size()-1;i>=0;i--){
            if (C.size() + P.size() <= maxSize) return;
            int v = P.get(i);
            C.add(v);
            ArrayList<Integer> newP = new ArrayList<Integer>();
            for (int w : P) if (A[v][w] == 1) newP.add(w);
            if (newP.isEmpty() && C.size() > maxSize) saveSolution(C);
            if (!newP.isEmpty()) expand(C,newP);
            C.remove((Integer)v);
            P.remove((Integer)v);
        }
    }

    void saveSolution(ArrayList<Integer> C){
        Arrays.fill(solution,0);
        for (int i : C) solution[i] = 1;
        maxSize = C.size();
    }
}
```

2.1.1. MC in Java

Listing 1 can be compared with Algorithm 1 in [4]. The constructor, lines 14 to 22, takes three arguments: n the number of vertices in the graph, A the adjacency matrix where $A[i][j]$ equals 1 if and only if vertex i is adjacent to vertex j, and $degree$ where $degree[i]$ is the number of vertices adjacent to vertex i (and is the sum of $A[i]$). The variables $nodes$ and $cpuTime$ are used as measures of search performance, $timeLimit$ is a bound on the run-time, $maxSize$ is the size of the largest clique found so far, $style$ is used as a flag to customise the algorithm with respect to ordering of vertices (and is not used till we get to MCQ), and the array $solution$ is the largest clique found such that $solution[i]$ is equal to 1 if and only if vertex i is in the largest clique found.

The method $search()$ finds a largest clique or terminates when having exceeded the allocated $timeLimit$. Two sets are produced: The *candidate set* P and the *current clique* C. Vertices from P may be selected and added to the growing clique C. Initially all vertices are added to P and C is empty (lines 27 to 29). The sets P and C are represented using Java's ArrayList, a resizable-array implementation of the List interface. Adding an item is an $O(1)$ operation but removing an arbitrary item is of $O(n)$ cost. This might appear to be a damning indictment of this simple data structure, but as we will see, it is the cost we pay if we want to maintain order in P, and in many cases we can work around this to enjoy $O(1)$ performance.

The search is performed in method $expand$. In line 34, a test is performed to determine if the CPU time limit has been exceeded, and if so search terminates. Otherwise we increment the number of nodes, *i.e.*, a count of the size of the backtrack search tree explored. The method then iterates over the vertices in P (line 36), starting with the last vertex in P down to the first vertex in P. This form of iteration over the ArrayList, getting entries with a specific index, is necessary when entries are deleted (line 45) as part of that iteration. A vertex v is selected from P (line 38), added to C (line 39), and a new candidate set $newP$ is then created (line 40) where $newP$ is the set of vertices in P that are adjacent to vertex v (line 41). Consequently all vertices in $newP$ are adjacent to all vertices in C and all pairs of vertices in C are adjacent (*i.e.*, C is a clique). If $newP$ is empty C is maximal and if it is the largest clique found it is saved (line 42). If $newP$ is not empty then C is not maximal and search can proceed via a recursive call to $expand$ (line 43). On returning from the recursive call v is removed from P and from C (lines 44 and 45).

There is one "trick" in $expand$ and that is at line 37: If the combined size of the current clique and the candidate set cannot unseat the champion, this branch of the backtrack tree can be abandoned. This is the simplest upper bound cut-off and corresponds to line 3 from Algorithm 1 in [4]. The method $saveSolution$ saves off the current maximal clique and records its size.

2.1.2. Observations on MC

There are several points of interest. First, there is the search process itself. If we commented out lines 37 and changed line 41 to add to $newP$ all vertices in P other than v, method $expand$ would produce the power set of P and at each depth k in the backtrack tree we would have $\binom{n}{k}$ calls to $expand$. That is, $expand$ produces a *binomial backtrack search tree* of size $O(2^n)$ (see pages 6 and 7 of [17]). This can be compared to a bifurcating search process where on one side we take an element and make a recursive call, and on the other side reject it and make a recursive call, terminating when P is empty (*i.e.*, generating a binary backtrack tree such as in [6,8,18]). This generates the power set on the leaf nodes of the backtrack tree and explores $2^{n+1} - 1$ nodes. This is also $O(2^n)$ but in practice is often twice as slow as the binomial search. In Figure 2 we see a binomial search produced by a simplification of MC, generating the power set of $\{0, 1, 2, 3\}$. Each node in the tree contains two sets: The set that will be added to the power set and the set that can be selected from at the next level. We see 16 nodes and at each depth k we have $\binom{n}{k}$ nodes. The corresponding tree for the bifurcating search (not shown) has 31 nodes with the power set appearing on the 16 leaf nodes at depth 4.

Figure 2. A binomial search tree producing the power set of $\{0, 1, 2, 3\}$.

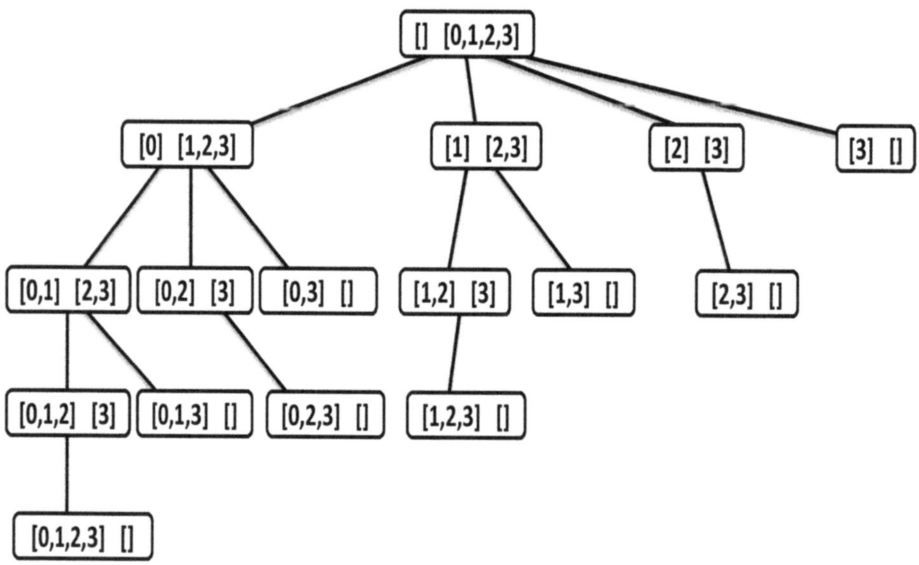

The second point of interest is the actual Java implementation. Java gives us an elegant construct for iterating over collections, the for-each loop, used in line 41 of Listing 1. This is rewritten in class MC0 (extending MC, overwriting the $expand$ method) Listing 2 lines 15 to 18: One line of code is replaced with 4 lines. MC0 gets the jth element of P, calls it w (line 16 of Listing 2) and if it is adjacent to v it is added to $newP$ (line 17 of Listing 2). In MC (line 41 of Listing 1) the for-each statement implicitly creates an iterator object and uses that for selecting elements. This typically results in a 10% reduction in runtime for MC0.

Our third point is how we create our sets. In MC0 line 14 the new candidate set is created with a capacity of i. Why do that when we can just create $newP$ with no size and let Java work it out dynamically? And why size i?

Listing 2. Inelegant but 50% faster, MC0 extends MC.

```
1  import java.util.*;
2
3  public class MC0 extends MC {
4
5      MC0 (int n,int[][]A,int[] degree) {super(n,A,degree);}
6
7      void expand(ArrayList<Integer> C, ArrayList<Integer> P){
8          if (timeLimit > 0 && System.currentTimeMillis() - cpuTime >= timeLimit) return;
9          nodes++;
10         for (int i=P.size()-1;i>=0;i--){
11             if (C.size() + P.size() <= maxSize) return;
12             int v = P.get(i);
13             C.add(v);
14             ArrayList<Integer> newP = new ArrayList<Integer>(i);
15             for (int j=0;j<=i;j++){
16                 int w = P.get(j);
17                 if (A[v][w] == 1) newP.add(w);
18             }
19             if (newP.isEmpty() && C.size() > maxSize) saveSolution(C);
20             if (!newP.isEmpty()) expand(C,newP);
21             C.remove(C.size()-1);
22             P.remove(i);
23         }
24     }
25 }
```

In the loop of line 10 i counts down from the size of the candidate set, less one, to zero. Therefore at line 14 P is of size $i + 1$ and we can set the maximum size of $newP$ accordingly. If we do not set the size Java will give $newP$ an initial size of 10 and when additions exceed this $newP$ will be re-sized. By grabbing this space we avoid that. This results in yet another measurable reduction in run-time.

Our fourth point is how we remove elements from our sets. In MC we remove the current vertex v from C and P (lines 44 and 45) whereas in MC0 we remove the *last element* in C and P (lines 21 and 22). Clearly v will always be the last element in C and P. The code in MC results in a sequential scan to find and then delete the last element, *i.e.*, $O(n)$, whereas in MC0 it is a simple $O(1)$ task. This raises another question: P and C are really stacks so why not use a Java Stack? The Stack class is represented using an ArrayList and cannot be initialised with a size, but has a default initial size of 10. When the stack grows and exceeds its current capacity, the capacity is doubled and the contents are copied across. Experiments showed that using a Stack increased run time by a few percentage points.

Typically MC0 is 50% faster than MC. In many cases a 50% improvement in run time would be considered a significant gain, usually brought about by changes in the algorithm. Here, such a gain can be achieved by moderately careful coding. And this is our first lesson: When comparing published results, we need to be cautious as we may be comparing programmer ability as much as differences in algorithms.

The fifth point is that MC makes more recursive calls than it needs to. At line 37 $|C| + |P|$ is sufficient to proceed but at line 43 it is possible that $|C| + |newP|$ is actually too small and will generate a failure at line 37 in the next recursive call. We should have a richer condition at line 43 but as we will soon see, the algorithms that follow do not need this.

The sixth point is a question of space: Why is the adjacency matrix an array of integers when we could have used booleans, surely that would have been more space efficient? In Java a boolean is represented as an integer with 1 being true, everything else false. Therefore there is no saving in space and only a minuscule saving in time (more code is generated to test if $A[i][j]$ equals 1 than to test if a boolean is true). Furthermore, by representing the adjacency matrix as integers, we can sum a row to get the degree of a vertex.

Finally, Listing 1 shows *exactly* what is measured. Our run time starts at line 25, at the start of search. This will include the times to set up the data structures peculiar to an algorithm, and any reordering of vertices. It does not include the time to read in the problem or the time to write out a solution. There is also no doubt about what we mean by a *node*: A call to $expand$ counts as one more node.

2.1.3. A Trace of MC

We now present two views of the MC search process over a simple problem. The problem is referred to as g10–50, and is a randomly generated graph with 10 vertices with edge probability 0.5. This is shown in Figure 3 and has at top a cartoon of the search process, to be read from left to right and top to bottom. Green coloured vertices are in P, blue vertices are those in C and red vertices are those removed from P and C in lines 44 and 45 of Listing 1. Also shown is the backtrack tree. The boxes correspond to calls to $expand$ and contain C and P. On arcs we have numbers with a down arrow $\downarrow$ if that vertex is added to C and an up arrow $\uparrow$ if that vertex is removed from C and P, therefore C represent the path from the root to the current node. A clear white box is a call to $expand$ that is an *interior* node of the backtrack tree leading to further recursive calls or the creation of a new champion. The green "shriek!" is a champion clique and a red "shriek!" is a failure because $|C| + |P|$ was too small to unseat the champion. The blue boxes correspond to calls to $expand$ that fail first time on entering the loop at line 36 of Listing 1. By looking at the backtrack tree we get a feel for the nature of binomial search.

2.2. MCQ and MCR

We now present Tomita's algorithm MCQ [12] as Listings 3–7. MCQ is at heart an extension of MC, performing a binomial search, with two significant advances. First, the graph induced by the candidate set is coloured using a greedy sequential colouring algorithm. This gives an upper bound on the size of the clique in P that can be added to C. Vertices in P are then selected in decreasing colour order, that is, P is ordered in non-decreasing colour order (highest colour last). And this is the second advance. Assume we select the ith entry in P and call it v. We then know that we can colour all the vertices in P corresponding to the 0th entry up to and including the ith entry using no more than the colour number of v. Consequently that sub-graph can contain a clique no bigger than the colour number of v, and if this is too small to unseat the largest clique, the search can be abandoned.

Figure 3. Cartoon, trace and backtrack-tree for MC on graph g10–50.

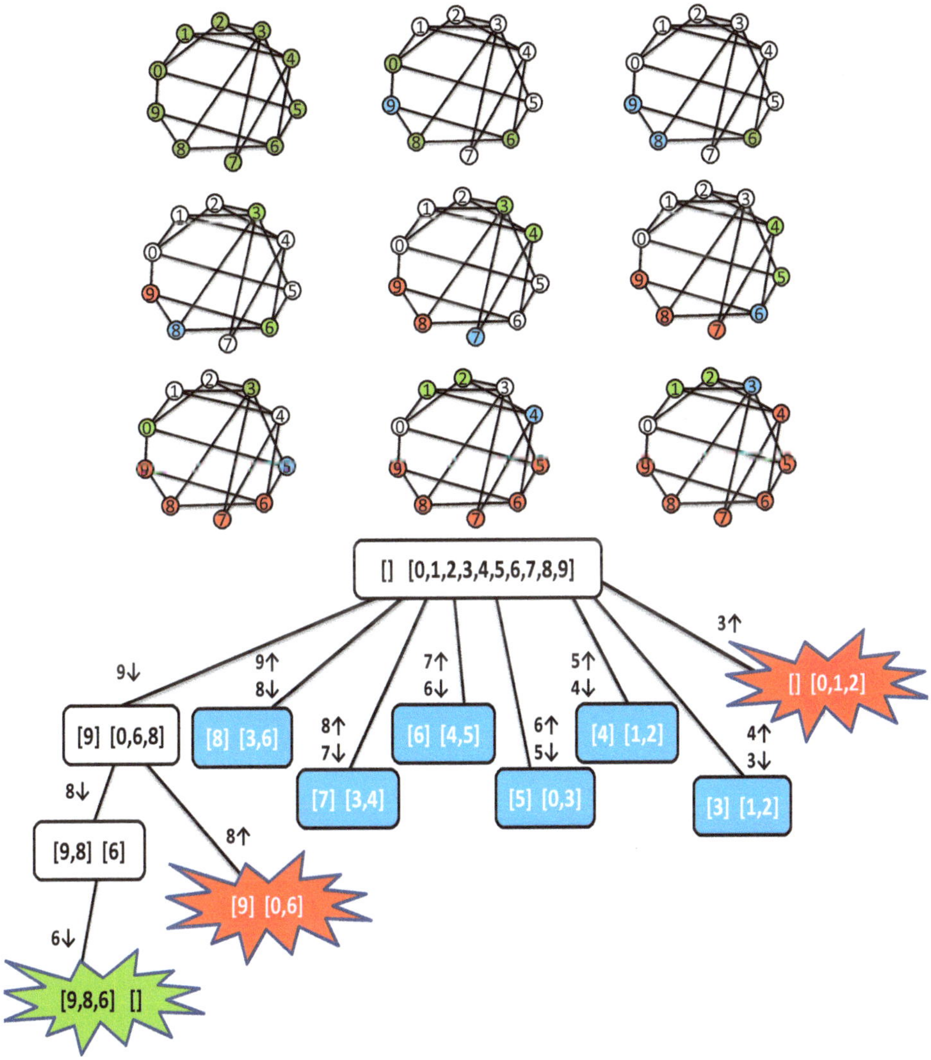

2.2.1. MCQ in Java

MCQ extends MC, Listing 3 line 3, and has an additional instance variable $colourClass$ (line 5) such that $colourClass[i]$ is an ArrayList of integers (line 15) and will contain all the vertices of colour $i + 1$ and is used when sorting vertices by their colour (lines 45 to 64, Listing 4). At the top of search (method $search$, lines 12 to 21, Listing 3) vertices are sorted (call to $orderVertices(P)$ at line 19) into some order, and this is described later.

Method $expand$ (line 23 to 43 Listing 3) corresponds to the method of the same name in Figure 2 of [12]. The array $colour$ is local to the method and holds the colour of the ith vertex in P. The candidate set P is then sorted in non-decreasing colour order by the call to $numberSort$ in line 28, and $colour[i]$

is then the colour of integer vertex $P.get(i)$. The search then begins in the loop at line 29. We first test to see if the combined size of the candidate set plus the colour of vertex v is sufficient to unseat the champion (line 30). If it is insufficient, the search terminates. Note that the loop starts at $m-1$ (line 29), the position of the last element in P, and counts down to zero. The ith element of P is selected and assigned to v. As in MC we create a new candidate set $newP$, the set of vertices (integers) in P that are adjacent to v (lines 33 to 37). We then test to see if C is maximal (line 38) and if it unseats the champion. If the new candidate set is not empty, we recurse (line 39). Regardless, v is removed from P and from C (lines 40 and 41).

Listing 3. MCQ (part 1), Tomita 2003.

```
1  import java.util.*;
2
3  class MCQ extends MC {
4
5      ArrayList[] colourClass;
6
7      MCQ (int n,int[][]A,int[] degree,int style) {
8          super(n,A,degree);
9          this.style = style;
10     }
11
12     void search(){
13         cpuTime                        = System.currentTimeMillis();
14         nodes                          = 0;
15         colourClass                    = new ArrayList[n];
16         ArrayList<Integer> C           = new ArrayList<Integer>(n);
17         ArrayList<Integer> P           = new ArrayList<Integer>(n);
18         for (int i=0;i<n;i++) colourClass[i] = new ArrayList<Integer>(n);
19         orderVertices(P);
20         expand(C,P);
21     }
22
23     void expand(ArrayList<Integer> C, ArrayList<Integer> P){
24         if (timeLimit > 0 && System.currentTimeMillis() - cpuTime >= timeLimit) return;
25         nodes++;
26         int m = P.size();
27         int[] colour = new int[m];
28         numberSort(C,P,P,colour);
29         for (int i=m-1;i>=0;i--){
30             if (C.size() + colour[i] <= maxSize) return;
31             int v = P.get(i);
32             C.add(v);
33             ArrayList<Integer> newP = new ArrayList<Integer>(i);
34             for (int j=0;j<=i;j++){
35                 int u = P.get(j);
36                 if (A[u][v] == 1) newP.add(u);
37             }
38             if (newP.isEmpty() && C.size() > maxSize) saveSolution(C);
39             if (!newP.isEmpty()) expand(C,newP);
40             C.remove(C.size()-1);
41             P.remove(i);
42         }
43     }
```

Listing 4. MCQ (part 1 continued), Tomita 2003.

```
    void numberSort(ArrayList<Integer> C, ArrayList<Integer> ColOrd, ArrayList<Integer> P, int[] colour){
        int colours = 0;
        int m = ColOrd.size();
        for (int i=0;i<m;i++) colourClass[i].clear();
        for (int i=0;i<m;i++){
            int v = ColOrd.get(i);
            int k = 0;
            while (conflicts(v,colourClass[k])) k++;
            colourClass[k].add(v);
            colours = Math.max(colours,k+1);
        }
        P.clear();
        int i = 0;
        for (int k=0;k<colours;k++)
            for (int j=0;j<colourClass[k].size();j++){
                int v = (Integer)(colourClass[k].get(j));
                P.add(v);
                colour[i++] = k+1;
            }
    }

    boolean conflicts(int v, ArrayList<Integer> colourClass){
        for (int i=0;i<colourClass.size();i++){
            int w = colourClass.get(i);
            if (A[v][w] == 1) return true;
        }
        return false;
    }
```

Listing 5. Vertex.

```
import java.util.*;

public class Vertex implements Comparable<Vertex> {

    int index, degree, nebDeg;

    public Vertex (int index,int degree) {
        this.index  = index;
        this.degree = degree;
        nebDeg      = 0;
    }

    public int compareTo(Vertex v){
        if (degree < v.degree || degree == v.degree && index > v.index) return 1;
        return -1;
    }
}
```

Listing 6. MCRComparator.

```
import java.util.*;

public class MCRComparator implements Comparator {

    public int compare(Object o1, Object o2){
        Vertex u = (Vertex) o1;
        Vertex v = (Vertex) o2;
        if (u.degree < v.degree ||
            u.degree == v.degree && u.nebDeg < v.nebDeg ||
            u.degree == v.degree && u.nebDeg == v.nebDeg && u.index > v.index) return 1;
        return -1;
    }
}
```

Listing 7. MCQ (part 2), Tomita 2003.

```

    void orderVertices(ArrayList<Integer> ColOrd){
        Vertex[] V = new Vertex[n];
        for (int i=0;i<n;i++) V[i] = new Vertex(i,degree[i]);
        for (int i=0;i<n;i++)
            for (int j=0;j<n;j++)
                if (A[i][j] == 1) V[i].nebDeg = V[i].nebDeg + degree[j];
        if (style == 1) Arrays.sort(V);
        if (style == 2) minWidthOrder(V);
        if (style == 3) Arrays.sort(V,new MCRComparator());
        for (Vertex v : V) ColOrd.add(v.index);
    }

     void minWidthOrder(Vertex[] V){
        ArrayList<Vertex> L = new ArrayList<Vertex>(n);
        Stack<Vertex> S = new Stack<Vertex>();
        for (Vertex v : V) L.add(v);
        while (!L.isEmpty()){
            Vertex v = L.get(0);
            for (Vertex u : L) if (u.degree < v.degree) v = u;
            S.push(v); L.remove(v);
            for (Vertex u : L) if (A[u.index][v.index] == 1) u.degree--;
        }
        int k = 0;
        while (!S.isEmpty()) V[k++] = S.pop();
    }
}
```

Method $numberSort$ (Listing 4) can be compared to the method of the same name in Figure 3 of [12]. $numberSort$ takes as arguments the current clique C, an ordered $ArrayList$ of integers $ColOrd$ corresponding to vertices to be coloured in that order, an $ArrayList$ of integers P that will correspond to the coloured vertices in non-decreasing colour order, and an array of integers $colour$ such that if $v = P.get(i)$ (v is the ith vertex in P) then the colour of v is $colour[i]$. Lines 45 to 64 (Listing 4) differs from Tomita's NUMBER-SORT method because we use the additional arguments $ColOrd$ and the growing clique C as this allows us to easily implement our next algorithm MCS (clique C is not used in $numberSort$ until we get to MCSb, therefore we carry it for convenience only.)

Rather than assigning colours to vertices explicitly, $numberSort$ places vertices into colour classes, *i.e.*, if a vertex is not adjacent to any of the vertices in $colourClass[i]$ then that vertex can be placed into that class and given colour number $i + 1$ ($i + 1$ so that colours range from 1 upwards). The vertices can then be sorted into colour order via a pigeonhole sort, where colour classes are the pigeonholes.

$numberSort$ starts by clearing out the colour classes that might be used (line 48). In lines 49 to 55 vertices are selected from $ColOrd$ and placed into the first colour class in which there are no conflicts, *i.e.*, a class in which the vertex is not adjacent to any other vertex in that class (lines 51 to 53, and method $conflicts$). The variable $colours$ records the number of colours used. Lines 56 to 63 is a pigeonhole sort, starting by clearing P and then iterating over the colour classes (loop start at line 58) and in each colour class adding those vertices into P (lines 59 to 63). The boolean method $conflicts$, lines 66 to 72, takes a vertex v and an ArrayList of vertices $colourClass$ where vertices in $colourClass$ are not pair-wise adjacent and have the same colour, *i.e.*, the vertices are an independent set. If vertex v is adjacent to any vertex in $colourClass$, the method returns true (lines 67 to 70), otherwise false. Note that if vertex v needs to be added into a new colour class in $numberSort$, the size of that $colourClass$ will be zero, and the for loop of lines 67 to 70 will not be performed and $conflicts$ returns true. The complexity of $numberSort$ is quadratic in the size of P.

Vertices need to be sorted at the top of search, line 19. To do this we use the class Vertex in Listing 5 and the comparator MCRComparator in Listing 6. If i is a vertex in P then the corresponding Vertex v has an integer $index$ equal to i. The Vertex also has attributes $degree$ and $nebDeg$. $degree$ is the degree of the vertex $index$ and $nebDeg$ is the sum of the degrees of the vertices in the neighbourhood of vertex $index$. Given an array V of class Vertex, this can be sorted using Java's $Arrays.sort(V)$ method in $O(n.\log(n))$ time, and is ordered by default using the $compareTo$ method in class Vertex. Our method forces a strict ordering of V by non-increasing degree, tie-breaking on $index$. This ensures reproducibility of results. If we allowed the $compareToMethod$ to deliver 0 when two vertices have the same degree, then $Arrays.sort$ would break ties. If the sort method was unstable, *i.e.*, it did not maintain the relative order of objects with equal keys [19], results may be unpredictable.

The class MCRComparator (Listing 6) allows us to sort vertices by non-increasing degree, tie breaking on the sum of the neighbourhood degree $nebDeg$ and then on $index$, giving again a strict order. This is the MCR order given in [15], where MCQ uses the simple degree ordering and MCR is MCQ with tie-breaking on neighbourhood degree.

Vertices can also be sorted into a minimum-width order. Given an ordered set of vertices, the width of a vertex is the number of edges that lead from that vertex to previous vertices in the order, and the width of the ordering is the maximum width of its vertices. The minimum width order (mwo) was proposed by Freuder [20] and also by Matula and Beck [21] where it was called "smallest last", and more recently in [16] as a *degeneracy ordering*. The method $minWidthOrder$, lines 86 to 98 of Listing 7, sorts the array V of Vertex into an "mwo". The vertices of V are copied into an ArrayList L (lines 87 and 89). The while loop starting at line 90 selects the vertex in L with smallest degree (lines 91 and 92) and calls it v. Vertex v is pushed onto the stack S and removed from L (line 93) and all vertices in L that are adjacent to v have their degree reduced (line 94). On termination of the while loop, vertices are popped off the stack and placed back into V, giving a minimum width (smallest last) ordering.

Method $orderVertices$ (Listing 7 lines 74 to 84) is then called once, at the top of search. The array of Vertex V is created for sorting in lines 75 and 76, and the sum of the neighbourhood degrees is computed in lines 77 to 79. $ColOrd$ is then sorted in one of three orders: $style == 1$ in non-increasing degree order, $style == 2$ in minimum width order, $style == 3$ in non-increasing degree tie-breaking on sum of neighbourhood degree. MCQ then uses the ordered candidate set P for colouring, initially in one of the initial orders, thereafter in the order resulting from $numberSort$ and that is non-decreasing colour order. In [12] it is claimed that this is an improving order (however, no evidence was presented for this claim). In [15] Tomita proposes a new algorithm, MCR, where MCR is MCQ with a different initial ordering of vertices, *i.e.*, MCQ with $style == 3$.

2.2.2. A Trace of MCQ

Figure 4 shows a cartoon and trace of MCQ over graph g10-50. Print statements were placed immediately after the call to $expand$ (Listing 3 line 24), after the selection of a vertex v (line 31) and just before v is rejected from P and C (line 40). Each picture in the cartoon gives the corresponding line numbers in the trace immediately below. Line 0 of the trace is a print-out of the ordered array V just after line 83 in method $orderVertices$ in Listing 7. This shows for each vertex the pair $< index, degree >$: the first call to $expand$ has $P = \{3, 0, 4, 6, 1, 2, 5, 8, 9, 7\}$, *i.e.*, non-decreasing degree order. MCQ makes 3 calls to $expand$ whereas MC makes 9 calls, and the MCQ colour bound cut-off in line 30 of Listing 3 is satisfied twice (Figure 4 lines 9 and 11).

Figure 4. Trace of MCQ1 on graph g10–50.

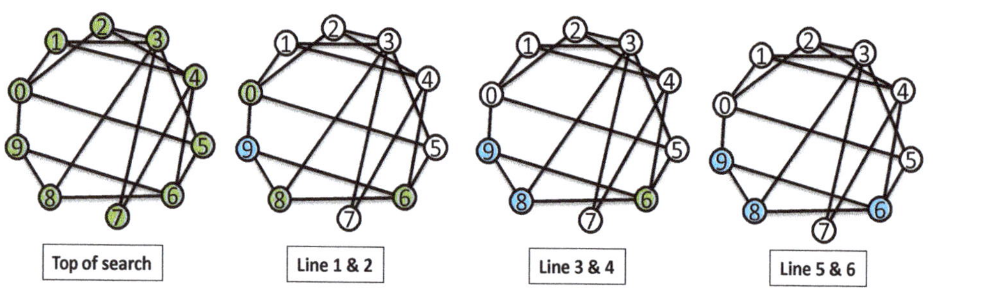


```
 0 <3,5> <0,4> <4,4> <6,4> <1,3> <2,3> <5,3> <8,3> <9,3> <7,2>
 1 > expand(C:[],P:[3, 0, 4, 6, 1, 2, 5, 8, 9, 7]
 2 > select 9 C:[] P:[3, 0, 4, 6, 1, 2, 7, 5, 8, 9] -> C:[9] & newP:[0, 6, 8]
 3 > > expand(C:[9],P:[0, 6, 8]
 4 > > select 8 C:[9] P:[0, 6, 8] -> C:[9, 8] & newP:[6]
 5 > > > expand(C:[9, 8],P:[6]
 6 > > > select 6 C:[9, 8] P:[6] -> SAVE: [9, 8, 6]
 7 > > > reject 6 C:[9, 8, 6] P:[6]
 8 > > reject 8 C:[9, 8] P:[0, 6, 8]
 9 > > select 6 C:[9] P:[0, 6] -> FAIL: vertex 6 colour too small (colour = 1)
10 > reject 9 C:[9] P:[3, 0, 4, 6, 1, 2, 7, 5, 8, 9]
11 > select 8 C:[] P:[3, 0, 4, 6, 1, 2, 7, 5, 8] -> FAIL: vertex 8 colour too small (colour = 3)
```

2.2.3. Observations on MCQ

We noted above that MC can make recursive calls that immediately fail. Can this happen in MCQ? Looking at lines 39 of Listing 3, $|C| + |newP|$ must be greater than $maxSize$. Since the colour of the vertex selected $colour[i]$ was sufficient to satisfy the condition of line 30, it must be that integer vertex v (line 31) is adjacent to at least $colour[i]$ vertices in P and thus in $newP$, therefore the next recursive call will not immediately fail. Consequently each call to $expand$ corresponds to an internal node in the backtrack tree.

We also see again exactly what is measured as CPU time: It includes the creation of our data structures, the reordering of vertices at the top of search and all recursive calls to $expand$ (lines 12 to 20).

Why is $colourClass$ an ArrayList[] rather than an ArrayList<ArrayList<Integer>>? That would have done away with the explicit cast in line 60. When using an ArrayList<ArrayList<Integer>> Java generates an implicit cast, so nothing is gained—it is merely syntactic sugar.

Tomita's presentation of MCQ [12] differs from Listing 3 in that it initially colours the sorted vertices prior to calling $expand$ and thereafter colour-sorts the new candidate set immediately before making a recursive call to $expand$. Appendix 1 explains this in detail and investigates the effect on performance.

2.3. MCS

In [13] MCS is presented as two modifications to MCQ. The first modification is to use "... an adjunct ordered set of vertices for approximate coloring". This is an ordered list of vertices to be used in the sequential colouring, and was called V_a. This order is static, set at the top of search. Therefore, rather than using the order in the candidate set P for colouring the vertices in P, the vertices in P are coloured in the order of vertices in V_a.

The second modification is to use a repair mechanism when colouring vertices (this is called a Re-NUMBER in Figure 1 of [13]). When colouring vertices, an attempt is made to reduce the colours used by performing exchanges between vertices in different colour classes. In [13] a recolouring of a vertex v occurs when a new colour class is about to be opened for v and that colour class exceeds the search bound, *i.e.*, if the number of colours can be reduced, this could result in search being cut off. In the context of colouring, I will say that vertex u and v *conflict* if they are adjacent, and that v *conflicts* with a colour class C if there exists a vertex $u \in C$ that is in *conflict* with v. Assume vertex v is in colour class C_k. If there exists a lower colour class C_i $(i < k - 1)$ and v conflicts with only a single vertex $w \in C_i$ and there also exists a colour class C_j, where $i < j < k$, and w does not conflict with any vertex in C_j, then we can place v in C_i and w in C_j, freeing up colour class C_k. This is given in Figure 1 of [13] and the procedure is named Re-NUMBER.

Figure 5 illustrates this procedure. The boxes correspond to colour classes i, j and k where $i < j < k$. The circles correspond to vertices in that colour class and the red arrowed lines as conflicts between pairs of vertices. Vertex v has just been added to colour class k, v conflicts only with w in colour class i, and w has no conflicts in colour class j. We can then move w up to colour class j and v down to colour class i.

Figure 5. A repair scenario with colour classes i, j and k.

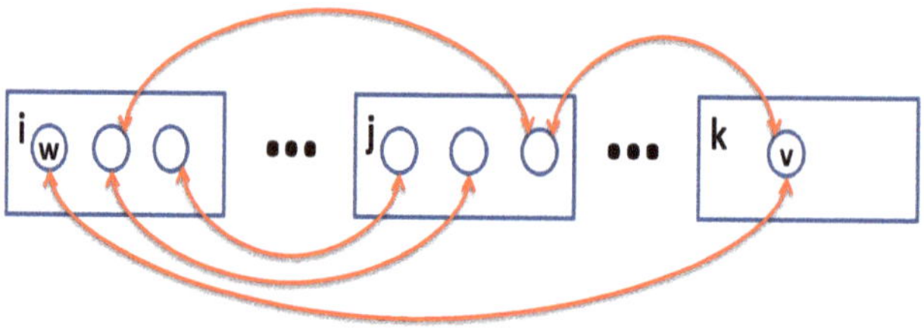

Experiments were then presented in [13] comparing MCR against MCS in which MCS is always the champion. But it is not clear where the advantage of MCS comes from: Does it come from the static colour order (the "adjunct ordered set") or does it come from the colour repair mechanism?

I now present two versions of MCS. The first, which I call MCSa, uses the static colouring order. The second, MCSb, uses the static colouring ordering *and* the colour repair mechanism (so MCSb *is* Tomita's MCS). Consequently, we will be able to determine where the improvement in MCS comes from: Static colour ordering or colour repair.

2.3.1. MCSa in Java

In Listing 8 we present MCSa as an extension to MCQ. Method $search$ creates an explicit colour ordering $ColOrd$ and the $expand$ method is called with this in line 18 (compare this to line 20 of MCQ). Method $expand$ now takes three arguments: The growing clique C, the candidate set P and the colouring order $ColOrd$. In line 26 $numberSort$ is called using $ColOrd$ (compare with line 28 in MCQ) and lines 27 to 45 are essentially the same as lines 29 to 42 in MCQ with the exception that $ColOrd$ must also be copied and updated (lines 32, 36 and 37) prior to the recursive call to $expand$ (line 40) and then down-dated after the recursive call (line 43). Therefore, MCSa is a simple extension of MCQ and, like MCQ, has three styles of ordering.

2.3.2. MCSb in Java

In Listing 9 we present MCSb as an extension to MCSa: The difference between MCSb and MCSa is in $numberSort$, with the addition of lines 10 and 20. At line 10 we compute $delta$ as the minimum number of colour classes required to match the search bound. At line 20, if we have exceeded the number of colour classes required to exceed the search bound and a new colour class k has been opened for vertex v and we can repair the colouring such that one less colour class is used, we can decrement the number of colours used. This repair is done in the boolean method $repair$ of lines 43 to 57. The $repair$ method returns true if vertex v in colour class k can be recoloured into a lower colour class, false otherwise, and can be compared to Tomita's Re-NUMBER procedure. We search for a colour class i, where $i < k - 1$, in which there exists only one vertex in conflict with v and we call this w (line 45). The method $getSingleConflictVariable$, lines 32 to 41, searches for such a vertex. It takes as arguments a vertex v and a colour class $colourClass$. If v is adjacent to only one vertex in $colourClass$ the index of that vertex is returned (line 40), where $0 \leq conflicVar < n$, otherwise a negative number is returned (line 39). The $repair$ method then proceeds at line 46 if a single conflicting vertex w was found, searching for a colour class j *above* i (for loop of line 47) in which there are no conflicts with w. If that was found (line 48), vertex v is removed from colour class k, w is removed from colour class i, v is added to colour class i and w to colour class j (lines 49 to 52), and $repair$ delivers $true$ (line 53). Otherwise, no repair occurred (line 56).

Listing 8. MCSa, Tomita 2010.

```
import java.util.*;

class MCSa extends MCQ {

    MCSa (int n,int[][]A,int[] degree,int style) {
        super(n,A,degree,style);
    }

    void search(){
        cpuTime                         = System.currentTimeMillis();
        nodes                           = 0;
        colourClass                     = new ArrayList[n];
        ArrayList<Integer> C            = new ArrayList<Integer>(n);
        ArrayList<Integer> P            = new ArrayList<Integer>(n);
        ArrayList<Integer> ColOrd       = new ArrayList<Integer>(n);
        for (int i=0;i<n;i++) colourClass[i] = new ArrayList<Integer>(n);
        orderVertices(ColOrd);
        expand(C,P,ColOrd);
    }

    void expand(ArrayList<Integer> C, ArrayList<Integer> P, ArrayList<Integer> ColOrd){
        if (timeLimit > 0 && System.currentTimeMillis() - cpuTime >= timeLimit) return;
        nodes++;
        int m = ColOrd.size();
        int[] colour = new int[m];
        numberSort(C,ColOrd,P,colour);
        for (int i=m-1;i>=0;i--){
            int v = P.get(i);
            if (C.size() + colour[i] <= maxSize) return;
            C.add(v);
            ArrayList<Integer> newP      = new ArrayList<Integer>(i);
            ArrayList<Integer> newColOrd = new ArrayList<Integer>(i);
            for (int j=0;j<=i;j++){
                int u = P.get(j);
                if (A[u][v] == 1) newP.add(u);
                int w = ColOrd.get(j);
                if (A[v][w] == 1) newColOrd.add(w);
            }
            if (newP.isEmpty() && C.size() > maxSize) saveSolution(C);
            if (!newP.isEmpty()) expand(C,newP,newColOrd);
            C.remove(C.size()-1);
            P.remove(i);
            ColOrd.remove((Integer)v);
        }
    }
}
```

Listing 9. MCSb, Tomita 2010.

```
import java.util.*;

class MCSb extends MCSa {

    MCSb (int n,int[][]A,int[] degree,int style) {
        super(n,A,degree,style);
    }

    void numberSort(ArrayList<Integer> C, ArrayList<Integer> ColOrd, ArrayList<Integer> P,int[] colour){
        int delta   = maxSize - C.size();
        int colours = 0;
        int m       = ColOrd.size();
        for (int i=0;i<m;i++) colourClass[i].clear();
        for (int i=0;i<m;i++){
            int v = ColOrd.get(i);
            int k = 0;
            while (conflicts(v,colourClass[k])) k++;
            colourClass[k].add(v);
            colours = Math.max(colours,k+1);
            if (k+1 > delta && colourClass[k].size() == 1 && repair(v,k)) colours--;
        }
        P.clear();
        int i = 0;
        for (int k=0;k<colours;k++)
            for (int j=0;j<colourClass[k].size();j++){
                int v = (Integer)(colourClass[k].get(j));
                P.add(v);
                colour[i++] = k+1;
            }
    }

    int getSingleConflictVariable(int v,ArrayList<Integer> colourClass){
        int conflictVar = -1;
        int count       = 0;
        for (int i=0;i<colourClass.size() && count<2;i++){
            int w = colourClass.get(i);
            if (A[v][w] == 1){conflictVar = w; count++;}
        }
        if (count > 1) return -count;
        return conflictVar;
    }

    boolean repair(int v, int k){
        for (int i=0;i<k-1;i++){
            int w = getSingleConflictVariable(v,colourClass[i]);
            if (w >= 0)
                for (int j=i+1;j<k;j++)
                    if (!conflicts(w,colourClass[j])){
                        colourClass[k].remove((Integer)v);
                        colourClass[i].remove((Integer)w);
                        colourClass[i].add(v);
                        colourClass[j].add(w);
                        return true;
                    }
        }
        return false;
    }
}
```

2.3.3. Observations on MCS

Tomita did not investigate where MCS's improvement comes from and neither did [2], coding up MCS in Python in one piece. However San Segundo did [10], incrementally adding colour repair to BBMC. We can also *tune* MCS. In MCSb we repair colourings when we open a new colour class that exceeds the search bound. We could instead repair unconditionally every time we open a new colour class, attempting to maintain a compact colouring. We do not investigate this here.

2.4. BBMC

San Segundo's BB-MaxClique algorithm [11] (BBMC) is similar to the earlier algorithms in that vertices are selected from the candidate set to add to the current clique in non-increasing colour order, with a colour cut-off within a binomial search. BBMC is at heart a bit-set encoding of MCSa with the following features.

1. The "BB" in "BB-MaxClique" is for "Bit Board". Sets are represented using bit strings.
2. BBMC colours the candidate set using a static sequential ordering, the ordering set at the top of search, the same as MCSa.
3. BBMC represents the neighbourhood of a vertex and its inverse neighbourhood as bit strings, rather than using a row of an adjacency matrix and its complement.
4. When colouring takes place, a colour class perspective is taken, determining what vertices can be placed in a colour class together, before moving on to the next colour class. Other algorithms (e.g., [12,13]) takes a vertex perspective, deciding on the colour of a vertex.

2.4.1. BBMC in Java

We implement sets using Java's BitSet class (a vector of bits with associated methods) and from now on we refer to P as *the candidate BitSet* and an ordered array of integers U as the *ordered candidate set*. In Listing 10, lines 5 to 7, we have an array of BitSet N for representing neighbourhoods, $invN$ as the inverse neighbourhoods (the complement of N) and V an array of Vertex. $N[i]$ is then a BitSet representing the neigbourhood of the ith vertex in the array V, and $invN[i]$ as its complement. The array V is used at the top of search for renaming vertices (and we discuss this later).

The $search$ method (lines 16 to 30) creates the candidate BitSet P, current clique (as a BitSet) C, and Vertex array V. The $orderVertices$ method renames the vertices and will be discussed later. The method $BBMaxClique$ corresponds to the procedure in Figure 3 of [11] and can be compared to the $expand$ method in Listing 8. In a BitSet we use $cardinality$ rather than $size$ (line 35, 40 and 44). The integer array U (same name as in [11]) is essentially the colour ordered candidate set such that if $v = U[i]$ then $colour[i]$ corresponds to the colour given to v and $colour[i] \leq colour[i + 1]$. The method call of line 38 colours the vertices and delivers those colours in the array $colour$ and the sorted candidate set in U. The for loop, lines 39 to 47 (again, counting down from $m - 1$ to zero), first tests to see if the colour cut-off occurs (line 40) and if it does the method returns.

Listing 10. San Segundo's BB-MaxClique in Java (part 1).

```
1  import java.util.*;
2
3  public class BBMC extends MCQ {
4
5      BitSet[] N;     // neighbourhood
6      BitSet[] invN;  // inverse neighbourhood
7      Vertex[] V;     // mapping bits to vertices
8
9      BBMC (int n,int[][]A,int[] degree,int style) {
10         super(n,A,degree,style);
11         N    = new BitSet[n];
12         invN = new BitSet[n];
13         V    = new Vertex[n];
14     }
15
16     void search(){
17         cpuTime  = System.currentTimeMillis();
18         nodes    = 0;
19         BitSet C = new BitSet(n);
20         BitSet P = new BitSet(n);
21         for (int i=0;i<n;i++){
22             N[i]    = new BitSet(n);
23             invN[i] = new BitSet(n);
24             V[i]    = new Vertex(i,degree[i]);
25         }
26         orderVertices();
27         C.set(0,n,false);
28         P.set(0,n,true);
29         BBMaxClique(C,P);
30     }
31
32     void BBMaxClique(BitSet C, BitSet P){
33         if (timeLimit > 0 && System.currentTimeMillis() - cpuTime >= timeLimit) return;
34         nodes++;
35         int m = P.cardinality();
36         int[] U = new int[m];
37         int[] colour = new int[m];
38         BBColour(P,U,colour);
39         for (int i=m-1;i>=0;i--){
40             if (colour[i] + C.cardinality() <= maxSize) return;
41             BitSet newP = (BitSet)P.clone();
42             int v = U[i];
43             C.set(v,true); newP.and(N[v]);
44             if (newP.isEmpty() && C.cardinality() > maxSize) saveSolution(C);
45             if (!newP.isEmpty()) BBMaxClique(C,newP);
46             P.set(v,false); C.set(v,false);
47         }
48     }
```

Otherwise a new candidate BitSet is created, $newP$ on line 41, as a clone of P. The current vertex v is then selected (line 42) and in line 43 v is added to the growing clique C and $newP$ becomes the BitSet corresponding to the vertices in the candidate BitSet that are in the neighbourhood of v. The operation $newP.and(N[v])$ (line 43) is equivalent to the for loop in lines 34 to 37 of Listing 3 of MCQ. If the current clique is both maximal and a maximum, it is saved via BBMC's specialised save method (described later), otherwise if C is not maximal (*i.e.*, $newP$ is not empty) a recursive call is made to

$BBMaxClique$. Regardless, v is removed from the current candidate BitSet and the current clique (line 46) and the for loop continues.

Method $BBColour$ (Listing 11) corresponds to the procedure of the same name in Figure 2 of [11] but differs in that it does not explicitly represent colour classes and therefore does not require a pigeonhole sort as in San Segundo's description. Our method takes the candidate BitSet P (see line 38), ordered candidate set U and array of $colour$ as parameters. Due to the nature of Java's BitSet the and operation is not functional but actually modifies bits, consequently cloning is required (line 51 Listing 11) and we take a copy of P. In line 52 $colourClass$ records the current colour class, initially zero, and i is used as a counter for adding coloured vertices into the array U. The while loop, lines 54 to 64, builds up colour classes whilst consuming vertices in $copyP$. The BitSet Q (line 56) is the candidate BitSet as we are about to start a new colour class. The while loop of lines 57 to 64 builds a colour class: The first vertex in Q is selected (line 58) and is removed from the candidate BitSet $copyP$ (line 59) and BitSet Q (line 60), Q then becomes the set of vertices that are in the current candidate BitSet (Q) and in the inverse neighborhood of v (line 61), *i.e.*, Q becomes the BitSet of vertices that can join the same colour class with v. We then add v to the ordered candidate set U (line 62), record its colour and increment our counter (line 63). When Q is exhausted (line 57) the outer while loop (line 54) starts a new colour class (lines 55 to 64).

Listing 11. San Segundo's BB-MaxClique in Java (part 1 continued).

```
49
50      void BBColour(BitSet P,int[] U,int[] colour){
51          BitSet copyP      = (BitSet)P.clone();
52          int colourClass  = 0;
53          int i            = 0;
54          while (copyP.cardinality() != 0){
55              colourClass++;
56              BitSet Q = (BitSet)copyP.clone();
57              while (Q.cardinality() != 0){
58                  int v = Q.nextSetBit(0);
59                  copyP.set(v,false);
60                  Q.set(v,false);
61                  Q.and(invN[v]);
62                  U[i] = v;
63                  colour[i++] = colourClass;
64              }
65          }
66      }
```

Listing 12 shows how the candidate BitSet is renamed/reordered. In fact it is not the candidate BitSet that is reordered, rather it is the description of the neighbourhood N and its inverse $invN$ that is reordered. Again, as in MCQ and MCSa, a Veretx array is created (lines 69 to 73) and is sorted into one of three possible orders (lines 74 to 76). Once sorted, a bit in position i of the candidate BitSet P corresponds to the integer vertex $v = V[i].index$. The neighbourhood and its inverse are then reordered in the loop of lines 77 to 83. For all pairs (i, j), we select the corresponding vertices u and v from V (lines 79 and 80) and if they are adjacent then the jth bit of $N[i]$ is set true, otherwise false (line 81). Similarly, the inverse neighbourhood is updated in line 82. The loop could be made twice as fast by exploiting symmetries in the adjacency matrix A. In any event, this method is called once at the top of search and is generally an insignificant contribution to run time.

Listing 12. San Segundo's BB-MaxClique in Java (part 2).

```
67
68      void orderVertices(){
69          for (int i=0;i<n;i++){
70              V[i] = new Vertex(i,degree[i]);
71              for (int j=0;j<n;j++)
72                  if (A[i][j] == 1) V[i].nebDeg = V[i].nebDeg + degree[j];
73          }
74          if (style == 1) Arrays.sort(V);
75          if (style == 2) minWidthOrder(V);
76          if (style == 3) Arrays.sort(V,new MCRComparator());
77          for (int i=0;i<n;i++)
78              for (int j=0;j<n;j++){
79                  int u = V[i].index;
80                  int v = V[j].index;
81                  N[i].set(j,A[u][v] == 1);
82                  invN[i].set(j,A[u][v] == 0);
83              }
84      }
85
86      void saveSolution(BitSet C){
87          Arrays.fill(solution,0);
88          for (int i=0;i<C.size();i++) if (C.get(i)) solution[V[i].index] = 1;
89          maxSize = C.cardinality();
90      }
91  }
```

BBMC requires its own $saveSolution$ method (lines 86 to 90 of Listing 12) due to C being a BitSet. Again the solution is saved into the integer array $solution$ and again we need to use the Vertex array V to map bits to vertices. This is done in line 88: If the ith bit of C is true then integer vertex $V[i].index$ is in the solution. This explains why V is global to the $BBMC$ class.

2.4.2. Observations on BBMC

In our Java implementation, we might expect a speedup if we did away with the in-built BitSet and did our own bit-string manipulations explicitly. It is also worth noting that in [10] comparisons are made with Tomita's results in [13] by rescaling tabulated results, *i.e.*, Tomita's code was not actually run, but this is not unusual.

2.5. *Summary of MCQ, MCR, MCS and BBMC*

Putting aside the chronology [11–13,15], MCSa is the most general algorithm presented here. BBMC is in essence MCSa with a BitSet encoding of sets. MCQ is MCSa except that we do away with the static colour ordering and allow MCQ to colour and sort the candidate set using the candidate set, somewhat in the manner of Uroborus the serpent that eats itself. And MCSb is MCSa with an additional colour repair step.

3. Exact Algorithms for Maximum Clique: A Brief History

We now present a brief history of complete algorithms for the maximum clique problems, starting from 1990. The algorithms are presented in chronological order.

1990: In 1990 [3] Carraghan and Pardalos present a branch and bound algorithm. Vertices are ordered in non-decreasing degree order at each depth in the binomial search with a cut-off based on the size of the largest clique found so far. Their algorithm is presented in Fortran 77 along with code to generate random graphs; consequently, their empirical results are entirely reproducible. Their algorithm is similar to MC (Listing 1) but sorts the candidate set P using current degree in each call to $expand$.

1992: In [8] Pardalos and Rodgers present a zero-one encoding of the problem where a vertex v is represented by a variable x_v that takes the value 1 if search decides that v is in the clique and 0 if it is rejected. Pruning takes place via the constraint $\neg adjacent(u,v) \rightarrow x_u + x_v \leq 1$ (Rule 4). In addition, a candidate vertex adjacent to all vertices in the current clique is forced into the clique (Rule 5) and a vertices of degree too low to contribute to the growing clique is rejected (Rule 7). The branch and bound search selects variables dynamically based on current degree in the candidate set: A *non-greedy* selection chooses a vertex of lowest degree and *greedy* selects highest degree. The computational results showed that greedy was good for (easy) sparse graphs and non-greedy was good for (hard) dense graphs.

1994: In [22] Pardalos and Xue reviewed algorithms for the enumeration problem (counting maximal cliques) and exact algorithms for the maximum clique problem. Although dated, it continues to be an excellent review.

1997: In [14] graph colouring and fractional colouring is used to bound search. Comparing again to MC (Listing 1) the candidate set is coloured greedily, and if the size of the current clique plus the number of colours used is less than or equal to the size of the largest clique found so far, that branch of search is cut off. In [14] vertices are selected in non-increasing degree order, the opposite of that proposed by [8]. We can get a similar effect to [14] in MC if we allow free selection of vertices, colour $newP$ between lines 42 and 43 and make the recursive call to $expand$ in line 43 conditional on the colour bound.

2002: Patric R. J. Östergård proposed an algorithm that has a dynamic programming flavour [7]. The search process starts by finding the largest clique containing vertices drawn from the set $S_n = \{v_n\}$ and records it size in $c[n]$. Search then proceeds to find the largest clique in the set $S_i = \{v_i, v_{i+1}, ..., v_n\}$ using the value in $c[i+1]$ as a bound. The vertices are ordered at the top of search in colour order, *i.e.*, the vertices are coloured greedily and then ordered in non-decreasing colour order, similar to that in $numberSort$ Listing 4. Östergård's algorithm is available as Cliquer [7]. In the same year, Torsten Fahle [4] presented a simple algorithm (Algorithm 1) that is essentially MC but with a free selection of vertices rather than the fixed iteration in line 36 of Listing 1 and dynamic maintenance of vertex degree in the candidate set. This is then enhanced (Algorithm 2) with forced accept and forced reject steps similar to Rules 4, 5 and 7 of [8] and the algorithm is named *DF* (*D*omain *F*iltering). DF is then enhanced to incorporate a colouring bound, similar to that in Wood [14].

2003: Jean-Charles Régin proposed a constraint programming model for the maximum clique problem [9]. His model uses a matching in a duplicated graph to deliver a bound within search, a *Not Set* as used in the Bron Kerbosch enumeration Algorithm 457 [23] and vertex selection using the pivoting strategy similar to that in [16,23–25]. That same year Tomita reported MCQ [12].

2004: Faisal N. Abu-Khzam *et al.* [26] presented a number of *kernelization* steps to reduce a graph before and during search in the vertex cover problem, where a minimum vertex cover of the complement graph is a maximal clique in the original graph. Some of the kernelization steps are similar to the pruning rules in [4,8] although *Crown Reduction* appears to be novel and effective.

2007: Tomita proposed MCR [15] and in the same year Janez Konc and Dušanka Janežič proposed the *MaxCliqueDyn* algorithm [5]. The algorithm is essentially MCQ [12] with dynamic reordering of vertices in the candidate set, using current degree, prior to colouring. This reordering is expensive and takes place high up in the backtrack tree and is controlled by a parameter T_{limit}. Varying this parameter influences the cost of the search process and T_{limit} must be tuned on an instance-by-instance basis.

2010: Pablo San Segundo and Cristóbal Tapia presented an early version of BBMC (BB-MCP) [27] and Tomita presented MCS [13]. In the same year Li and Quan proposed new max-SAT encodings for maximum clique [6,18].

2011: Pablo San Segundo proposed BBMC [11] and BBMCR [10], where BBMCR includes a colour repair step. In [10] it is noted that in [13] "... the concrete contribution of recolouring is unfortunately not made explicit." San Segundo's colour repair, BB_ReCol differs from that in Listing 9 in that a *single swap* can occur after a double swap (as in lines 49 to 52 of Listing 9). This cannot occur in Listing 9 because $repair$ (line 43) is called only when a new colour class k is opened for vertex v (line 20); consequently v must have been adjacent to at least one vertex in each colour class less than k and therefore $count$ (line 34) cannot be equal to zero at line 40.

2012: Renato Carmo and Alexandre P. Züge [2] reported an empirical study of 8 algorithms including those from [3] and [4] along with MCQ, MCR, MCS and MaxCliqueDyn. The claim is made that the Bron Kerbosch algorithm provides a unified framework for all the algorithms studied, although a Not Set is not used. Neither do they use pivoting as described in [16,23–25]. All algorithms are coded in Python, therefore the study is *objective* (the authors include none of their own algorithms) and *fair* (all algorithms are coded by the authors and run in the same environment). BBMC is not include in the study, MCS is not broken into its constituent parts (MCSa and MCSb), and the study uses only the DIMACS benchmarks.

4. The Computational Study

The computational study attempts to answer the following questions.

1. Where does the improvement in MCS come from? By comparing MCQ with MCSa we can measure the contribution due to static colouring, and by comparing MCSa with MCSb we can measure the contribution due to colour repair.
2. How much benefit can be obtained from the BitSet encoding? We compare MCSa with BBMC over a variety of problems.
3. We have three possible initial orderings (styles). Is any one of them better than the others and is this algorithm independent?
4. Most papers use only random problems and the DIMACS benchmarks. What other problems might we use in our investigation?
5. Is it safe to recalibrate published results?

Throughout our study we use a reference machine (named Cyprus), a machine with two Intel E5620 2.4 GHz quad-core processors with 48 GB memory, running Linux CentOS 5.3 and Java version 1.6.0_07.

4.1. MCQ vs. *MCS: Static Ordering and Colour Repair*

Is MCS faster than MCQ, and if so, why? MCSa is MCQ with a static colour ordering set at the top of search, and MCSb is MCSa with the colour repair mechanism. By comparing these algorithms, we can determine if indeed MCSb is faster than MCQ and where that gain comes from—the static colouring order or the colour repair. We start our investigation with Erdős–Rënyi random graphs $G(n, p)$ where n is the number of vertices and each edge is included in the graph with probability p independent from every other edge.

The first experiments are on random $G(n, p)$, first with $n = 100$, $0.40 \leq p \leq 0.99$, p varying in steps of 0.01, sample size of 100, then with $n = 150$, $0.50 \leq p \leq 0.95$, p varying in steps of 0.05, sample size of 100, and $n = 200$, $0.55 \leq p \leq 0.95$, p varying in steps of 0.05, sample size of 100. Unless otherwise stated, all experiments are carried out on our reference machine. The algorithms MCQ, MCSa and MCSb all use $style = 1$ (*i.e.*, MCQ1, MCSa1, MCSb1). Figure 6 shows on the left the average number of nodes against the edge probability and on the right the average run time in milliseconds against the edge probability, for MCQ1, MCSa1 and MCSb1. The top row has $n = 100$, middle row $n = 150$ and bottom row $n = 200$. For MCQ1 the sample size at $G(200, 0.95)$ was reduced to 28, *i.e.*, the MCQ1-200 job was terminated after 60 hours. As we apply the modifications to MCQ, we see a reduction in nodes with MCSb1 exploring less states than MCSa1 and MCSa1 less than MCQ1. However, on the right we see that reduction in search space does not always result in reduction in run time. MCSb1 is always slower than MCSa1, *i.e.*, the colour repair is too expensive and when $n = 100$ MCSb1 is often more expensive to run than MCQ! Therefore, it appears that MCS gets its advantage just from the static colour ordering and that the colour repair slows it down.

Figure 6. $G(n, p)$, sample size 100. MCQ *vs.* MCS, where is the win? (left) Search effort in nodes visited (*i.e.*, decisions made by the search process); (right) run time in milliseconds.

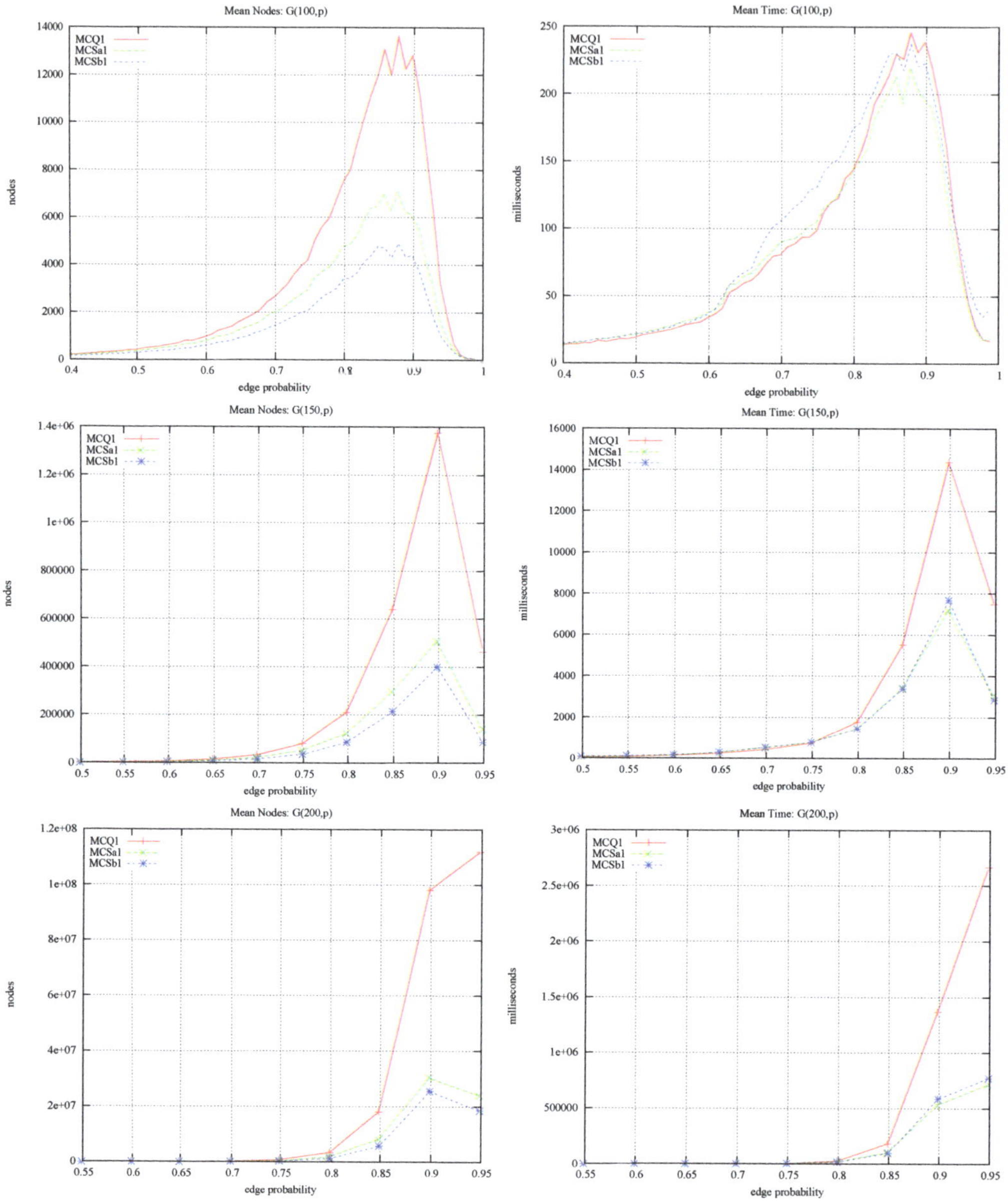

Table 1. DIMACS instances: MCQ *vs.* MCS, nodes, run time in seconds and (clique size).

instance	MCQ1			MCSa1			MCSb1		
brock200-1	868,213	7	(21)	524,723	4	(21)	245,146	**3**	(21)
brock400-1	342,473,950	4,471	(27)	198,359,829	2,888	(27)	142,253,319	**2,551**	(27)
brock400-2	224,839,070	2,923	(29)	145,597,994	2,089	(29)	61,327,056	**1,199**	(29)
brock400-3	194,403,055	2,322	(31)	120,230,513	1,616	(31)	70,263,846	**1,234**	(31)
brock400-4	82,056,086	1,117	(33)	54,440,888	**802**	(33)	68,252,352	1,209	(33)
brock800-1	1,247,519,247	—	**(23)**	1,055,945,239	—	**(23)**	911,465,283	—	(21)
brock800-2	1,387,973,191	—	(21)	1,171,057,646	—	**(24)**	914,638,570	—	(21)
brock800-3	1,332,309,827	—	(21)	1,159,165,900	—	(21)	914,235,793	—	(21)
brock800-4	804,901,115	—	(26)	640,444,536	**12,568**	(26)	659,145,642	13,924	(26)
hamming10-4	636,203,658	—	**(40)**	950,939,457	—	(37)	858,347,653	—	(37)
johnson32-2-4	10,447,210,976	—	(16)	8,269,639,389	—	(16)	7,345,343,221	—	(16)
keller5	603,233,453	—	(27)	596,150,386	—	(27)	523,346,613	—	(27)
keller6	285,704,599	—	(48)	226,330,037	—	(52)	240,958,450	—	**(54)**
MANN-a27	38,019	9	(126)	38,019	**6**	(126)	38,597	8	(126)
MANN-a45	2,851,572	4,989	(345)	2,851,572	**3,766**	(345)	2,545,131	4,118	(345)
MANN-a81	550,869	—	(1100)	631,141	—	(1100)	551,612	—	(1100)
p-hat1000-1	237,437	2	(10)	176,576	2	(10)	151,033	2	(10)
p-hat1000-2	466,616,845	—	(45)	34,473,978	**1,401**	(46)	166,655,543	7,565	(46)
p-hat1000-3	440,569,803	—	(52)	345,925,712	—	(55)	298,537,771	—	**(56)**
p-hat1500-1	1,642,981	16	(12)	1,184,526	14	(12)	990,246	14	(12)
p-hat1500-2	414,514,960	—	(52)	231,498,292	—	**(60)**	259,771,137	—	(57)
p-hat1500-3	570,637,417	—	(56)	220,823,126	—	(69)	176,987,047	—	(69)
p-hat300-3	3,829,005	74	(36)	624,947	**13**	(36)	713,107	21	(36)
p-hat500-2	1,022,190	23	(36)	114,009	**3**	(36)	137,568	5	(36)
p-hat500-3	515,071,375	—	(47)	39,260,458	**1,381**	(50)	104,684,054	4,945	(50)
p-hat700-2	18,968,155	508	(44)	750,903	**27**	(44)	149,0522	74	(44)
p-hat700-3	570,423,439	—	(48)	255,745,746	—	(62)	243,836,191	—	(62)
san1000	302,895	20	(15)	150,725	10	(15)	53,215	**3**	(15)
san200-0.9-2	1,149,564	20	(60)	229,567	5	(60)	62,776	**1**	(60)
san200-0.9-3	8,260,345	154	(44)	6,815,145	111	(44)	1,218,317	**32**	(44)
san400-0.7-1	55,010	**1**	(40)	119,356	2	(40)	134,772	3	(40)
san400-0.7-2	606,159	**14**	(30)	889,125	19	(30)	754,146	16	(30)
san400-0.7-3	582,646	11	(22)	521,410	10	(22)	215,785	**5**	(22)
san400-0.9-1	523,531,417	—	(56)	4,536,723	422	(100)	582,445	**54**	(100)
sanr200-0.7	206,262	1	(18)	152,882	1	(18)	100,977	1	(18)
sanr200-0.9	44,472,276	892	(42)	14,921,850	283	(42)	9,730,778	**245**	(42)
sanr400-0.5	380,151	2	(13)	320,110	2	(13)	190,706	2	(13)
sanr400-0.7	101,213,527	979	(21)	64,412,015	711	(21)	46,125,168	**650**	(21)

We also see a region where problems are hard for all our algorithms, at $n = 100$ and $n = 150$, both in terms of nodes and run time, and in [10] it is suggested that this behaviour is a "... phase transition to triviality ...". However at $n = 200$ there is a different picture. We see a hard region in terms of nodes but an ever-increasing run time. That is, even though nodes are falling, CPU time is climbing. This agrees with the tabulated results in [11] (Tables 4 and 5 on page 580) for BB-MaxClique. It is a conjecture that run time increases because the cost of each node (call to expand) incurs more cost in the colouring of the relatively larger candidate set. In going from $G(200, 0.90)$ to $G(200, 0.95)$, the maximum clique size increased on average from 41 to 62, a 50% increase, and for MCSa1 the average number of nodes fell by 20% (30% for MCSb1). The search space has fallen and the clique size has increased, which increases the cost of colouring and results in an overall increase in run time. Therefore it does not appear to be a phase transition in the sense of [28–30], *i.e.*, a feature of the problem that is algorithm independent.

We now report on the 66 DIMACS instances [31] in Table 1. For each algorithm, we have 3 entries: The number of nodes, CPU time in seconds, and in brackets the size of the largest clique found. Each algorithm was allowed 14,400 CPU seconds and if that was exceeded we have a table entry of "—". The best CPU time in a row is in **bold** font, and when CPU time limit is exceeded, the largest maximum clique size is **emboldened**. Easy instances are not tabulated, *i.e.*, those that took less than a second. Overall, we see that MCQ1 is rarely the best choice with MCSa1 or MCSb1 performing better. There are 11 problems where MCSb1 beats MCSa1 and 9 problems where MCSa1 beats MCSb1. Therefore, the DIMACS benchmarks do not significantly separate the behaviour of these two algorithms.

These results conflict somewhat with those in [10]. There it is claimed that colour repair, when added to BBMC, results in a performance gain in dense graphs ($p \geq 0.8$). Results are presented for a subset of the DIMACS instances with some of the difficult instances absent (brock800-*, hamming10-4, keller5, keller6, johnson32-2-4, MANN-a81, p-hat1000-3, p-hat1500-2, p-hat1500-3) and for random graphs with a sample size of 10.

4.2. BBMC vs. *MCSa: A Change of Representation*

What advantage is to be obtained from the change of representation between MCSa and BBMC, *i.e.*, representing sets as $ArrayList$ in MCSa and as a BitSet in BBMC? MCSa and BBMC are at heart the same algorithm. They both produce the same colourings, order the candidate set in the same way and explore the same backtrack tree.

Figure 7. Run time of MCSa1 against BBMC1, on the left $(G100, p)$ and on the right $G(200, p)$.

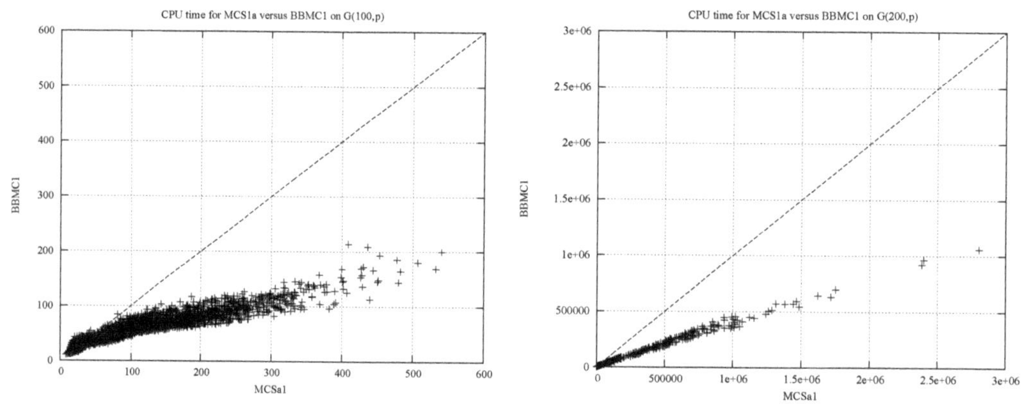

Figure 7 shows on the left the run time of MCSa1 (x-axis) against the run time of BBMC1 (y-axis) in milliseconds on each of the $G(100, p)$ random instances and on the right for $G(200, p)$. The dotted line is the reference $x = y$. If points are below the line then BBMC1 is faster than MCSa1. BBMC1 is typically twice as fast as MCSa1.

In Table 2 we tabulate *Goldilocks* instances from the DIMACS benchmark suite: We remove the instances that are too easy (take less than a second) and those that are too hard (take more than 4 h), leaving those that are "just right" for both algorithms. Under each algorithm, we have: Nodes visited (and this is the same for both algorithms), run time (in seconds), and in brackets the size of the maximum clique. The column on the far right is the ratio of MCSa1's run time over BBMC1's run time, and a value greater than 1 shows that BBMC1 was faster by that amount. Again, we see similar behaviour to that observed over the random problems: BBMC1 is typically twice as fast as MCSa1.

Table 2. DIMACS *Goldilocks* instances: MCSa1 *vs.* BBMC1, nodes, run time in seconds and clique size.

instance	MCSa1			BBMC1			MCSa1/BBMC1
brock200-1	524,723	4	(21)	524,723	2	(21)	2.03
brock400-1	198,359,829	2,888	(27)	198,359,829	1,421	(27)	2.03
brock400-2	145,597,994	2,089	(29)	145,597,994	1,031	(29)	2.03
brock400-3	120,230,513	1,616	(31)	120,230,513	808	(31)	2.00
brock400-4	54,440,888	802	(33)	54,440,888	394	(33)	2.03
brock800-4	640,444,536	12,568	(26)	640,444,536	6,908	(26)	1.82
MANN-a27	38,019	6	(126)	38,019	1	(126)	4.12
MANN-a45	2,851,572	3,766	(345)	2,851,572	542	(345)	6.94
p-hat1000-1	176,576	2	(10)	176,576	1	(10)	1.80
p-hat1000-2	34,473,978	1,401	(46)	34,473,978	720	(46)	1.95
p-hat1500-1	1,184,526	14	(12)	1,184,526	9	(12)	1.52
p-hat300-3	624,947	13	(36)	624,947	5	(36)	2.36
p-hat500-2	114,009	3	(36)	114,009	1	(36)	2.56
p-hat500-3	39,260,458	1,381	(50)	39,260,458	606	(50)	2.28
p-hat700-2	750,903	27	(44)	750,903	12	(44)	2.20
san1000	150,725	10	(15)	150,725	5	(15)	1.76
san200-0.9-2	229,567	5	(60)	229,567	2	(60)	2.36
san200-0.9-3	6,815,145	111	(44)	6,815,145	50	(44)	2.20
san400-0.7-1	119,356	2	(40)	119,356	1	(40)	2.04
san400-0.7-2	889,125	19	(30)	889,125	9	(30)	2.12
san400-0.7-3	521,410	10	(22)	521,410	5	(22)	2.10
san400-0.9-1	4,536,723	422	(100)	4,536,723	125	(100)	3.37
sanr200-0.9	14,921,850	283	(42)	14,921,850	123	(42)	2.30
sanr400-0.5	320,110	2	(13)	320,110	1	(13)	1.85
sanr400-0.7	64,412,015	711	(21)	64,412,015	365	(21)	1.95

Figure 8. The effect of style on MCQ, MCSa and MCSb. On the left $G(100, p)$ and on the right $G(150, p)$. Plotted is search effort in nodes against edge probability. The top two plots are for MCQ, middle plots MCSa and bottom MCSb.

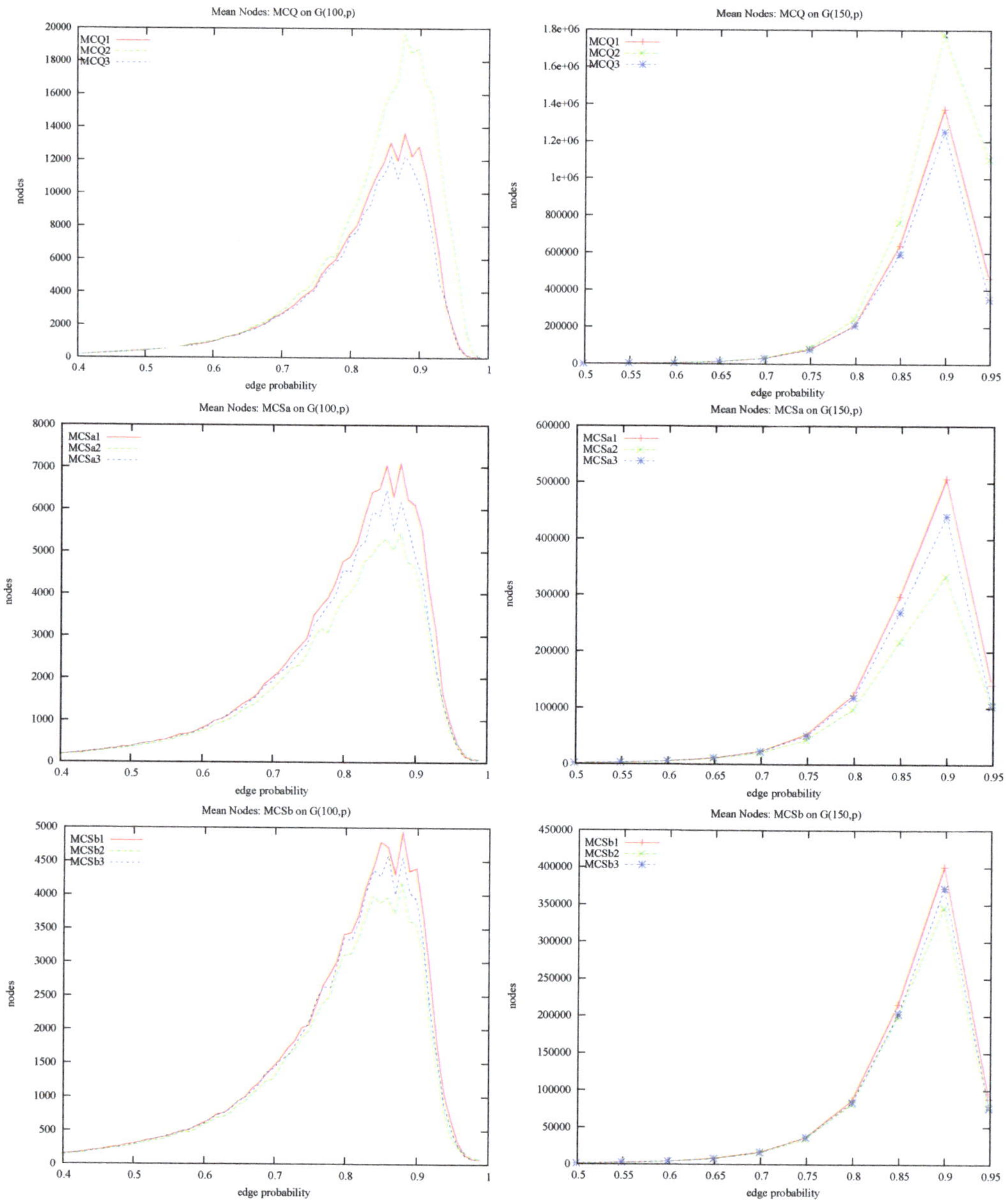

4.3. MCQ and MCS: The Effect of Initial Ordering

What effect does the initial ordering of vertices have on performance? First, we investigate MCQ, MCSa and MCSb with our three orderings: Style 1 being non-decreasing degree, style 2 a minimum width ordering, style 3 non-decreasing degree tie-breaking on the accumulated degree of neighbours. At this stage, we do not consider BBMC, as it is just a BitSet encoding of MCSa. We use random problems $G(n, p)$ with n equal to 100 and 150 with a sample size of 100. This is shown graphically in Figure 8: On the left $G(100, p)$ and on the right $G(150, p)$ with average nodes visited plotted against edge probability. Plots on the first row are for MCQ, middle row MCSa and bottom MCSb. For MCQ style 3 is the winner and style 2 is worst, whereas in MCSa and MCSb style 2 is always best. Why is this? In MCQ, the candidate set is ordered as the result of colouring and this order is then used in the next colouring. Therefore, MCQ gradually disrupts the initial minimum width ordering, but MCSa and MCSb do not (and neither does BBMC). The minimum width ordering (style 2) is best for MCSa, MCSb and BBMC. Note that MCQ3 *is* Tomita's MCR [15] and our experiments on $G(n, p)$ show that MCR (MCQ3) beats MCQ (MCQ1).

Table 3. DIMACS instances: The effect of style on run time in seconds.

	MCQ			MCSa			MCSb			BBMC		
instance	s_1	s_2	s_3	s_1	s_2	s_3	s_1	s_2	s_3	s_1	s_2	s_3
brock200-1	7	5	4	4	3	3	3	3	3	2	1	1
brock400-1	4,471	**3,640**	5,610	2,888	**1,999**	3,752	**2,551**	3,748	2,152	1,421	**983**	1,952
brock400-2	2,923	4,573	**1,824**	2,089	2,415	**1,204**	**1,199**	2,695	2,647	1,031	1,230	**616**
brock400-3	2,322	2,696	**1,491**	1,616	1,404	**1,027**	**1,234**	2,817	2,117	808	711	**534**
brock400-4	1,117	**574**	1,872	802	**338**	1,283	1,209	1,154	**607**	394	**158**	651
brock800-1	—	—	—	—	—	—	—	—	—	—	—	—
brock800-2	—	—	—	—	—	—	—	—	—	—	—	—
brock800-3	—	—	—	—	—	—	—	—	—	—	**9,479**	12,815
brock800-4	—	—	—	**12,568**	13,502	—	**13,924**	—	—	**6,908**	7,750	12,992
hamming10-4	—	—	—	—	—	—	—	—	—	—	—	—
johnson32-2-4	—	—	—	—	—	—	—	—	—	—	—	—
keller5	—	—	—	—	—	—	—	—	—	—	—	—
keller6	—	—	—	—	—	—	—	—	—	—	—	—
MANN-a27	9	9	9	6	7	6	8	7	8	1	1	1
MANN-a45	**4,989**	5,369	4,999	3,766	**3,539**	3,733	4,118	**3,952**	4,242	**542**	580	554
MANN-a81	—	—	—	—	—	—	—	—	—	—	—	—
p-hat1000-1	2	2	1	2	2	2	2	2	2	1	1	1
p-hat1000-2	—	—	—	1,401	**861**	1,481	7,565	8,459	**6,606**	720	**431**	763
p-hat1000-3	—	—	—	—	—	—	—	—	—	—	—	—
p-hat1500-1	16	16	15	14	15	15	14	14	16	9	9	10
p-hat1500-2	—	—	—	—	—	—	—	—	—	—	—	—
p-hat300-3	74	127	**69**	13	**10**	12	21	24	**18**	5	**4**	5
p-hat500-3	—	—	—	1,381	**660**	1,122	**4,945**	6,982	5,167	606	**282**	500
p-hat700-2	508	551	**353**	27	25	**24**	**74**	93	108	12	11	11
p-hat700-3	—	—	—	—	**12,244**	—	—	—	—	6,754	**5,693**	7,000
san1000	20	19	18	10	10	10	3	3	3	5	5	5
san200-0.9-2	**20**	73	35	5	**1**	5	1	1	1	2	**0**	2
san200-0.9-3	154	**4**	59	111	**0**	65	32	**3**	8	50	**0**	27
san400-0.7-1	1	5	2	2	17	4	3	0	1	1	8	1
san400-0.7-2	**14**	47	16	**19**	26	23	16	9	**4**	**9**	11	10
san400-0.7-3	**11**	38	41	**10**	22	39	**5**	13	19	**5**	9	18
san400-0.9-1	—	—	—	**422**	—	8,854	54	**0**	—	**125**	—	3,799
sanr200-0.7	1	2	1	1	1	1	1	1	1	0	0	0
sanr200-0.9	**892**	1,782	1,083	283	**229**	364	245	**227**	444	123	**104**	164
sanr400-0.5	2	2	2	2	2	2	2	2	2	1	1	1
sanr400-0.7	979	1,075	**975**	711	**608**	719	**650**	660	674	365	**326**	369

We now report on the 66 DIMACS instances [31], Tables 3 and 4. Table 3 gives run times in seconds. An entry of "—" corresponds to the CPU time limit of 14,400 s being exceeded and the search terminating early. Problems that took less than a second have been excluded from the tables. For each algorithm we have three columns, one for each *style*: First column s_1 is style 1 with vertices in non-increasing degree order, s_2 is style 2 with vertices in minimum width order, s_3 is style 3 with vertices in non-increasing degree order tie-breaking on sum of neighbouring degrees.

Table 4. DIMACS instances: The effect of style on search nodes in 1,000,000's.

	MCQ			MCSa			MCSb			BBMC		
instance	s_1	s_2	s_3	s_1	s_2	s_3	s_1	s_2	s_3	s_1	s_2	s_3
brock200-1	0.86	0.59	0.51	50.52	0.30	0.32	**0.24**	0.26	0.27	0.52	0.30	0.32
brock400-1	342.5	266.2	455.3	198.4	132.8	278.9	142.3	208.6	**114.8**	198.4	132.8	278.9
brock400-2	224.8	381.9	125.2	145.6	178.5	76.4	**61.3**	151.8	154.3	145.6	178.5	76.4
brock400-3	194.4	214.0	114.7	120.2	101.6	72.8	**70.3**	163.5	125.5	120.2	101.6	72.8
brock400-4	82.1	36.5	148.3	54.4	**19.3**	90.9	68.3	62.7	31.9	54.4	**19.3**	90.9
brock800-1	—	—	—	—	—	—	—	—	—	—	—	—
brock800-2	—	—	—	—	—	—	—	—	—	—	—	—
brock800-3	—	—	—	—	—	—	—	—	—	—	**949.4**	1,369.1
brock800-4	—	—	—	**640.4**	773.3	—	659.1	—	—	**640.4**	773.3	1,440.8
hamming10-4	—	—	—	—	—	—	—	—	—	—	—	—
johnson32-2-4	—	—	—	—	—	—	—	—	—	—	—	—
keller5	—	—	—	—	—	—	—	—	—	—	—	—
keller6	—	—	—	—	—	—	—	—	—	—	—	—
MANN-a27	0.038	0.038	0.038	0.038	0.038	0.038	0.038	**0.034**	0.038	0.038	0.038	0.038
MANN-a45	2.9	2.9	2.9	2.9	2.9	2.8	2.5	**2.4**	2.5	2.9	2.9	2.8
MANN-a81	—	—	—	—	—	—	—	—	—	—	—	—
p-hat1000-1	2.4	2.5	2.4	1.8	1.7	1.8	1.5	**1.48**	**1.48**	1.8	1.7	1.8
p-hat1000-2	—	—	—	34.5	**19.2**	36.9	166.7	177.9	142.0	34.5	**19.2**	36.9
p-hat1000-3	—	—	—	—	—	—	—	—	—	—	—	—
p-hat1500-1	1.6	1.8	1.9	1.2	1.2	1.4	1.0	**0.9**	1.2	1.2	1.2	1.4
p-hat1500-2	—	—	—	—	—	—	—	—	—	—	—	—
p-hat300-3	3.8	7.1	4.0	0.62	**0.49**	0.64	0.71	0.82	0.64	0.62	**0.49**	0.64
p-hat500-3	—	—	—	39.3	**16.9**	30.9	104.7	152.8	111.6	39.3	**16.9**	30.9
p-hat700-2	18.9	19.0	12.8	0.75	0.63	**0.59**	1.5	1.9	2.2	0.75	0.63	**0.59**
p-hat700-3	—	—	—	—	**216.5**	—	—	—	—	282.4	**216.5**	297.1
san1000	0.30	0.31	0.29	0.15	0.15	0.15	0.05	**0.05**	**0.05**	0.15	0.15	0.15
san200-0.9-2	1.1	4.3	2.1	0.23	0.06	0.24	0.06	0.05	**0.03**	0.23	0.06	0.23
san200-0.9-3	8.3	0.23	3.2	6.8	**0.01**	3.6	1.2	0.12	0.24	6.8	**0.01**	3.6
san400-0.7-1	0.06	0.12	0.09	0.12	0.66	0.15	0.13	**0.01**	0.05	0.12	0.66	0.15
san400-0.7-2	0.61	1.7	0.67	0.89	0.88	0.93	0.75	0.31	**0.16**	0.89	0.88	0.93
san400-0.7-3	0.58	1.9	2.3	0.52	0.92	1.9	**0.22**	0.55	0.99	0.52	0.92	1.9
san400-0.9-1	—	—	—	4.5	—	220.2	0.58	**0.02**	—	4.5	—	220.2
sanr200-0.7	0.21	0.29	0.22	0.15	0.18	0.16	**0.10**	0,12	0.11	0.15	0.18	0.16
sanr200-0.9	44.5	101.0	62.2	14.9	12.5	20.6	9.7	**8.1**	19.0	14.9	12.5	20.6
sanr400-0.5	0.38	0.42	0.35	0.32	0.32	0.30	**0.19**	0.18	0.20	0.32	0.32	0.30
sanr400-0.7	101.2	106.7	101.5	64.4	54.4	64.1	46.1	**44.9**	48.7	64.4	54.4	64.1

Table 4 gives the number of nodes, in millions, for the experiments in Table 3. In Table 3 a **bold** entry is the best run time for that algorithm against the problem instance, and this is done only when run times differ significantly. For MCQ there is no particular style that is a consistent winner. This is a surprise as MCQ3 is Tomita's MCR and in [15] it is claimed that MCR was faster than MCQ. The evidence that supports this claim is Table 2 of [15], 8 of the 66 DIMACS instances. For MCSa and BBMC style 2 is best more often than not, and in MCSb style 1 is best more often than not. Overall we see that the BBMC2 is our best algorithm, *i.e.*, BBMC with a minimum width ordering.

4.4. More Benchmarks (not DIMACS)

In [16] experiments are performed on counting maximal cliques in exceptionally large sparse graphs, such as the Pajek data sets (graphs with hundreds of thousands of vertices) and SNAP data sets (graphs with vertices in the millions) [35]. Those graphs are out of the reach of the exact algorithms reported here. The initial reason for this is space consumption. To tackle such large sparse problems, we require a change of representation, away from the adjacency matrix and towards the adjacency lists as used in [16]. Therefore we explore large random instances as in [11,13] to further investigate ordering and the effect of the BitSet representation, the hard solvable instances in BHOSLIB to see how far we can go, and structured graphs produced via the SNAP (Stanford Network Analysis Project) graph generator. We start with BHOSLIB.

In Table 5 we have the only instances from the BHOSLIB suite (Benchmarks with Hidden Optimum Solutions [36]) that could be solved in 4 hours. Each instance has a maximum clique of size 30. A **bold** entry is the best run time. For this suite, we see that with respect to style there is no clear winner.

Table 5. BHOSLIB using BBMC: 1,000's of nodes and run time in seconds. Problems have 450 vertices and graph density 0.82.

instance	n	edges	BBMC1		BBMC2		BBMC3	
frb30-15-1	450	83,198	292,095	**3,099**	626,833	6,503	361,949	3,951
frb30-15-2	450	83,151	557,252	5,404	599,543	6,136	436,110	**4,490**
frb30-15-3	450	83,126	167,116	1,707	265,157	2,700	118,495	**1,309**
frb30-15-4	450	83,194	991,460	9,663	861,391	**8,513**	1,028,129	9,781
frb30-15-5	450	83,231	282,763	2,845	674,987	7,033	281,152	**2,802**

Table 6 shows results on large random problems. Similar experiments are reported in Tables 4 and 5 of [11] and Table 2 in [13]. The first three columns are the nodes visited, and this is the same for MCSa and BBMC. Run times are then given in seconds for MCSa and BBMC using each of the three styles. Highlighted in **bold** is the search of fewest nodes and this is style 2 (minimum width ordering) in all but one case. Comparing the run times, we see that as problems get larger, involving more vertices, the relative speed difference between BBMC and MCSa diminishes, and at $n = 15,000$ the performances of MCSa and BBMC are essentially the same. This was also observed in [10] and is expected: As problems get larger the BitSet requires more words to represent the set, and with more words the number of iterations within the BitSet increases.

Table 6. Large random graphs, sample size 10.

instance		nodes			MCSa			BBMC		
n	p	s_1	s_2	s_3	s_1	s_2	s_3	s_1	s_2	s_3
1,000	0.1	4,536	**4,472**	4,563	0	0	0	0	0	0
	0.2	39,478	**38,250**	38,838	0	0	0	0	0	0
	0.3	400,018	**371,360**	404,948	4	4	4	2	2	2
	0.4	3,936,761	**3,780,737**	4,052,677	40	39	38	26	25	26
	0.5	79,603,712	**75,555,478**	80,018,645	860	910	859	570	574	604
3,000	0.1	144,375	**142,719**	145,487	3	3	3	2	2	2
	0.2	2,802,011	**2,723,443**	2,804,830	38	38	38	32	32	32
	0.3	73,086,978	**71,653,889**	73,354,584	964	960	978	926	930	931
10,000	0.1	5,351,591	**5,303,615**	5,432,812	236	252	245	212	216	214
15,000	0.1	22,077,212	21,751,100	**21,694,036**	1,179	1,117	1,081	1,249	1,235	1,208

The graphgen program was downloaded from the SNAP web site and modified to use a random seed so that generated graphs with the same parameters were actually different. This allows us to generate a variety of graphs, such as complete graphs, star graphs, 2D grid graphs, Erdós–Rënyi random graphs with an exact number of edges, k-regular graphs (each vertex with degree k), Albert–Barbasi graphs, power law graphs, Klienberg copying model graphs and small-world graphs. Finding maximum cliques in a complete graph, star graph and 2D grid graph is trivial. Similarly, and surprisingly, small scale experiments suggested that Albert–Barbasi and Klienberg's graphs are also easy with respect to maximum clique. However k-regular and small world are a challenge.

Figure 9. k-Regular SNAP instances $KR(200, k)$, $130 \leq k \leq 160$, sample size 20.

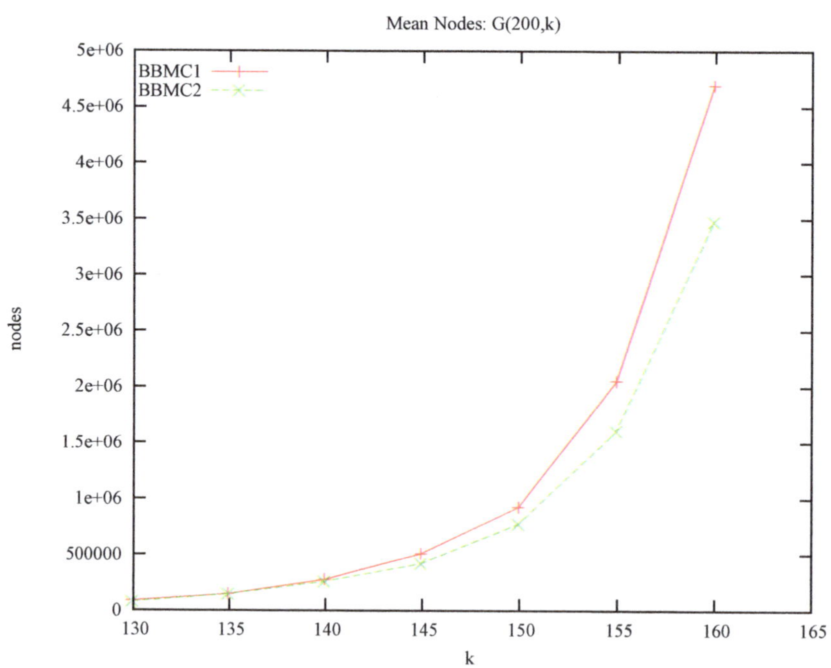

The SNAP graphgen program was used to generated k-regular graphs $KR(n,k)$, *i.e.*, random graphs with n vertices each with degree k. Graphs were generated with $n = 200$ and $50 \leq k \leq 160$, with k varying in steps of 5, 20 instances at each point. BBMC1 and BBMC2 were then applied to each instance. Obviously, with style equal to 1 or 3, there is no heuristic information to be exploited at the top of search. But would a minimum width ordering, style 2, have an advantage? Figure 9 shows average search effort in nodes plotted against uniform degree k. We see that minimum width ordering does indeed have an advantage. What is also of interest is that $KR(n,k)$ instances tend to be harder than their $G(n,p)$ equivalents. For example, we can compare $KR(200,160)$ with $G(200,0.8)$ in Figure 6: MCSa1 took on average 1.9 million nodes for $G(200,0.8)$ and BBMC1 took on average 4.7 million nodes on the twenty $KR(200,160)$ instances.

Figure 10. Small world graphs $SW(200,k,p)$: (upper) search effort, (lower) maximum clique size.

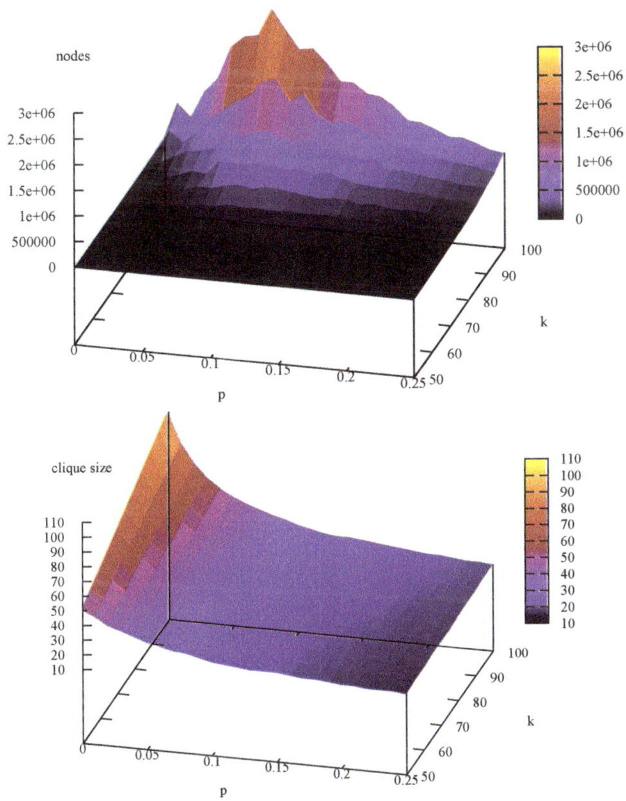

Small-World graphs $SW(n,k,p)$ were then generated using graphgen. This takes three parameters: n the number of vertices, k where each vertex is connected to k nearest neighbours to the right in a ring topology (*i.e.*, vertices start with uniform degree $2k$), and p a rewiring probability. This corresponds to the graphs in Figure 1 of [32]. Small-World graphs were generated with $n = 1{,}000$, $50 \leq k \leq 100$ in steps of 5, $0.0 \leq p \leq 0.25$ in steps of 0.01, 10 graphs at each point. BBMC1 was then applied to each instance to investigate how difficulty of finding a maximum clique varies with respect to k and p and also how size of maximum clique varies, *i.e.*, this is an investigation of the problem. The results are shown as three dimensional plots in Figure 10: The graph above is average search effort and below average maximum clique size. Looking at the graph above: When $p = 0.0$ problems are easy; as p increases and randomness is introduced, the problems quickly get hard, but as p continues to increase the graphs tend to become predominantly random and behave more like large sparse random graphs and get easier. We also see that as neighbourhood size k increases, the problems get harder. We can compare the $SW(1000, 100, p)$ to the graphs $G(1000, 0.2)$ in Table 6: $G(1000, 0.2)$ took on average 39,478 nodes whereas $SW(1000, 100, 0.01)$ took 709,347 nodes, $SW(1000, 100, 0.08)$ took 2,702,199 nodes and $SW(1000, 100, 0.25)$ 354,430 nodes. Clearly small-world instances are relatively hard. Looking at the graph below (average maximum clique size), we see that as rewiring probability p increases maximum cliques size decreases, and as k increases so too does maximum clique size.

4.5. Calibration of Results

To compare computational results across publications a standard C program, dfmax, is compiled and run against a set of benchmarks. These run times are then used as a conversion factor, and the results are then taken from one publication, scaled accordingly, and then included in another publication. Recent examples of this are [7] including rescaled results from [33]; [9] including rescaled results from [7], [14] and [4]; [15] including rescaled results from [7] and [33]; [11] including rescaled results from [5]; [10] including rescaled results from [11]; [6] including rescaled results from [9,15]. Is this procedure safe?

To test this we take two additional machines, Fais and Daleview, and calibrate them with respect to our reference machine Cyprus. We then run experiments on each machine using the Java implementations of the algorithms implemented here against some of the DIMACS benchmarks. These results are then rescaled. If the rescaling gives substantially different results from those on the reference machine, this would suggest that this technique is not safe.

Table 7. Conversion factors using dfmax on three machines: Cyprus, Fais and Daleview.

machine	r100.5	r200.5	r300.5	r400.5	r500.5	Intel(R)	GHz	cache	Java	scaling factor
Cyprus	0.0	0.02	0.24	1.49	5.58	Xeon(R) E5620	2.40	12,288KB	1.6.0_07	1
Fais	0.0	0.08	0.58	3.56	13.56	XEON(TM) CPU	2.40	512KB	1.5.0_06	0.41
Daleview	0.0	0.09	0.53	3.00	10.95	Atom(TM) N280	1.66	512KB	1.6.0_18	0.50

Table 7 gives a "Rosetta Stone" for the three machines used in this study. The standard program dfmax [37] was compiled using gcc and the -O2 compiler option on each machine and then run on the benchmarks r* on each machine. Run times in seconds are tabulated for the five benchmark instances, each machine's /proc/cpuinfo is given and a conversion factor relative to the reference machine Cyprus is then computed in the same manner as that reported in [11] ("... the first two graphs from the benchmark were removed (user time was considered too small) and the rest of the times averaged ..."). Therefore when rescaling the run times from Fais, we multiply the actual run time by 0.41 and for Daleview by 0.50.

Table 8 shows the results of the calibration experiments. Tabulated are a subset of DIMACS instances that took more than 1 s and less than 2 h to solve using MCSa1 on our second slowest machine (Fais).

Run times are tabulated in milliseconds (in brackets) and the actual ratio of Cyprus-time over Fais-time (expected to be 0.41) is given as well as Cyprus-time over Daleview-time (expected to be 0.50) for each data point. Two algorithms are used, MCSa1 and BBMC1. The last row of Table 8 gives the relative performance ratios computed using the sum of the run times in the table. Referring back to Table 7 we expect a Cyprus/Fais ratio of 0.41 but empirically get 0.12 when using MCSa1 and 0.14 when using BBMC1. We expect a Cyprus/Daleview ratio of 0.50 but empirically get an average 0.26 with MCSa1 and 0.10 with BBMC1. The conversion factors in Table 7 consistently overestimate the speed of Fais and Daleview. For example, we would expect MCSa1 applied to brock200-1 on Fais to have a run time of $19,343 \times 0.41 = 7,930$ milliseconds on Cyprus. In fact it takes 4,777 milliseconds. If we use the derived ratio in the last row of Table 8 we get $19,343 \times 0.12 = 2,321$ milliseconds. As another example, consider san1000 using BBMC1 on Daleview. We would expect this to take $54,816 \times 0.50 = 27,408$ milliseconds on Cyprus. In fact it takes 5,927 milliseconds! If we use the conversion ratio from the last row of Table 8, we get a more accurate estimate $54,816 \times 0.10 = 5,481$ milliseconds.

Table 8. Calibration experiments using 3 machines, 2 algorithms and a subset of DIMACS.

	MCSa1						BBMC1					
instance	**Fais**		**Daleview**		**Cyprus**		**Fais**		**Daleview**		**Cyprus**	
brock200-1	0.25	(19,343)	0.27	(17,486)	1.00	(4,777)	0.15	(15,365)	0.09	(25,048)	1.00	(2,358)
brock200-4	0.40	(1,870)	0.43	(1,765)	1.00	(755)	0.20	(1,592)	0.13	(2,464)	1.00	(321)
hamming10-2	0.18	(1,885)	0.14	(2,299)	1.00	(333)	0.25	(608)	0.21	(710)	1.00	(151)
hamming8-4	0.24	(1,885)	0.28	(1,647)	1.00	(455)	0.23	(1,625)	0.19	(1,925)	1.00	(367)
johnson16-2-4	0.35	(2,327)	0.38	(2,173)	1.00	(823)	0.26	(1,896)	0.14	(3,560)	1.00	(495)
MANN-a27	0.21	(32,281)	0.22	(31,874)	1.00	(6,912)	0.14	(12,335)	0.10	(16,491)	1.00	(1,676)
p-hat1000-1	0.25	(8,431)	0.28	(7,413)	1.00	(2,108)	0.14	(8,359)	0.12	(9,389)	1.00	(1,169)
p-hat1500-1	0.19	(77,759)	0.22	(66,113)	1.00	(14,421)	0.11	(90,417)	0.10	(92,210)	1.00	(9,516)
p-hat300-3	0.25	(53,408)	0.26	(51,019)	1.00	(13,486)	0.14	(41,669)	0.09	(60,118)	1.00	(5,711)
p-hat500-2	0.27	(13,400)	0.30	(12,091)	1.00	(3,659)	0.14	(10,177)	0.11	(13,410)	1.00	(1,428)
p-hat700-1	0.40	(1,615)	0.51	(1,251)	1.00	(641)	0.29	(1,169)	0.24	(1,422)	1.00	(344)
san1000	0.11	(94,107)	0.12	(89,330)	1.00	(10,460)	0.10	(57,868)	0.11	(54,816)	1.00	(5,927)
san200-0.9-1	0.29	(4,918)	0.31	(4,705)	1.00	(1,444)	0.18	(4,201)	0.11	(6,588)	1.00	(748)
san200-0.9-2	0.22	(23,510)	0.25	(20,867)	1.00	(5,240)	0.15	(14,572)	0.09	(23,592)	1.00	(2,218)
san400-0.7-1	0.25	(10,230)	0.27	(9,607)	1.00	(2,573)	0.15	(8,314)	0.12	(10,206)	1.00	(1,260)
san400-0.7-2	0.23	(84,247)	0.27	(72,926)	1.00	(19,565)	0.13	(71,360)	0.11	(87,325)	1.00	(9,219)
san400-0.7-3	0.24	(45,552)	0.27	(40,792)	1.00	(10,839)	0.13	(39,840)	0.11	(46,818)	1.00	(5,162)
sanr200-0.7	0.31	(5,043)	0.33	(4,676)	1.00	(1,548)	0.19	(4,079)	0.12	(6,652)	1.00	(795)
sanr200-0.9	0.23	(1,249,144)	0.23	(1,211,762)	1.00	(283,681)	0.15	(844,487)	0.09	(1,409,428)	1.00	(123,461)
sanr400-0.5	0.28	(9,898)	0.31	(8,754)	1.00	(2,745)	0.16	(9,177)	0.12	(12,658)	1.00	(1,484)
sanr400-0.7	0.10	(7,292,771)	0.28	(2,544,196)	1.00	(711,861)	0.14	(2,698,444)	0.10	(3,737,833)	1.00	(365,629)
ratio (total)	0.12	(9,033,624)	0.26	(4,202,746)	1.00	(1,098,326)	0.14	(3,937,554)	0.10	(5,622,663)	1.00	(539,439)

But maybe this is because we have used a C program (dfmax) to calibrate a Java program. Would we get a reliable calibration if a C program was used? Östergård's Cliquer program was downloaded and compiled on our three machines and run against DIMACS benchmarks, *i.e.*, the experiments in Table 8 were repeated using Cliquer and dfmax with a different, and easier, set of problems. The results are shown in Table 9 were an entry "—" was a run of dfmax that was terminated after 2 minutes. What we see is an actual scaling factor of 0.62 for Cliquer on Fais when dfmax predicts 0.41 and for Cliquer on Daleview 0.26 when we expect 0.50; again we see that the rescaling procedure fails. The last three columns show a dfmax calibration using problems other than the r* benchmarks and here we see an error of about 5% on Fais (expected 0.41, actual 0.39) and about 16% on Daleview (expected 0.50, actual 0.43). Therefore, it appears that rescaling results using dfmax and the five r* benchmarks is not a safe procedure and can result in wrong conclusions being drawn regarding the relative performance of algorithms.

4.6. Relative Algorithmic Performance on Different Machines

But is it even safe to draw conclusions on our algorithms when we base those conclusions on experiments performed on a single machine? Previously, in Table 2 we compared MCSa against BBMC on our reference machine Cyprus and concluded that BBMC was typically twice as fast as MCSa. Will that hold on Fais and on Daleview? Table 10 takes the data from Table 8 and divides the run time of MCSa by BBMC for each instance on our three machines. On Fais BBMC is rarely more than 50% faster than MCSa and on Daleview BBMC is slower than MCSa more often than not! If experiments were performed only on Daleview using only the DIMACS instances, we might draw entirely different conclusions and claim that BBMC is slower than MCSa. This change in relative algorithmic ordering has been observed on five different machines (four using the Java 1.6.0) using all of the algorithms. The -server and -client options were also tried. The -server option sometimes gave speedups of a factor of 2, sometimes a factor of 0.5, and this can also affect relative algorithmic performance.

Table 9. Calibration experiments for Cliquer and dfmax using 3 machines.

	Cliquer						dfmax					
instance	Fais		Daleview		Cyprus		Fais		Daleview		Cyprus	
brock200-1	0.66	(9,760)	0.43	(18,710)	1.00	(6,490)	0.39	(25,150)	0.42	(23,020)	1.00	(9,730)
brock200-4	0.64	(690)	0.47	(1,190)	1.00	(440)	0.41	(1,510)	0.46	(1,360)	1.00	(620)
p-hat1000-1	0.62	(1,750)	0.36	(3,020)	1.00	(1,090)	0.41	(1,680)	0.45	(1,540)	1.00	(690)
p-hat700-1	0.67	(150)	0.37	(270)	1.00	(100)	—	—	—	—	—	—
san1000	0.75	(120)	0.30	(300)	1.00	(90)	—	—	—	—	—	—
san200-0.7-1	0.48	(1,750)	0.20	(4,220)	1.00	(840)	—	—	—	—	—	—
san200-0.9-2	0.61	(18,850)	0.21	(53,970)	1.00	(11,530)	—	—	—	—	—	—
san400-0.7-3	0.62	(6,800)	0.26	(16,100)	1.00	(4,230)	—	—	—	—	—	—
sanr200-0.7	0.65	(2,940)	0.36	(5,270)	1.00	(1,900)	0.40	(5,240)	0.44	(4,770)	1.00	(2,080)
sanr400-0.5	0.62	(1,490)	0.38	(2,420)	1.00	(930)	0.41	(3,550)	0.47	(3,080)	1.00	(1,460)
ratio (total)	0.62	(44,300)	0.26	(105,470)	1.00	(27,640)	0.39	(37,130)	0.43	(33,770)	1.00	(14,580)

5. Conclusions

We have seen that small implementation details (in MC) can result in large changes in performance. Modern programming languages with rich constructs and large libraries of utilities make it easier for the programmer to do this. We have also drifted away from the days when algorithms were presented along with their implementation code (examples here are [8,23]) to presenting algorithms only in pseudo-code. Fortunately we are moving into a new era where code is being made publicly available (examples here are Östergård's Cliquer and Konc and Janežič's MaxCliqueDyn) via the web. Hopefully this will grow and allow Computer Scientist to be better able to perform reproducible empirical studies.

Tomita [13] presented MCS as an improvement on MCR brought about via two modifications: (1) a static colour ordering and (2) a colour repair step. Our study has shown that modification (1) improves performance and (2) degrades performance, *i.e.*, MCSa is better than MCSb.

Table 10. Calibration experiment part 2, does hardware affect relative algorithmic performance? Values greater than 1 imply BBMC is faster than MCSa, and values less than 1 imply MCSa is faster.

instance	Fais	Daleview	Cyprus
brock200-1	1.26	0.70	2.03
brock200-4	1.17	0.72	2.35
hamming10-2	3.10	3.24	2.21
hamming8-4	1.16	0.86	1.24
johnson16-2-4	1.23	0.61	1.66
MANN-a27	2.62	1.93	4.12
p-hat1000-1	1.01	0.79	1.80
p-hat1500-1	0.86	0.72	1.52
p-hat300-3	1.28	0.85	2.36
p-hat500-2	1.32	0.90	2.56
p-hat700-1	1.38	0.88	1.86
san1000	1.63	1.63	1.76
san200-0.9-1	1.17	0.71	1.93
san200-0.9-2	1.61	0.88	2.36
san400-0.7-1	1.23	0.94	2.04
san400-0.7-2	1.18	0.84	2.12
san400-0.7-3	1.14	0.87	2.10
sanr200-0.7	1.24	0.70	1.95
sanr200-0.9	1.48	0.86	2.30
sanr400-0.5	1.08	0.69	1.85
sanr400-0.7	2.70	0.68	1.95

BBMC is algorithm MCSa with sets represented as bit strings, *i.e.*, BitSet is used rather than ArrayList. Experiments on the reference machine showed a speedup typically of a factor of 2. The three styles of ordering were investigated. The orderings were quickly disrupted by MCQ, but in the other algorithms minimum width ordering was the best in random problems, whereas in the DIMACS instances there was no clear winner.

New benchmark problems (*i.e.*, problems rarely investigated by the maximum clique community) were investigated such as BHOSLIB, k-regular and small-world graphs. Motivation for this study was partly to compare algorithms but also to explore these problems to determine if and when they are hard.

Finally, we demonstrated that the standard procedure for calibrating machines and rescaling results is unsafe, and that running our own code on different machines can lead to different relative algorithmic performance. This is disturbing. First, it suggests that to perform a fair and reliable empirical study we should not rescale others' results: We must either code up the algorithms ourselves, as done here and also by Carmo and Züge [2], or download and run code on our machines. Secondly, we should run our experiments on different machines.

All the codes used in this study are available online [34] along with instructions on how to run the code, the DIMACS instances, random problem generator and runtime results.

Appendix

At the top of MCQ's search, Tomita [12] sorts vertices in non-increasing degree order and the first Δ vertices are given colours 1 to Δ respectively, where Δ is the maximum degree in the graph, thereafter vertices are given colour $\Delta + 1$. This is done to *prime* the candidate set for the initial call to EXPAND. Thereafter Tomita calls NUMBER-SORT immediately before the recursive call to EXPAND. A simpler option is taken here: colouring and sorting of the candidate set is done only at the start of *expand*. Using graph g10–50 as an example, in Figure 2 of [12] vertices would initially be selected in the order [7,9,8,5,2,1,6,4,0,3] with colours respectively [6,6,6,6,6,5,4,3,2,1], *i.e.*, using 6 colours. Here vertices are selected in order [9,8,5,7,2,1,6,4,0,3] with colours [4,3,3,2,2,2,2,1,1,1], *i.e.*, using 4 colours, a tighter upper bound and vertices no longer in degree order.

Figure 11. The effect of Tomita's initial colour ordering.

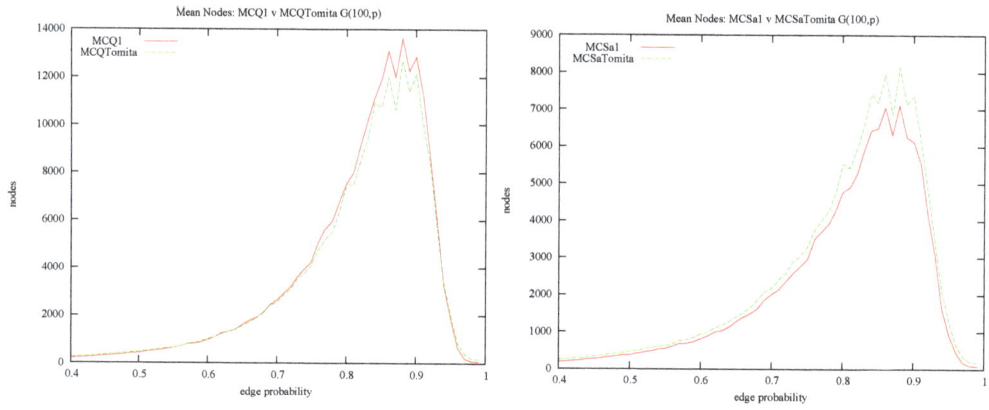

Listing 13 presents a Java implementation of MCQ as described in [12] but in our framework. Lines 18 to 20 give an initial colour to the sorted vertices. Method $numberSort$ is now called *after* the selection of a vertex (line 40). A similar change was made to MCSa. Figure 11 shows the effect of the initial colour ordering, using $G(100, p)$ on calls to *expand* (nodes). We see on the left that Tomita's MCQ is marginally better than MCQ1 and on the right that MCSa1 is better than Tomita's equivalent (and we see a similar improvement in BBMC1). In conclusion, the approach adopted here is simpler, using a single colour-ordering procedure. In MCQ1 the effect on performance is detrimental but small, and in MCSa1 (and BBMC1a) it is beneficial.

Acknowledgements

I would like to thank Pablo San Segundo, Jeremy Singer, Ciaran McCreesh and my reviewers.

Listing 13. MCQTomita.

```
import java.util.*;

class MCQTomita extends MC {

    MCQTomita (int n,int[][]A,int[] degree,int style) {
        super(n,A,degree,style);
    }

    void search(){
        cpuTime                                = System.currentTimeMillis();
        nodes                                  = 0;
        colourClass                            = new ArrayList[n];
        ArrayList<Integer> C                   = new ArrayList<Integer>(n);
        ArrayList<Integer> P                   = new ArrayList<Integer>(n);
        for (int i=0;i<n;i++) colourClass[i] = new ArrayList<Integer>(n);
        orderVertices(P);
        int[] colour = new int[P.size()];
        int maxDeg = degree[P.get(0)];
        for (int i=0;i<maxDeg;i++) colour[i] = i+1;
        for (int i=maxDeg;i<n;i++) colour[i] = maxDeg+1;
        expand(C,P,colour);
    }

    void expand(ArrayList<Integer> C, ArrayList<Integer> P,int[] colour){
        if (timeLimit > 0 && System.currentTimeMillis() - cpuTime >= timeLimit) return;
        nodes++;
        int m = P.size();
        for (int i=m-1;i>=0;i--){
            if (C.size() + colour[i] <= maxSize) return;
            int v = P.get(i);
            C.add(v);
            ArrayList<Integer> newP = new ArrayList<Integer>(i);
            for (int j=0;j<=i;j++){
                int u = P.get(j);
                if (A[u][v] == 1) newP.add(u);
            }
            if (newP.isEmpty() && C.size() > maxSize) saveSolution(C);
            if (!newP.isEmpty()){
                int[] newColour = new int[newP.size()];
                numberSort(C,newP,newP,newColour);
                expand(C,newP,newColour);
            }
            C.remove(C.size()-1);
            P.remove(i);
        }
    }
}
```

References

1. Garey, M.R.; Johnson, D.S. *Computers and Intractability*; W.H. Freeman and Co.: New York, NY, USA, 1979.
2. Renato, C.; Alexandre P. Z. Branch and bound algorithms for the maximum clique problem under a unified framework. *J. Braz. Comp. Soc.* **2012**, *18*, pp. 137–151.

3. Randy, C.; Panos M.P. An exact algorithm for the maximum clique problem. *Oper. Res. Lett.* **1990**, *9*, 375–382.
4. Torsten, F. Simple and Fast: Improving a Branch-and-Bound Algorithm for Maximum Clique. In *Proceedings of the ESA 2002*, *LNCS 2461*, Rome, Italy, 17–21 September 2002; pp. 485–498.
5. Janez, K.; Dušanka, J. An improved branch and bound algorithm for the maximum clique problem. *MATCH Commun. Math. Comput. Chem.* **2007**, *58*, pp. 569–590. Available online: http://www.sicmm.org/ konc/ (accessed on 12 November 2012).
6. Chu, M.; Li, Z.Q. An Efficient Branch-and-Bound Algorithm Based on Maxsat for the Maximum Clique Problem. In *Proceedings of the AAAI'10*, Atlanta, GA, USA, 11–15 July 2010; pp. 128–133.
7. Östergård, P.R.J. A fast algorithm for the maximum clique problem. *Discret. Appl. Math.* **2002**, *120*, pp. 197–207. Available online: http://users.tkk.fi/pat/cliquer.html/ (accessed on 12 November 2012).
8. Pardalos, P.M.; Rodgers, G.P. A branch and bound algorithm for the maximum clique problem. *Comput. Oper. Res.* **1992**, *19*, pp. 363–375.
9. Régin, J.-C. Using Constraint Programming to Solve the Maximum Clique Problem. In *Proceedings CP 2003, LNCS 2833*, Kinsale, Ireland, 29 September–3 October 2003; pp. 634–648.
10. Segundo, P.S.; Matia, F.; Diego, R.-L.; Miguel, H. An improved bit parallel exact maximum clique algorithm. *Optim. Lett.* **2011**, doi:10.1007/s11590-011-0431-y.
11. Segundo, P.S.; Diego, R.-L.; Augustín, J. An exact bit-parallel algorithm for the maximum clique problem. *Comput. Oper. Res* **2011**, *38*, 571–581.
12. Tomita, E.; Sutani, Y.; Higashi, T.; Takahashi, S.; Wakatsuki, M. An Efficient Branch-and-Bound Algorithm for Finding a Maximum Clique. In *Proceedings of the DMTCS 2003, LNCS 2731*, Dijon, France, 7–12 July 2003; pp. 278–289.
13. Tomita, E.; Sutani, Y.; Higashi, T.; Takahashi, S.; Wakatsuki, M. A Simple and Faster Branch-and-Bound Algorithm for Finding Maximum Clique. In *Proceedings of the WALCOM 2010, LNCS 5942*, Dhaka, Bangladesh, 10–12 February 2010; pp. 191–203.
14. Wood, D.R. An algorithm for finding a maximum clique in a graph. *Oper. Res. Lett.* **1997**, *21*, 211–217.
15. Tomita, E.; Toshikatsu, K. An efficient branch-and-bound algorithm for finding a maximum clique and computational experiments. *J. Glob. Optim.* **2007**, *37*, 95–111.
16. David, E.; Darren, S. Listing all maximal cliques in large sparse real-world graphs. In *Experimental Algorithms, LNCS 6630. Comput. Sci.* **2011**, *6630*, 364–375.
17. Knuth, D.E. Generating all Combinations and Permutations. In *The Art of Computer Programming*; Pearson Education Inc.: Stoughton, MA, USA, January 2006; Volume 4, pp.1–3.
18. Li, C.M.; Quan, Z. Combining Graph Structure Exploitation and Propositional Reasoning for the Maximum Clique Problem. In *Proceedings of the ICTAI'10*; Arras, France, 27–29 October 2010; Volume 1, pp. 344–351.
19. Bentley, J.L.; McIlroy, M.D. Engineering a sort function. *Softw.-Pract. Exp.* **1993**, *23*, 1249–1265.
20. Eugene, C.F. A sufficient condition for backtrack-free search. *J. Assoc. Comput. Mach.* **1982**, *29*, 24–32.

21. David, W.M.; Beck, L.L. Smallest-Last ordering and clustering and graph coloring algorithms. *J. Assoc. Comput. Mach.* **1983**, *30*, 417–427.
22. Pardalos, P.M.; Xue, J. The maximum clique problem. *J. Glob. Optim.* **1994**, *4*, 301–324.
23. Bron, C.; Kerbosch, J. Algorithm 457: Finding all cliques of an undirected graph [h]. *Commun. ACM* **1973**, *16*, 575–579.
24. Akkoyunlu, E.A. The enumeration of maximal cliques of large graphs. *SIAM J. Comput.* **1973**, *2*, 1–6.
25. Tomita, E.; Tanaka, A.; Takahashi, H. The worst-case time complexity for generating all maximal cliques and computational experiments. *Theor. Comput. Sci.* **2006**, *363*, 28–42.
26. Abu-Khzam, F.N.; Collins, R.L.; Fellows, M.R.; Langston, M.A.; Suters, W.H.; Symons, C.T. Kernelization algorithms for the vertex cover problem: Theory and experiments. In *ALENEX/ANALC*; New Orleans, LA, USA, 10–13 January 2004; pp. 62–69.
27. Segundo, P.S.; Tapia, C. A New Implicit Branching Strategy for Exact Maximum Clique. In *Proceedings of ICTAI'10*; Arras, France, 27–29 October 2010; Volume 1, pp. 352–357.
28. Cheeseman, P.; Kanefsky, B.; Taylor, W.M. Where the Really Hard Problems are. In *Proceedings of the IJCAI'91*, Sidney, Australia, 24–30 August 1991; pp. 331–337.
29. Gent, I.P.; MacIntyre, E.; Prosser, P.; Walsh, T. The Constrainednss of Search. In *Proceedings of the AAAI'96*, Portland, OR, USA, 4–8 August 1996; pp. 246–252.
30. Zweig, K.A.; Palla, G.; Vicsek, T. What makes a phase transition? Analysis of the random satisfiability problem. *Physica A* **2010**, *389*, 1501–1511.
31. DIMACS instances. Available online: ftp://dimacs.rutgers.edu/pub/challenge/graph/benchmarks/clique (accessed on 12 November 2012).
32. Watts, D.J.; Strogatz, S.H. Collective dynamics of small world networks. *Nature* **1998**, *394*, 440–442.
33. Sewell, E.C. A branch and bound algorithm for the stability number of a sparse graph. *INFORMS J. Comput.* **1998**, *10*, 438–447.
34. Prosser, P. Maximum Clique Algorithms in Java. Available online: http://www.dcs.gla.ac.uk/ pat/-maxClique (accessed on 12 November 2012).
35. Stanford Large Network Dataset Collection. Available online: http://snap.stanford.edu/data/index.html (accessed on 12 November 2012).
36. Benchmarks with Hidden Optimum Solutions. Available online: http://www.nlsde.buaa.edu.cn/kexu/benchmarks/graph-benchmarks.htm (accessed on 12 November 2012).
37. Dfmax. Available online: ftp://dimacs.rutgers.edu/pub/dsj/clique (accessed on 12 November 2012).

Algorithms **2012**, *5*, 654-667; doi:10.3390/a5040654

OPEN ACCESS

algorithms

ISSN 1999-4893

www.mdpi.com/journal/algorithms

Article

Extracting Co-Occurrence Relations from ZDDs

Takahisa Toda

ERATO, MINATO Discrete Structure Manipulation System Project, JST, Sapporo-Shi 060-0814, Japan;
E-Mail: toda@erato.ist.hokudai.ac.jp or toda.takahisa@gmail.com

Received: 27 September 2012; in revised form: 4 December 2012 / Accepted: 6 December 2012 / Published: 13 December 2012

Abstract: A zero-suppressed binary decision diagram (ZDD) is a graph representation suitable for handling sparse set families. Given a ZDD representing a set family, we present an efficient algorithm to discover a hidden structure, called a co-occurrence relation, on the ground set. This computation can be done in time complexity that is related not to the number of sets, but to some feature values of the ZDD. We furthermore introduce a conditional co-occurrence relation and present an extraction algorithm, which enables us to discover further structural information.

Keywords: BDD; ZDD; partition; co-occurrence; data mining

---

1. Introduction

Enumerating a large number of sets and finding useful information from them have recently attracted the attention of many researchers. The data structure called a zero-suppressed binary decision diagram [1], ZDD for short, is known to be useful for compactly representing collections of sets and for efficiently manipulating them. ZDDs have been applied to various problems. In the analysis of transaction databases, Minato and Arimura [2,3] invented ZDD-based techniques for frequent itemset mining. Coudert [4] introduced a ZDD-based approach to solve many graph and set optimization problems. Sekine and Imai [5] developed a new paradigm of the exact computation for network reliability by means of binary decision diagrams (see [6,7]), BDDs for short. Recently, for multi-terminal binary decision diagrams, which are a well accepted technique for the state graph based quantitative analysis of large and complex systems, a zero-suppressed version has been studied by Lampka *et al.* [8]. Roughly speaking, an idea common to these is to compress a large number of sets into a ZDD (BDD) and manipulate them without decompression.

In this paper, we study the following basic problem of ZDDs: Given a ZDD representing a set family, extract a hidden structure, called a co-occurrence relation, over the ground set. This computation can be done in time complexity that is related not to the number of sets, but to some feature values of the ZDD representing the sets. Thus it is effective especially when a large number of sets are compressed into a small ZDD. Since we do not put any domain-specific assumption on the sets represented by a ZDD, our algorithm is widely applicable to ZDDs obtained from real-life data.

The co-occurrence relation is defined as follows: given a set S and a collection $\mathcal{C}$ of subsets of S, two elements $a, b \in S$ co-occur with each other for $\mathcal{C}$ if it holds that for all $T \in \mathcal{C}$, $a \in T$ if and only if $b \in T$. In a series of work for finding various useful information from databases [9–11], the co-occurrence relation was introduced, although an efficient extraction algorithm is not known. Clearly the co-occurrence relation is an equivalence relation and it induces the partition consisting of equivalence classes, called a co-occurrence partition. Since ZDDs represent collections of sets, co-occurrence relations and partitions are similarly defined for ZDDs. Since elements in the same block of a co-occurrence partition have the same behavior, when we want to find useful information from a ZDD, we need not distinguish between them and the ZDD can be compressed further.

This paper is organized as follows. In Section 2 we introduce some basic notions on ZDDs. We present algorithms in Section 3 and provide examples in Section 4. Concluding remarks are given in Section 5.

2. Basic Notions on ZDDs

Since we do not treat BDDs, we only introduce ZDDs. ZDDs are graph representations for set families. Figure 1(b) illustrates the ZDD representing the set family $\{\emptyset, \{e_1\}, \{e_2\}, \{e_3\}\}$. Whenever a ZDD is given, we always assume that a ground set S and the order of the elements are fixed. For simplicity, let $S := \{e_1, \ldots, e_n\}$, where the elements are numbered from 1 to n $(= |S|)$ and ordered in this order. The node at the top is called the root. Each internal node has the three fields V, LO and HI. The field V holds the index of an element in S. The fields LO and HI point to other nodes, which are called LO and HI children, respectively. The arc to a LO child is called a LO arc and illustrated by a dashed arrow, while the arc to a HI child is called a HI arc and illustrated by a solid arrow. There are only two non-internal nodes, denoted by $\bot$ and $\top$.

Figure 1. The two graph representations for the same set family $\{\emptyset, \{e_1\}, \{e_2\}, \{e_3\}\}$. (**a**) Binary Decision Tree; (**b**) ZDD.

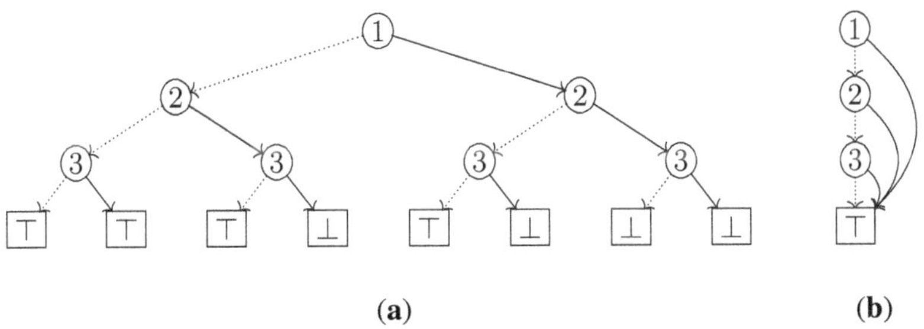

The following two conditions for ZDDs enable a unique and efficient representation. First, whenever an arc goes from an internal node f to an internal node g, a ZDD must satisfy $\mathrm{V}(f) < \mathrm{V}(g)$. Thus no nodes having the same index occur twice in a path. Second, a ZDD must be irreducible in the sense that the following reduction operations cannot be applied anymore.

1. For each internal node f whose HI child is $\bot$, redirect all the incoming arcs of f to the LO child of f, and then eliminate f (Figure 2(a)).
2. Share all equivalent subgraphs (Figure 2(b)).

Figure 2. The two reduction rules for ZDDs. (**a**) Node Elimination; (**b**) Node Sharing.

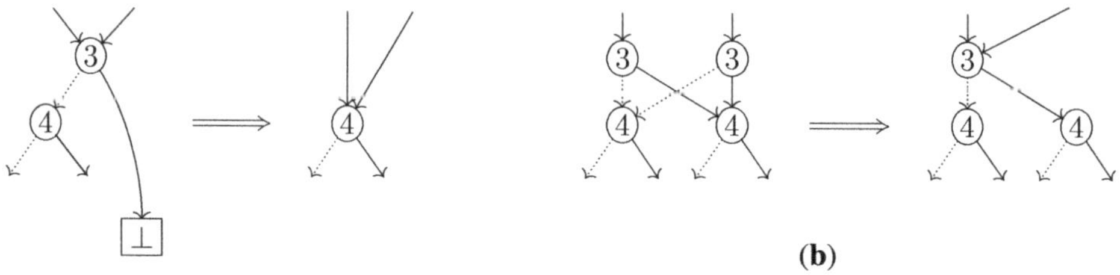

(**b**)

(**a**)

Now, let us see the correspondence between ZDDs and set families. Given a ZDD, for each path P from the root to $\top$, define a subset T_P of S such that $e_i \in T_P$ if the HI arc of an internal node f is selected (where $i = \mathrm{V}(f)$); otherwise, $e_i \notin T_P$. Note that if P contains no nodes of index i, then we can know that $e_i \notin T_P$ due to the node elimination rule. We obtain the set family $\{T_P \colon P \text{ is a path in the ZDD}\}$. Conversely, given a set family, construct the corresponding binary decision tree as is illustrated in Figure 1(a) and make it irreducible by applying the two reduction rules. Observe for example that Figure 1(b) is obtained from Figure 1(a). It is known (see [1,12] (§7.1.4), for details) that every set family has one and only one representation as a ZDD if the size of a ground set and the order of the elements are fixed.

For any node f in a ZDD, the graph consisting of all nodes accessible from f forms a ZDD whose root is f. The size of a ZDD is the total number of nodes in the ZDD, including non-internal nodes. The cardinality of a node is the total number of paths from the node to $\top$. Since in ZDDs we are interested in paths leading to $\top$, we mean by a branch node an internal node whose two children have paths leading to $\top$; in other words, the LO child is not $\bot$. Note that a branch node is not a synonym of an internal node.

3. Algorithms

We present an algorithm to extract a hidden structure, called a co-occurrence relation, from a ZDD. Our algorithm constructs a co-occurrence partition while traversing a ZDD. We first explain how to traverse a ZDD and then how to manipulate a partition efficiently in the traversal. We furthermore introduce the notion of a conditional co-occurrence relation and present an extraction algorithm.

3.1. Traversal Part

Let us first consider a naive method to compute a co-occurrence partition. Suppose that a ZDD represents a collection $\mathcal{C}$ of subsets of a set S. The co-occurrence partition is incrementally constructed as follows. We start with the partition $\{S\}$ consisting of the single block S. For each path P from the root to $\top$, we obtain a new partition from the current partition by separating each block b into the two parts $b \cap T_P$ and $b \cap (S \setminus T_P)$ if both parts are nonempty, where T_P denotes the set in $\mathcal{C}$ corresponding to P. This can be done by checking which arc is selected at each node of P. For example, let us see the ZDD given in Figure 3: If we first examine the path $1 \dashrightarrow 2 \dashrightarrow 3 \dashrightarrow 4 \rightarrow \top$, then the block S of the initial partition splits into the two parts $\{4\}$ and $S \setminus \{4\}$, since HI arc is selected only at the label 4 node. It can be easily verified that after all paths are examined, the co-occurrence partition induced by $\mathcal{C}$ is constructed. However, since this method depends on the number of paths (thus the size of $\mathcal{C}$), this is not effective for ZDDs which efficiently compress a large number of sets. It would be desirable if we could construct a co-occurrence partition directly from a ZDD.

Figure 3. The computing process of our algorithm for the ZDD that represents the set family $\{\{e_4\}, \{e_3, e_5\}, \{e_2, e_6\}, \{e_1, e_4\}, \{e_1, e_3, e_5\}, \{e_1, e_2, e_4, e_6\}\}$ is shown below. For example, in the third line from the bottom of the left column, the number 2 on the left side means that $\top$ was visited twice; the right arrow means that the state of e_2 changed from LO to HI; the left arrow means that the state of e_3 changed from HI to LO. In the bottom of the right column, the co-occurrence partition $\{\{e_1\}, \{e_2, e_6\}, \{e_3, e_5\}, \{e_4\}\}$ is obtained.

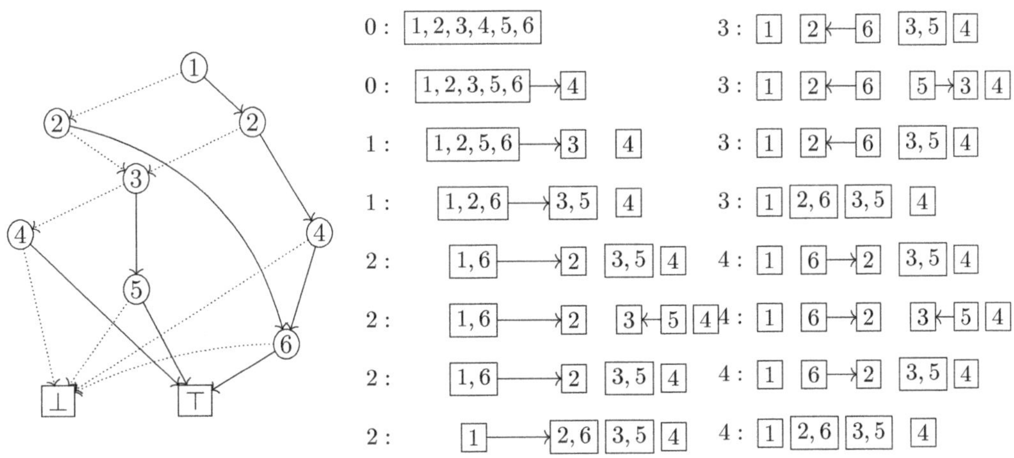

Our algorithm improves the naive method above by avoiding as many useless visits of nodes as possible. We traverse a ZDD basically in a depth-first order. In each node, we select the next node in a LO arc first order, *i.e.*, the LO child if the LO child is not $\bot$; otherwise, the HI child. After we arrive at $\top$, we go back to the most recent branch node and select the HI arc. Note that we need not go back to the root, since arc types do not change until the most recent branch node. For example, in Figure 3, after the first visit of $\top$, we go back to the label 3 node and go ahead along the path $3 \rightarrow 5 \rightarrow \top$.

The difference from the usual depth-first search is that when we visit an already visited node, we go down from the node to $\top$ by selecting only HI-arcs. This is essential because the usual depth-first search may fail to detect separable elements. For example, in Figure 4, the two elements e_3 and e_4 are separable, and in our traversal the third and fourth columns in the table 3b have different arc types thus we can know that they are really separated. On the other hand, in the usual depth-first search they are observed as if they had a common arc type: Since an already visited node is no longer visited, the arc type of e_4 in the table 3a is not updated, which means the type remains LO.

Figure 4. Each table on the center shows the change of selected arc types when the ZDD is traversed by the usual depth-first search. Similarly, the tables on the right correspond to the changes when traversed by our algorithm.

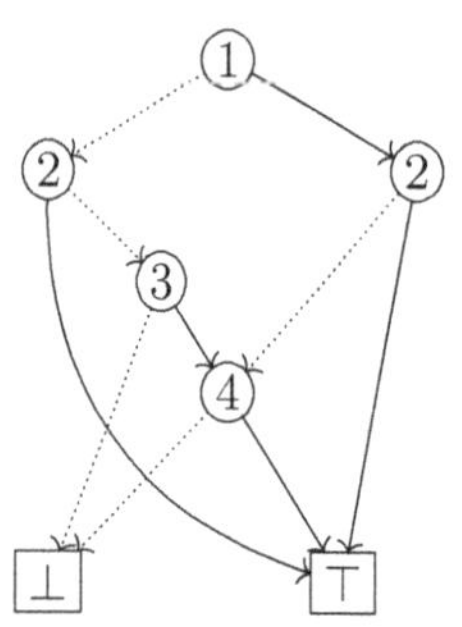

1a:

1	2	3	4
L	L	H	H

1b:

1	2	3	4
L	L	H	H

2a:

1	2	3	4
	H	L	L

2b:

1	2	3	4
	H	L	L

3a:

1	2	3	4
H	L	L	

3b:

1	2	3	4
H	L	L	H

4a:

1	2	3	4
	H	L	L

4b:

1	2	3	4
	H	L	L

Unlike the usual depth-first search, we do not skip necessary paths as the following lemma implies.

Lemma 3.1. *In each visit of a node g after the first, two elements get separated when traversing the subgraph whose root is g if and only if they get separated when going from g to $\top$ with only HI-arcs.*

Proof. Since the sufficiency is immediate, we only show the necessity. Suppose for contradiction that two elements e_i and e_j $(i < j)$ get separated when visiting all nodes below g, while they are not separated when only selecting HI-arcs. Let e_k denote the element corresponding to g. For the case $i < k$, there are two paths from g such that they have different arc types at e_j. However, in the first visit of g, we could trace both paths and know that e_i and e_j are separated, which is a contradiction. For the other case $k \leq i$, there is a path from g with different arc types at e_i and e_j, and we could trace this path in the first visit of g and reach a contradiction. □

The traversal part is formally described in Algorithm 1. We here explain some notation and terminology. Recall that in each internal node f, the next node of f in a LO arc first order is the LO child if f is a branch node, *i.e.*, an internal node whose two children have paths leading to $\top$; otherwise, the HI child. In order to traverse a ZDD, branch nodes are pushed onto the stack BRANCH, and visited nodes are contained in N_{visited}. The $\top$ is contained in N_{visited} in the initialization part, which reduces an exceptional case in the traversal part, *i.e.*, the loop block. For each step of the traversal, by invoking the function Update, we update the current partition p according to which arc is selected at the currently visited node f and whether there exist nodes hidden between f and the next node g due to the node elimination rule. To do this efficiently, we need the following things: The graph structure G defined on the blocks of p, the set B_{new} of blocks which have been created since the last visit of $\top$, and the set E_{HI} of elements whose arc types are HI. The set B_{new} is refreshed for each visit of $\top$. The function Update is explained in detail in the next subsection.

Algorithm 1 Calculate a co-occurrence partition from a ZDD defined on a set $S := \{e_1, \ldots, e_n\}$

```
Require: ZDD is neither ⊥ nor ⊤, and n > 0
  p ← the partition {S};
  G ← the digraph with no arc and one vertex corresponding to the unique block S of p;
  E_HI ← ∅; B_new ← ∅; Initialize BRANCH as an empty stack;
  f ← the root of ZDD;
  g ← the next node of f in a LO arc first order;
  N_visited ← {⊤, f};
  if f is a branch node then
      push f onto BRANCH;
  end if
  loop
      Update (f, g, p, G, B_new, E_HI);
      if g ∉ N_visited then
          f ← g;
          g ← the next node of f in a LO arc first order;
          N_visited ← N_visited ∪ {f};
          if f is a branch node then
              push f onto BRANCH;
          end if
      else
          while g ≠ ⊤ do
              f ← g;
              g ← HI (f);
              Update (f, g, p, G, B_new, E_HI);
          end while
          if BRANCH is empty then
              return p; // End of the traversal
          end if
          B_new ← ∅;
          f ← the node popped from BRANCH;
          g ← HI (f);
      end if
  end loop
```

3.2. Manipulation Part

In the traversal described in the previous subsection, whenever we visit a node f and select the next node g, we update the current partition p by invoking the function Update. Namely, when we find an element e_i which is separable from the other elements in the same block, we move e_i to an appropriate block so that each block consists of inseparable elements with respect to the information up to this time.

For example, let us see the computing process in Figure 3 step by step. Suppose that we arrive at the label 3 node after the first visit of $\top$. At this time $p = \{S \setminus \{e_4\}, \{e_4\}\}$. When we go to the label 5 node along the HI arc, the element e_3 becomes in a HI state while the other elements are in a LO state. Thus we create a new block and move e_3 into it. We furthermore memorize the arc from the previous block b, which e_3 was in, to the new block b', which now consists of only e_3. This is necessary because $e_5 \in b$ soon becomes in a HI state and we have to insert e_5 into b', not a new block. We then reach $\top$ and go back to the label 2 node on the left side. The element $e_2 \in b$ becomes in a HI state, but we never insert e_2 into b', since insertion is allowed only within the period from the creation of b' until the arrival at $\top$. Therefore, we create a new block b'' and move e_2 into it. We furthermore redirect the outgoing arc of b to the new block b''. In this way, we update the current partition p, the graph structure G on the blocks of p, and the set B_{new} of blocks created since the last visit of $\top$.

The function Update is formally described in Algorithm 2. Let e_i and e_j be the elements corresponding to the current node f and the next node g, respectively. We move e_i to another block only if the arc type of e_i changes from LO to HI or from HI to LO. Note that we need not move e_i in the other cases. This move operation for e_i is done in the former part of the function Update by invoking the function Move. The destination block of e_i is determined by means of the auxiliary data structures G and B_{new}. The G defines a parent-child relation between the blocks of the current partition p. That a block b is a parent of a block b' implies that b' is formed by elements which most recently went out from b. Moving elements of b to b' is allowed only within the period from the creation of b' until the arrival at $\top$, which can be decided by using B_{new}.

There may be some nodes hidden between the current node f and the next node g due to the node elimination rule. Let e_l be the element corresponding to such a hidden node. Since e_l is now in a LO state, it suffices to move e_l only if the previous arc type is HI. This computation is done in the latter part of the function Update.

We are now ready to state the time complexity of our algorithm. Recall that a branch node is an internal node whose two children have paths leading to $\top$.

Theorem 3.2. *Let k be the maximum number of HI arcs in a path from the root to $\top$. Let m be the number of branch nodes. Let n be the size of a ground set. Algorithm 1 correctly computes a co-occurrence partition. It can be implemented to run in time proportional to $n + km$.*

Proof. From Lemma 3.1 and the observations up to here, we can easily verify that Algorithm 1 correctly computes a co-occurrence partition. Throughout this proof, we mean by a period the time period from a visit of $\top$ to the next visit.

The time necessary to create the initial partition is proportional to n. We show that the function Update can be implemented so that the total time in a period is proportional to k. Partitions can be manipulated so that the function Move runs in constant time. Thus the latter part of the function Update

is the computational bottleneck. To compute this part efficiently, we implement E_{HI} as a doubly linked list (see Figure 5). For each step of the traversal, we memorize the position of the most recently inserted element into E_{HI}. Note that when we arrive at $\top$ and go back to the most recent branch node, we have to recover the corresponding position in some way e.g., by means of a stack. When we insert an element e_i into E_{HI}, we put e_i in the next position of the most recently inserted element. It can be easily verified that all elements placed before (respectively, after) the most recently inserted element are sorted in increasing order of their indices. Thus, in order to scan all elements $e_l \in E_{\text{HI}}$ with $i < l < j$, it suffices to search from the position of the most recently inserted element until the condition breaks. Since the total number of elements searched in a period is proportional to k, we obtain the time necessary to compute the function Update through a period.

Algorithm 2 Update the current partition p and the auxiliary data structures $G, B_{\text{new}}, E_{\text{HI}}$ according to the current node f, the selected arc type of f, and the next node g

function UPDATE($f, g, p, G, B_{\text{new}}, E_{\text{HI}}$)
  $i \leftarrow \mathrm{V}(f); j \leftarrow \mathrm{V}(g)$;
  if the HI arc of f is selected and $e_i \notin E_{\text{HI}}$ **then**
    $\mathrm{Move}(e_i, p, G, B_{\text{new}})$; $E_{\text{HI}} \leftarrow E_{\text{HI}} \cup \{e_i\}$;
  else if the LO arc of f is selected and $e_i \in E_{\text{HI}}$ **then**
    $\mathrm{Move}(e_i, p, G, B_{\text{new}})$; $E_{\text{HI}} \leftarrow E_{\text{HI}} \setminus \{e_i\}$;
  end if
  for all $e_l \in E_{\text{HI}}$ with $i < l < j$ **do**
    $\mathrm{Move}(e_l, p, G, B_{\text{new}})$; $E_{\text{HI}} \leftarrow E_{\text{HI}} \setminus \{e_l\}$;
  end for
end function

function MOVE($e_i, p, G, B_{\text{new}}$)
  $b \leftarrow$ the block of p which contains e_i;
  if the child of b is not in B_{new} **then**
    Add a new empty block b' to p;
    Add b' to G in such a way that b' has no child and the child of b is b';
    $B_{\text{new}} \leftarrow B_{\text{new}} \cup \{b'\}$;
  end if
  Move e_i to the block corresponding to the child of b;
  Delete b from p and G if b is empty;
end function

Let us consider the number of traversed nodes with repetition during the computation. Clearly the number of periods is $m + 1$. For each i $(0 \leq i \leq m)$, let P_i denote the path traced in the i-th period, which starts with a branch node and ends with $\top$. The number of HI arcs in P_i is bounded above by k. The head of each LO arc in P_i is a branch node, since the LO arc of a non-branch node is not selected in our traversal. The LO arc of any branch node is traversed exactly once. Thus the total number of LO arcs traversed during the computation is m. Therefore, $\sum_{0\leq i\leq m}|P_i| \leq (m+1)k+m$. We conclude that the time necessary to execute Algorithm 1 is proportional to $n + km$. □

Figure 5. For each step of the traversal of the ZDD given in Figure 3, the doubly linked list of HI-state elements is shown below, where the index denotes the number of times ⊤ was visited and the double box or circle denotes the position after which an element is inserted.

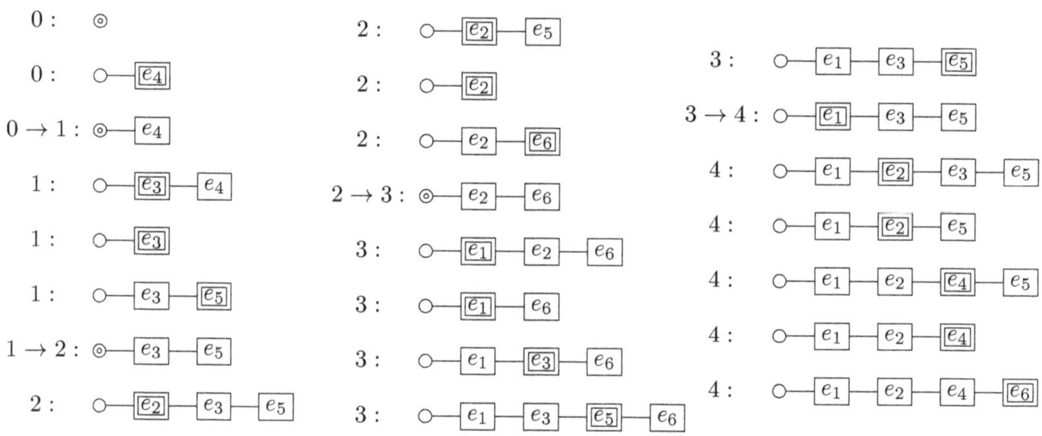

3.3. Conditional Co-occurrence Relations

Given a ZDD where every two elements are separable, Algorithm 1 cannot extract any useful information from the ZDD, but even so, we want to find some structural information hidden in the ground set. In this subsection we focus on the condition that enforces some elements always to be in a HI state and some elements always to be in a LO state.

Let $(\mathrm{ON}, \mathrm{OFF})$ be a pair of subsets of the ground set S of a ZDD. Two elements $e_i, e_j \in S$ are conditionally inseparable with respect to $(\mathrm{ON}, \mathrm{OFF})$ if they co-occur with each other for all paths that satisfy the condition: the HI arcs are always selected for all elements in ON; The LO arcs are always selected for all elements in OFF.

Before extracting this relation, we need a preprocessing so that we can trace only paths that satisfy the condition above. Recall that the cardinality of a node f is the number of paths from f to $\top$. It is known (see also Algorithm C and Exercise 208 in [12]) that given a ZDD, the cardinalities of all nodes in the ZDD can be computed in time proportional to the size of f. This computation can be done in a bottom-up fashion: The cardinalities of $\bot$ and $\top$ are 0 and 1, respectively; the cardinality of each internal node is the sum of the cardinalities of the two children. Given a pair $(\mathrm{ON}, \mathrm{OFF})$, it is easy to change to be able to compute the numbers of paths from all internal nodes f to $\top$ that satisfy the condition concerning $(\mathrm{ON}, \mathrm{OFF})$. For convenience we call these numbers conditional cardinalities with respect to $(\mathrm{ON}, \mathrm{OFF})$.

To construct a conditional co-occurrence partition, change Algorithm 1 as follows.

1. Return the initial partition if the conditional cardinality of the root is zero.
2. The next node g of the current node f is the LO child if the conditional cardinalities of the two children are nonzero; else if the conditional cardinality of the LO child is zero, the HI child; else, the LO child.
3. In the while block of Algorithm 1, the next node g is the LO child if the conditional cardinality of the HI child is zero; otherwise, the HI child.

Theorem 3.3. *Let m be the number of branch nodes. Let n be the size of a ground set. The computation for a conditional co-occurrence partition can be done in time proportional to mn.*

Proof. This theorem can be proved in a similar way to the proof in Theorem 3.2, but an upper bound for the number of the traversed nodes cannot be similarly calculated. Indeed, because of the change in the while block, we may have to select many LO arcs. At least we can say that the size of each path P_i is at most n and the number of periods is at most $m + 1$. Thus the time is proportional to mn. □

Thanks to this theorem, when selecting a pair $(\mathrm{ON}, \mathrm{OFF})$, there is no need to worry about a rapid increase of computation time. This is in contrast to the case where we arbitrarily select paths and compute a co-occurrence partition from the selected paths. These paths are no longer compressed, and even if they can be compressed in some way, the size is generally irrelevant to the size of the original ZDD, and thus we cannot give a similar guarantee.

4. Examples

In this section we provide two examples. First, we applied our algorithm to two datasets commonly used in frequent itemset mining. The datasets we used are mushroom and pumsb obtained from the Frequent Itemset Mining Dataset Repository. The mushroom dataset contains characteristics of various species of mushrooms and the pumsb dataset contains census data for population and housing. In both datasets, each record consists of distinct item IDs, which indicate characteristics of the record. Each record is considered as a set of items and a dataset as a set family, thus both datasets can be represented as ZDDs (see Table 1). The parameters n and k given in Theorem 3.2 correspond to the number of distinct items that appear in a dataset and the maximum number of items in a record, respectively. Although the maximum item ID in the pumsb dataset is 7116 and the minimum item ID is 0, there are only 2113 distinct item IDs. Thus we normalized the ground set to be the set $\{1, 2, \ldots, 2113\}$ such that each element i in the set corresponds to the i-th item ID that appears in the pumsb dataset.

Table 1. The used datasets, where n, k, m denote the parameters given in Theorem 3.2.

	#Records	**#Items (n)**	k	m	$n + km$	**#ZDD Nodes**
mushroom	8,124	119	23	288	6,743	791
pumsb	49,046	2,113	74	48,058	3,558,405	1,498,636

The computed partitions for the mushroom and the pumsb datasets are shown in Table 2, where the entries in the right table are shown as original pumsb item IDs. For example, in each record of the mushroom dataset, either elements 75 and 89 both appear or none of them do. Since items in the same block have the same behavior, when we want to find useful information from a ZDD, we need not distinguish between them. If the number of blocks is small, then various analyses on a ZDD can be efficiently performed on a small set of items by selecting one representative from each block. Thus our algorithm is useful. Unfortunately, without any constraints there are many blocks in both datasets; however, a few constraints may reduce the number of blocks significantly. For example, in the pumsb dataset, there are 2037 many blocks without any constraints, while the constraints $\mathrm{ON} = \{5065\}$ and $\mathrm{OFF} = \emptyset$ reduce the number to 71 (see Table 3 for other settings of constraints).

Table 2. The computed results for the mushroom dataset (left) and the pumsb dataset (right), where the blocks of single items are omitted in the left table and the blocks of at most two items are omitted in the right table. Each line corresponds to one block.

Blocks				
3	74	84	92	97
75	89			
73	83			

Blocks				
4409	4491	4494	4945	6866
49	1118	4163		
5945	6855	6865		
154	4497	4500		
4953	5946	6856		

Table 3. The numbers of blocks in various settings of constraints ON and OFF in the pumsb dataset. In the left table, each line in the first column contains one item chosen at random for ON, where $\mathrm{OFF} = \emptyset$; in the right table, each line in the first column contains five items chosen at random for OFF, where $\mathrm{ON} = \emptyset$. Items are shown as original pumsb item IDs.

ON	#Blocks
5065	71
98	330
208	408
52	45
5375	12

OFF					#Blocks
1	4744	4933	5894	6021	1,466
347	1469	4447	4503	4772	1,774
0	3280	4543	6052	6062	1,898
271	5695	6140	6405	7057	1,772
2421	4656	5949	6159	6299	2,031

As a second example, we applied the algorithm for the conditional case to a set of paths enumerated from the graph given in Figure 6. We considered paths from the vertex 01 to the vertex 47 of the graph such that no vertices are visited twice, which are called simple paths. Since simple paths can be identified with sets of edges, the set of all simple paths from 01 to 47 can be represented as a ZDD whose ground set corresponds to the edge set of the graph. The number of such simple paths turns out to be 14,144,961,271, while the corresponding ZDD in our ordering of the edge set has only 599 branch nodes (see Table 4). This is in contrast to the pumsb dataset in the previous example, where the number of branch nodes is roughly the same as the number of records represented by a ZDD. The ZDD of the present example can be quickly constructed in a top-down fashion. This technique has been described in the literature; see, e.g., [5,12], (Exercise 225 in §7.1.4). We analyzed which edges co-occur with each other for all simple paths with the constraints ON and OFF given in Figure 6. The computed partition is shown in the right table of Figure 6. As we showed in Theorem 3.3, once we obtain a small ZDD like in this case, we can quickly compute co-occurrence partitions in various settings of ON and OFF.

Figure 6. We considered simple paths from the vertex 01 to the vertex 47. When the edge set ON consists of bold edges and OFF consists of dashed edges, the blocks of the corresponding co-occurrence partition except for blocks of single edges are shown in the right table as the collections of edges separated by horizontal lines.

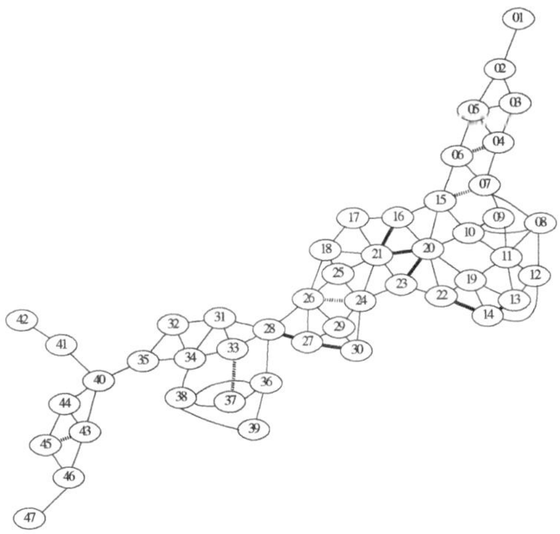

Blocks				
04–06	07–15	10–20	12–14	14–19
15–20	16–20	17–21	18–21	19–20
20–22	21–25	21–24	21–23	24–26
26–28	26–27	27–29	33–37	40–41
41–42	43–45			
01–02	13–14	14–22	16–21	20–23
20–21	27–30	27–28	35–40	46–47
15–16	19–22	23–24		
16–17	17–18	22–23		
36–39	37–38			
36–37	37–38			
28–36	34–38			
44–45	45–46			

Table 4. The ZDD representing simple paths from the vertex 01 to the vertex 47, where n, k, m denote the parameters given in Theorem 3.2.

Start	End	#Paths	#Edges (n)	k	m	$n + km$	#ZDD Nodes
01	47	14,144,961,271	92	44	599	26,448	1,085

In order to enumerate simple paths and construct ZDDs, we used the Stanford GraphBase, the simpath and the simpath-reduce programs by Knuth [13,14]. Furthermore, in both examples we used the Colorado University Decision Diagram Package by Somenzi [15].

5. Conclusions

We presented the following basic algorithm of ZDDs: Given a ground set S and a ZDD that represents a collection of subsets of S, the algorithm extracts a hidden structure, called a co-occurrence relation, on S from the ZDD. We furthermore introduced conditional co-occurrence relations and presented an extraction algorithm, which enables us to discover further structural information. We showed that these computations can be done in time complexity that is related not to the number of sets, but to some feature values of a ZDD. Our algorithms are effective especially when a large number of sets are compressed into a small ZDD.

References

1. Minato, S. Zero-Suppressed BDDs for Set Manipulation in Combinatorial Problems. In *Proceedings of 30th ACM/IEEE Design Autiomation Conference (DAC-93)*, Dallas, TX, USA, June 1993; pp. 272–277.
2. Minato, S.; Arimura, H. Efficient Method of Combinatorial Item Set Analysis Based on Zero-Suppressed BDDs. In *Proceedings of IEEE/IEICE/IPSJ International Workshop on Challenges in Web Information Retrieval and Integration (WIRI-2005)*, Tokyo, Japan, April 2005; pp. 3–10.
3. Minato, S.; Arimura, H. Frequent closed item set mining based on zero-suppressed BDDs. *Trans. Jpn. Soc. Artif. Intell.* **2007**, *22*, 165–172.
4. Coudert, O. Solving Graph Optimization Problems with ZBDDs. *In Proceedings of the 1997 European Conference on Design and Test*, Paris, France, March 1997; pp. 224–228.
5. Sekine, K.; Imai, H. A Unified Approach via BDD to the Network Reliability and Path Numbers. *Technical Report 95-09*, Department of Information Science, University of Tokyo, 1995.
6. Akers, S.B. Binary decision diagrams. *IEEE Trans. Comput.* **1978**, *27*, 509–516.
7. Bryant, R.E. Graph-Based algorithms for boolean function manipulation. *IEEE Trans. Comput.* **1986**, *35*, 677–691.
8. Lampka, K.; Siegle, M.; Ossowski, J.; Baier, C. Partially-Shared zero-suppressed multi-terminal BDDs: Concept, algorithms and applications. *Form. Methods Syst. Des.* **2010**, *36*, 198–222.
9. Minato, S. Finding Simple Disjoint Decompositions in Frequent Itemset Data Using Zero-Suppressed BDDs. In *Proceedings of IEEE ICDM Workshop on Computational Intelligence in Data Mining*, Houston, TX, USA, November 2005; pp. 3–11.
10. Minato, S.; Ito, K. Symmetric item set mining method using zero-suppressed bdds and application to biological data. *Trans. Jpn. Soc. Artif. Intell.* **2007**, *22*, 156–164.
11. Minato, S. A Fast Algorithm for Cofactor Implication Checking and Its Application for Knowledge Discovery. In *Proceedings of IEEE 8th International Conference on Computer and Information Technology (CIT 2008)*, Sydney, Australia, July 2008; pp. 53–58.
12. Knuth, D.E. *The Art of Computer Programming Volume 4a*; Addison-Wesley Professional: New Jersey, NJ, USA, 2011.
13. Knuth, D.E. The Stanford GraphBase. Available online: http://www-cs-faculty.stanford.edu/uno/sgb.html (accessed on 4 September 2012).
14. Knuth, D.E. SIMPATH and SIMPATH-REDUCE. Available online: http://www-cs-faculty.stanford.edu/uno/programs.html (accessed on 4 September 2012).

15. Somenzi, F. CUDD: CU Decision Diagram Package: Release 2.5.0. Available online: http://vlsi.colorado.edu/fabio/CUDD/ (accessed on 4 September 2012).

Algorithms **2013**, *6*, 1-11; doi:10.3390/a6010001

OPEN ACCESS

algorithms

ISSN 1999-4893

www.mdpi.com/journal/algorithms

Article

Maximum Disjoint Paths on Edge-Colored Graphs: Approximability and Tractability

Paola Bonizzoni [1], Riccardo Dondi [2,*] and Yuri Pirola [1]

[1] Department of Computer Systems and Communication, University of Milan-Bicocca, Viale Sarca 336, Milan, Italy; E-Mails: bonizzoni@disco.unimib.it (P.B.); pirola@disco.unimib.it (Y.P.)

[2] Department of Humanities and Social Sciences, University of Bergamo, Via Donizzetti 3, Bergamo, Italy

* Author to whom correspondence should be addressed; E-Mail: riccardo.dondi@unibg.it; Tel.: +39-03520-52423

Received: 31 October 2012; in revised form: 13 December 2012 / Accepted: 18 December 2012 / Published: 27 December 2012

Abstract: The problem of finding the maximum number of vertex-disjoint uni-color paths in an edge-colored graph has been recently introduced in literature, motivated by applications in social network analysis. In this paper we investigate the approximation and parameterized complexity of the problem. First, we show that, for any constant $\varepsilon > 0$, the problem is not approximable within factor $c^{1-\varepsilon}$, where c is the number of colors, and that the corresponding decision problem is W[1]-hard when parametrized by the number of disjoint paths. Then, we present a fixed-parameter algorithm for the problem parameterized by the number and the length of the disjoint paths.

Keywords: social networks; disjoint paths; fixed-parameter algorithms; hardness of approximation

---

1. Introduction

Social networks are usually represented and studied as graphs. Vertices represent the elements analyzed (e.g., individuals), while edges represent a binary relation between the considered elements. Among the different properties considered to study such graphs, one of the most relevant is the vertex connectivity of two given vertices. Vertex connectivity is a measure of the information flowing from one vertex to the other, and it has many applications. For example, it is used for the identifications of important structural properties of a social network, like group cohesiveness and centrality [1,2]. A classical result of graph theory, known as Menger's theorem, states that vertex connectivity is equivalent to the maximum number of disjoint paths between two given vertices.

While a lot of interest has been put in the study of networks that represent a single type of relation, a natural extension that has been recently introduced in literature [3] is to consider multi-relational social networks, that is social networks where more than one kind of relation between elements of the network is considered. In order to investigate vertex connectivity in multi-relational social networks, the combinatorial problem known as *Maximum Colored Disjoint Paths* (MAX CDP) has been introduced in [3]. MAX CDP asks for the maximum number of vertex-disjoint uni-color paths in an edge-colored graph, where the different edge-colors represent different kinds of relation.

The computational and approximation complexity of MAX CDP has been investigated in [3]. When the input graph contains exactly one color, MAX CDP is polynomial time solvable (it can be reduced to the maximum flow problem), while it has been shown to be NP-hard when the edges of the graph are colored. Moreover, MAX CDP is shown to be approximable within factor c, where c is the number of colors of the edges of the input graph, but not approximable within factor $2 - \varepsilon$, for any $\varepsilon > 0$, even when c is a fixed constant.

In [3], it is also investigated a variant of the problem, denoted as ℓ-LCDP, where the length of the paths in the solution are (upper) bounded by an integer $\ell \geq 1$. The ℓ-LCDP problem is NP-hard, for $\ell \geq 4$, while it admits a polynomial time algorithm when $\ell \leq 3$. This variant of the problem can be approximated in polynomial time within factor $(\ell - 1)/2 + \varepsilon$.

In this paper we investigate the approximation and parameterized complexity of MAX CDP and ℓ-LCDP. First, we show in Section 3 that MAX CDP is not approximable within factor $c^{1-\varepsilon}$, for any constant $\varepsilon > 0$, and that the corresponding decision problem (CDP) is W[1]-hard when parametrized by the number p of disjoint uni-color paths. Then, in Section 4, we give a fixed-parameter algorithm for ℓ-LCDP, when ℓ and the number of disjoint uni-color paths are considered as parameters. Table 1 summarizes the results known about the complexities of these problems along with the new results presented in this work.

Table 1. Complexity status of MAX CDP.

Problem	Parameter	Status	Ref.
MAX CDP	c	NP-hard for any $c \geq 2$, c-approximable	[3]
		Inapprox. within $c^{1-\varepsilon}$	new
CDP	p	W[1]-hard	new
ℓ-LCDP	ℓ	NP-hard for $\ell \geq 4$	[3]
		Poly-time for $\ell \leq 3$	[3]
ℓ-LCDP$_p$	(ℓ, p)	FPT	new

2. Definitions

In this section we give some preliminary definitions that will be useful in the rest of the paper. First, in this paper, we will consider only undirected graphs. Consider a set of colors $C = \{1, \ldots, c\}$. In the paper we denote by c the cardinality of C. A C-edge-colored graph (or simply an edge-colored graph when the set of colors is clear from the context) is defined as $G = (V, \mathcal{E})$, where V denotes the set of vertices of G and $\mathcal{E} = \{E_1, \ldots, E_c\}$ denotes a collection of edge sets, where the set E_i, with $i \in C$, represents the set of edges colored with color i. Notice that, for a given pair of vertices v_i, v_j, there may exist more than one edge between v_i and v_j (each of these edges is associated with a distinct color of C).

A path π in G is called a *uni-color* path if all the edges of π have the same color, that is they belong to the same set E_i (for some $i \in C$). Given two vertices $x, y \in V$, an xy-path is a path between vertices x and y. Two paths π' and π'' are *internally disjoint* (or, simply, *disjoint*) if they do not share any internal vertex, while a set of paths are internally disjoint if they are pairwise internally disjoint.

Next, we introduce the formal definitions of the problems we deal with in this paper, namely the optimization problem MAX CDP, the decision problem (CDP) naturally associated with MAX CDP, and the corresponding length-bounded variants ℓ-LCDP and ℓ-LCDP$_p$.

Problem 1. MAXIMUM COLORED DISJOINT PATHS (MAX CDP).
Input: a set C of colors, a C-edge-colored graph $G = (V, \mathcal{E})$, and two vertices $s, t \in V$.
Output: the maximum number of disjoint uni-color st-paths.

Problem 2. COLORED DISJOINT PATHS (CDP).
Input: a set C of colors, a C-edge-colored graph $G = (V, \mathcal{E})$, a non-negative integer p, and two vertices $s, t \in V$.
Output: Do there exist at least p disjoint uni-color st-paths in G?

The ℓ-LENGTH COLORED DISJOINT PATHS (ℓ-LCDP) problem is a variant of MAX CDP where the length of the paths in the solution is bounded by an integer $\ell \geq 1$. The ℓ-LCDP$_p$ problem is the decision version of ℓ-LCDP which asks if there exists a solution of ℓ-LCDP with cardinality at least p.

3. Approximation and Parameterized Complexity of MAX CDP

In this section, we present a reduction from MAXIMUM INDEPENDENT SET to MAX CDP. Since the reduction preserves the solution cost, it implies that MAX CDP is not approximable within factor $c^{1-\varepsilon}$, for any $\varepsilon > 0$, and that CDP is W[1]-hard when the parameter is the size p of the solution.

Given an undirected graph $G_I = (V_I, E_I)$, the MAXIMUM INDEPENDENT SET (MAX INDSET) problem asks for an independent set $I \subseteq V_I$ of maximum cardinality, *i.e.*, a maximum-cardinality set I such that if $v', v'' \in I$ then $\{v', v''\} \notin E_I$. In the following, starting from a graph G_I, we construct a gadget (an edge-colored graph) G_C, such that finding an independent set I of cardinality k in G_I is equivalent to finding k disjoint uni-color st-paths in G_C. First, we describe the edge-colored graph G_C associated with a generic graph G_I, then we prove some properties of the computed gadget.

Description of the gadget. Let $G_I = (V_I, E_I)$ be an undirected graph, with $V = \{v_1, \ldots, v_n\}$ and $E_I = \{e_1, \ldots, e_m\}$. Without loss of generality, we assume that G_I is connected, since a maximum independent set of a non-connected graph is the union of the maximum independent sets of its connected components. Let Π_{E_I} be an ordered list of the edges of G_I, based on some ordering. We construct an edge-colored graph $G_C = (V_C, E_1, \ldots, E_n)$ associated with G_I as follows. Informally, the vertex set V_C is composed by two distinguished vertices s and t and a vertex for each edge of G_I, while each set E_i, $1 \leq i \leq c$, is composed connecting the vertices associated with edges of G_I incident to v_i in the same order as they appear in Π_{E_I}. Formally, the set of colors is:

$$C = \{1, \ldots, n\}$$

Now, we define the vertex set V_C:

$$V_C = \{s, t\} \cup \{u_{i,j} \mid \{v_i, v_j\} \in E_I\}$$

Finally, we define the edge set E_i, $1 \leq i \leq n$:

$$\begin{aligned} E_i = &\{\{u_{i,x}, u_{i,y}\} \mid \text{no edge } \{v_i, v_z\} \text{ appears between } \{v_i, v_x\} \text{ and } \{v_i, v_y\} \text{ in the list } \Pi_{E_I}\} \cup \\ &\{\{s, u_{i,j}\} \mid u_{i,j} \text{ is the first edge incident in } v_i \text{ of the list } \Pi_{E_I}\} \cup \\ &\{\{u_{i,j}, t\} \mid u_{i,j} \text{ is the last edge incident in } v_i \text{ of the list } \Pi_{E_I}\} \end{aligned}$$

Figure 1 represents an example of an undirected graph G_I and of the edge-colored graph G_C associated with it.

Figure 1. An example of a graph G_I and the edge-colored graph G_C associated with it. For convenience, we labelled the edges of G_I such as they correspond to the vertices in G_C. The colors of the edges in G_C are indicated by numbers placed near the edges, while the two distinguished vertices s and t are highlighted in grey. The order Π_{E_I} of the edges of G_I is simply the lexicographic order of their labels.

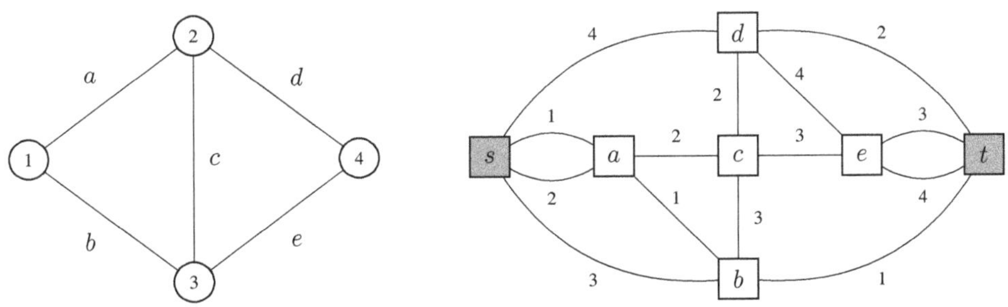

(a) G_I (b) G_C

Given a graph G_I with n vertices and m edges, the associated edge-colored graph G_C has $m + 2$ vertices, $O(mn)$ edges, and n colors, *i.e.*, $c = n$.

Properties of the gadget. First, we introduce the following properties of the gadget.

Remark 1. *A uni-color st-path of color i, with $1 \leq i \leq c$, contains each vertex $u_{i,x}$ of G_C associated with an edge incident in $v_i \in V_I$.*

Proof. The proof follows by construction, since the edges of color i, with $1 \leq i \leq c$, induce a st-path that contains each vertex $u_{i,x}$ of G_C associated with an edge incident in $v_i \in V_I$ ordered as in list Π_{E_I}. □

Next, we prove the two main results of the reduction from MAX INDSET to MAX CDP.

Lemma 2. *Let $G_I = (V_I, E_I)$ be an undirected graph and $I \subseteq V_I$ be an independent (vertex) set for G_I. Then, we can compute in polynomial time (at least) $|I|$ disjoint uni-color st-paths in the edge-colored graph G_C associated with G_I.*

Lemma 3. *Let $G_I = (V_I, E_I)$ be an undirected graph and G_C be the edge-colored graph associated with G_I. If there exist k disjoint uni-color st-paths in G_C, then we can compute in polynomial time an independent set $I \subseteq V_I$ for G_I, with $|I| = k$.*

The first lemma is easily proved by showing that the uni-color st-paths associated with the vertices of the independent set I are pairwise disjoint. Conversely, the second lemma can be proved by showing that the vertices of G_I associated with the k uni-color st-paths of G_C form an independent set for G_I.

Proof of Lemma 2. By construction, in G_C there exists a uni-color st-path associated with each vertex v of the original graph G_I. We will show that the set P of paths of G_C associated with each vertex $v \in I$ are internally disjoint. Let π_i and π_j be two paths of P associated with vertices v_i and v_j, respectively, of I. Notice that the two paths π_i and π_j connect the vertices which represent the edges of G_I incident to v_i and v_j, respectively. Since I is an independent set in G_I, no edge $e' \in E_I$ is incident to both v_i and v_j (i.e., $u_{i,j} \notin E_I$), thus π_i and π_j are (internally) disjoint. □

Proof of Lemma 3. Let P be the set of k disjoint uni-color st-paths of G_C. Since each color is (bi-univocally) associated with a single path in G_C which, in turn, is (bi-univocally) associated with a single vertex of G_I, we can define a set $I \subseteq V_I$ that consists of the vertices of G_I associated with a path of P. Clearly, $|I| = |P| = k$. We claim that I is an independent vertex set for G_I. Suppose that I is not an independent set, thus there exist two vertices $v_i, v_j \in I$ such that $\{v_i, v_j\} \in E_I$. Let $u_{i,j}$ be the vertex of G_C representing edge $\{v_i, v_j\}$. Since $v_i, v_j \in I$, then there exist two paths π_i, π_j in P associated with v_i and v_j. By Remark 1, both paths must contain vertex $u_{i,j}$ as an internal vertex, since edge $\{v_i, v_j\}$ is incident to both v_i and v_j. Hence paths π_i and π_j are not internally disjoint, which contradicts our assumption and thus I is an independent set for G_I. □

Consequences. Lemmas 2 and 3 prove the existence of an L-reduction [4] from MAX INDSET to MAX CDP with constants $\beta = \gamma = 1$. Hence, considering that, unless P = NP, MAX INDSET cannot be approximated in polynomial time within factor $|V_I|^{1-\varepsilon}$ for any constant $\varepsilon > 0$ [5], and that $|V_I| = c$, the following theorem holds.

Theorem 4. *For any constant $\varepsilon > 0$,* MAX CDP *cannot be approximated within factor $c^{1-\varepsilon}$ in polynomial time unless* P = NP.

This result greatly improves the previous inapproximability factor $2 - \varepsilon$ for MAX CDP [3] and, given the c-approximation algorithm presented in [3], it is the asymptotically optimal inapproximability ratio for MAX CDP. However, notice that the inapproximability factor $2 - \varepsilon$ for MAX CDP given in [3] holds even if c is a fixed constant, while in our reduction c is not fixed.

From the parameterized complexity point of view, the reduction also implies the W[1]-hardness of the decision problem CDP, as stated in the following theorem.

Theorem 5. CDP *is* W*[1]-hard when parameterized by the number* p *of disjoint uni-color* st*-paths.*

Proof. The reduction presented by Lemmas 2 and 3 is also a parameterized reduction [6] from INDEPENDENT SET (the decision problem naturally associated with MAX INDSET) to CDP (indeed the size of an independent set of G_I is identical to the number of disjoint uni-color st-path in G_C). Since INDEPENDENT SET is W[1]-hard when the parameter is the size of the required independent set [7], then also CDP is W[1]-hard when parametrized by number p of disjoint uni-color st-paths. □

4. A Fixed-Parameter Algorithm for ℓ-LCDP$_p$

In this section, we study ℓ-LCDP$_p$, the length-bounded (decision) version of MAX CDP, which asks if there exist p uni color disjoint st-paths of length at most ℓ. We show that ℓ-LCDP$_p$ is fixed-parameter tractable when the parameters are ℓ and p by presenting a parameterized algorithm based on the *color coding* technique [8]. For an introduction to parameterized complexity see [6]. Notice that ℓ-LCDP$_p$ is unlikely to admit fixed-parameter tractable algorithms when parameterized only by p or only by ℓ. Indeed in the latter case, ℓ-LCDP$_p$ is already NP-hard when $\ell = 4$ [3]. In the former case, we have proved in the previous section that CDP (hence ℓ-LCDP$_p$, when $\ell = n$) is W[1]-hard when parameterized by p.

Color coding is a technique initially introduced to design fixed-parameter algorithms for various restrictions of the subgraph isomorphism problem. It then gained popularity and it has been successfully applied to tackle the computational hardness of various problems on networks and graphs [9–11], on strings [12,13], and problems of subset selection [14,15]. The basic idea of the color coding technique applied on graph problems is, first, to "color" the vertices of the graph from a set of k colors (for an appropriate choice of the number k of colors), and, then, to find a solution of the given problem with the additional constraint that the vertices of the solution are colored with distinct colors (called a "colorful" or "color coded" solution), if such a solution exists. The process is re-iterated with a different coloring if a colorful solution is not found.

The key theoretical result, which allows to obtain deterministic algorithms based on the color coding technique, is the deterministic construction of k-perfect families of hash functions. A family F of hash functions from a set U (the vertex set in the traditional applications of color coding) to the set $\{1, \ldots, k\}$ of colors is *k-perfect* if, for each subset U' of U such that $|U'| = k$, there exists a hash function f in F such that U' is colorful w.r.t. f, *i.e.*, f assigns a distinct label to each element of U'. In fact, if the given problem has a solution S of size k, then there exists a hash function in F such that solution S is colorful. Hence, it suffices to test if there exists a colorful solution for one of the colorings given by the hash functions of the k-perfect family in order to guarantee the existence of a solution of the original problem, if such a solution exists. Crucial to the overall running time is the size of a k-perfect family and the time required to enumerate and evaluate the hash functions of the family. Currently, the best bounds (such as [8,16,17]) are, in general, explicit constructions of families of size $2^{O(k)} \log^{O(1)}(|U|)$ in time proportional to their size.

The description of the parameterized algorithm for the ℓ-LCDP$_p$ problem is divided into two parts. First, we present a procedure that, given an edge-colored graph G_C and a vertex-coloring function λ, verifies if in G_C there exist p disjoint uni-color st-paths long at most ℓ and with the additional constraint that the inner vertices of the p paths are colored with distinct colors. Then, we show that, by exploiting well-known properties of families of perfect hash functions, the previous procedure can be used to solve the ℓ-LCDP$_p$ problem in polynomial time (if p and ℓ are parameters). In the following, to avoid ambiguities between vertex's and edge's colors, function λ will be called *vertex-labelling* function (or, simply, a *labelling* function) instead of the traditional term of coloring function.

A dynamic-programming procedure for the $\mathcal{L}$-labelled ℓ-LCDP$_p$ problem. Let $G_C = (V, E_1, \ldots, E_c)$ be a C-edge-colored graphs with two distinguished vertices s and t, and let λ be a labelling function which maps each vertex v of $V \setminus \{s,t\}$ to a label $\lambda(v)$ belonging to a set $\mathcal{L}$ (we assume that λ assigns a distinct label to each vertex of a solution of ℓ-LCDP$_p$). Let $L \subseteq \mathcal{L}$ be a fixed set of labels. A simple path π in G_C is *L-labelled* if and only if the labels of its vertices (with the exclusion of s and t) are contained in L and are pairwise distinct. A set $\{\pi_1, \ldots, \pi_k\}$ of simple paths is *L-labelled* if and only if there exists a partition $\{L_1, \ldots, L_k\}$ of L such that each π_i is L_i-labelled. We say that a path π is *g-colored*, with $g \in C$, if all of its edges belong to set E_g. The $\mathcal{L}$-labelled ℓ-LCDP$_p$ problem, given G_C and $\lambda : V \to \mathcal{L}$ with $|\mathcal{L}| = (\ell - 1)p$, asks if there exists an $\mathcal{L}$-labelled solution for the ℓ-LCDP$_p$ problem on G_C. We solve the $\mathcal{L}$-labelled ℓ-LCDP$_p$ problem by combining two dynamic-programming recurrences. The first one, $M[L, v, g]$, tests if, for a set of labels $L \subseteq \mathcal{L}$, there exists an L-labelled g-colored path from vertex s to a vertex v different from t. The second one, $P[L]$, tests if, for a set of labels $L \subseteq \mathcal{L}$ such that $|L| = (\ell - 1)q$ for some integer $q \in [0, p]$, there exists a partition $\{L_1, \ldots, L_q\}$ of L in q subsets such that each set L_i labels a g_i-colored st-path of length $l \leq \ell$.

Recurrence for $M[L, v, g]$ is defined as follows (where $\uplus$ represents the disjoint union operator):

$$M[L, v, g] = \begin{cases} 1 & \text{if } v = s \\ 0 & \text{if } L = \varnothing \text{ and } v \neq s \\ \max\left\{M[L', u, g] \mid L = L' \uplus \{\lambda(v)\} \wedge \{u, v\} \in E_g\right\} & \text{otherwise} \end{cases} \tag{4.1}$$

Correctness of the previous recurrence is proved by the following lemma.

Lemma 6. $M[L, v, g]$ *is* true *if and only if there exists an L-labelled g-colored path from s to v.*

Proof. The proof is by induction on the cardinality of L. If $|L| = 0$, the base cases apply and a path which does not use any label exits if and only if $v = s$. Now, assume that $M[L, v, g]$ is correct for any L such that $|L| \leq k$ (for some k) and we will prove the correctness of $M[L', v, g]$ for all L' such that $|L'| = k + 1$. Moreover, assume that $v \neq s$, since, otherwise, the first base case applies which is clearly correct. Then, an L'-labelled g-colored path from s to $v \neq s$ exists if and only if (*i*) $\lambda(v) \in L$ and (*ii*) there exists an L''-labelled g-colored path π from s to a vertex u such that $\{u, v\} \in E_g$ and $L'' = L' \setminus \{\lambda(v)\}$. Since $|L''| = |L'| - 1 = k$, path π exists if and only if $M[L'', u, g]$ is true. The inductive case of Equation 4.1 tests the above mentioned conditions, hence $M[L', v, g]$ is correct also for sets of labels L such that $|L| = k + 1$, concluding the proof. □

Clearly, M can be used to test if there exists an $\mathcal{L}$-labelled g-colored st-path, as illustrated by the following corollary.

Corollary 7. *The existence of an $\mathcal{L}$-labelled g-colored st-path can be tested in time $O(2^{|\mathcal{L}|}\,|E_g|)$.*

Proof. By Lemma 6, to test the existence of an $\mathcal{L}$-labelled g-colored st-path, it suffices to test the existence of a vertex v such that $\{v,t\} \in E_g$ and $M[\mathcal{L}, v, g]$ is true. For a fixed color g and a fixed set L of labels, the time needed to evaluate $M[L, v, g]$ for all $v \in V$ is $O(|E_g|)$ since each edge is considered only a constant number of times (twice, indeed). Since there exist $2^{|\mathcal{L}|}$ distinct subsets of $\mathcal{L}$, the overall time is $O(2^{|\mathcal{L}|}\,|E_g|)$. □

The second recurrence, $P[L]$, which, given an integer $q \in [0,p]$ and a subset $L \subseteq \mathcal{L}$ such that $|L| = (\ell-1)q$, solves the L-labelled ℓ-LCDP$_q$ problem, is defined as follows:

$$P[L] = \begin{cases} 1 & \text{if } L = \varnothing \\ \max\{P[L'] \wedge M[L'', v, g] \mid \\ \qquad L = L' \uplus L'' \wedge |L''| = (\ell-1) \wedge g \in C \wedge \{v,t\} \in E_g\} & \text{otherwise} \end{cases} \tag{4.2}$$

Notice that we implicitly assume that the solution of the $\varnothing$-labelled ℓ-LCDP$_0$ problem is always YES (*i.e.*, $P[\varnothing] = 1$).

Correctness of Equation 4.2, as proved in the following lemma, derives from Corollary 7, from the bound on the cardinality of L'', and from the disjointness of L' and L''.

Lemma 8. *Given an edge-colored graph G_C and a vertex-labelling function $\lambda : V \to \mathcal{L}$ with $|\mathcal{L}| = (\ell-1)p$, then there exists an $\mathcal{L}$-labelled set $\mathcal{S}$ of p disjoint uni-color st-paths of length at most ℓ if and only if $P[\mathcal{L}]$ is true.*

To prove this lemma, we first prove some intermediate results.

Property 9. *Let L_i and L_j be two disjoint subsets of $\mathcal{L}$, let v_i and v_j be two distinct vertices, and g_i and g_j be two (possibly equal) colors. Then $M[L_i, v_i, g_i]$ and $M[L_j, v_j, g_j]$ are both true if and only if there exist two disjoint uni-color paths π_i and π_j from s to v_i and v_j, respectively.*

Proof. By Lemma 6, since both $M[L_i, v_i, g_i]$ and $M[L_j, v_j, g_j]$ are true, paths π_i and π_j exist labelled with set L_i and L_j, respectively. Since L_i and L_j are disjoint, there could not exist a common vertex v (different from s), otherwise $\lambda(v)$ would belong to both L_i and L_j. Hence, π_i and π_j are disjoint. □

Property 10. *The length of an L-labelled path π from s to a vertex $v \neq t$ is, at most, $|L|$.*

Proof. All the vertices (but s, which is not labelled) of π are labelled with distinct labels in L, hence there could be at most $|L|+1$ vertices in π. □

Proof of Lemma 8. We prove the correctness of P by induction on the number of paths p. If $p = 0$, then $|\mathcal{L}| = (\ell-1)p = 0$. Thus, the base case applies and, since we assume that 0 paths always exist, it is also correct. Let us assume that P is correct for any $p \leq k$ and let us prove its correctness for $p = k+1$. First, we prove that if $P[\mathcal{L}]$ is true, then a solution $\mathcal{S}$ for ℓ-LCDP$_p$ can be built. Notice that the second case of Equation 4.2 tries every possible bi-partition of set $\mathcal{L}$ in two sets L' and L'' of cardinality $|\mathcal{L}| - (\ell-1)$ and $\ell - 1$, respectively. If function $P[\mathcal{L}]$ is true, then at least one of the bi-partitions verifies the given conditions. Notice that $|L'| = |\mathcal{L}| - (\ell - 1) = (\ell - 1)(k+1) - (\ell - 1) = (\ell - 1)k$. Hence, by induction hypothesis, since $P[L']$ is true, there exists an L'-labelled set $\mathcal{S}'$ of k disjoint uni-color st-paths. The other conditions, as shown in the proof of Corollary 7, test the existence of an L''-labelled g-colored st-path π for some color $g \in C$. Thus, if there exists a bi-partition which satisfies all the conditions, then there exits an L-labelled set $\mathcal{S} = \mathcal{S}' \uplus \{\pi\}$ of $k+1$ uni-color st-paths. Moreover, since L' and L'' are disjoint, by Property 9, path π and any path of $\mathcal{S}$ are disjoint. Furthermore, since $|L''| = \ell - 1$, by Property 10, the length of π is, at most, ℓ (in particular, $\ell - 1$ from s to vertex v, plus 1 from v to t). As a consequence, $\mathcal{S}$ is an $\mathcal{L}$-labelled set of $p = k+1$ disjoint uni-color st-paths of length, at most, ℓ.

Now, we prove that if there exists an $\mathcal{L}$-labelled set $\mathcal{S}$ of $(k+1)$ disjoint uni-color st-paths, then $P[\mathcal{L}]$ is true. For each path $\pi \in \mathcal{S}$, let L_i be the set of labels labelling π_i. Since the paths in $\mathcal{S}$ are disjoint, also the sets $L_1, \ldots, L_{k+1}$ are disjoint. Moreover, since the length of each path is at most ℓ, we have that $|L_i| \leq (\ell - 1)$. Notice that $|\mathcal{L}|$ is $(\ell - 1)(k+1)$, thus it is possible to find a partition of $\mathcal{L}$ in p sets $L'_1, \ldots L'_{k+1}$ of cardinality $\ell - 1$ such that each L_i is a subset of L'_i. Let us consider a generic path π_i. Since π_i is a uni-color st-path (of length at most ℓ), then there exists a vertex v and a color g such that $M[L'_i, v, g]$ is true and $\{v, t\} \in E_g$ (Corollary 7). Finally, since $\bar{L}'_i = L \setminus L'_i$ is a set of labels of cardinality $(\ell - 1)k$ and $\mathcal{S} \setminus \{\pi_i\}$ is an $\bar{L}'_i$-labelled set of k disjoint uni-color st-paths of length at most ℓ, by induction hypothesis we have that $P[\bar{L}'_i]$ is true. Therefore, the bi-partition $\{L'_i, \bar{L}'_i\}$ satisfies all the condition of Equation 4.2 and $P[\mathcal{L}]$ is true. □

An immediate consequence is that the $\mathcal{L}$-labelled ℓ-LCDP$_p$ problem can be solved in polynomial time when ℓ and p are parameters.

Corollary 11. *The $\mathcal{L}$-labelled ℓ-LCDP$_p$ problem can be solved in time $O(2^{2\ell p} m)$, where $m = \sum_{g \in C} |E_g|$.*

Proof. The evaluation of M needs $O(2^{|\mathcal{L}|} m)$ time. For a fixed $L \subseteq \mathcal{L}$, the evaluation of $P[L]$ requires $O(2^{|L|} m)$ and, since there are $2^{|\mathcal{L}|}$ possible subsets of $\mathcal{L}$, the time needed to evaluate P is $O(2^{|\mathcal{L}|}) + O(2^{|\mathcal{L}|} 2^{|\mathcal{L}|} m) = O(2^{2\ell p} m)$. □

The algorithm for ℓ-LCDP$_p$. As explained before, it is possible to explicitly construct a k-perfect family F of hash functions, that is a set F of hash functions from a universal set U to the set of integers $\{1, \ldots, k\}$ such that for each $U' \subseteq U$ of cardinality k there exists a hash function $f \in F$ which assigns distinct integers to the elements of U'. It has been shown (see, for example, [8,16,17]) that a k-perfect family of hash functions of size $2^{O(k)} \log^{O(1)} |U|$ can be explicitly constructed in time proportional to its size. As a consequence, the ℓ-LCDP$_p$ problem can be solved by solving the $\mathcal{L}$-labelled ℓ-LCDP$_p$ problem for all the labelling functions given by the hash functions of a $(\ell - 1)p$-perfect family (where $U = V$) in time $2^{O(\ell p)} O(m \log^{O(1)} |V_C|)$. We remark that this algorithm is mainly of theoretical interest, since the running times are impractical even with modest choices of the parameters ℓ and p. However, as formalized by the following theorem, it settles the parameterized complexity of the ℓ-LCDP$_p$ problem for the parameters ℓ and p.

Theorem 12. *The ℓ-LCDP$_p$ problem parameterized by the bound on the path length ℓ and the number p of disjoint uni-color st-paths is in* FPT.

5. Conclusions

In this paper we have considered the MAX CDP problem, a combinatorial problem motivated by applications in social network analysis that, given an edge-colored graph G_C, asks for the maximum number of disjoint uni-color paths in G_C. We have shown that the problem is not approximable within factor $c^{1-\varepsilon}$, for any constant $\varepsilon > 0$, and that the corresponding decision problem (CDP) is W[1]-hard when parametrized by the number p of disjoint uni-color paths. Then, we have given a fixed-parameter algorithm for ℓ-LCDP$_p$, a restriction of the problem where the length of the disjoint paths are bounded by a parameter. An interesting open problem is to improve the time complexity of the fixed-parameter algorithm for ℓ-LCDP$_p$. Moreover, kernelization complexity issues are still completely unexplored.

Acknowledgments

Paola Bonizzoni and Riccardo Dondi have been supported by the PRIN 2010/11 grant "Automi e Linguaggi Formali: Aspetti Matematici e Applicativi".

References

1. Hanneman, R.; Riddle, M. Introduction to Social Network Methods. In *The SAGE Handbook of Social Network Analysis*; Scott, J., Carrington, P.J., Eds.; SAGE Publications Ltd.: Thousand Oaks, CA, USA, 2011; pp. 340–369.
2. Wasserman, S.; Faust, K. *Social Network Analysis: Methods and Applications (Structural Analysis in the Social Sciences)*; Cambridge University Press: Cambridge, UK, 1994.
3. Wu, B.Y. On the maximum disjoint paths problem on edge-colored graphs. *Discret. Optim.* **2012**, *9*, 50–57.
4. Ausiello, G.; Crescenzi, P.; Gambosi, V.; Kann, G.; Marchetti-Spaccamela, A.; Protasi, M. *Complexity and Approximation: Combinatorial Optimization Problems and their Approximability Properties*; Springer-Verlag: Berlin/Heidelberg, Germany, 1999.
5. Zuckerman, D. Linear Degree Extractors and the Inapproximability of Max Clique and Chromatic Number. In *Proceedings of the 38th Annual ACM Symposium on Theory of Computing*; ACM: New York, NY, USA, 2006; pp. 681–690.
6. Niedermeier, R. *Invitation to Fixed-Parameter Algorithms*; Oxford University Press: Oxford, UK, 2006.
7. Downey, R.G.; Fellows, M.R. Fixed-parameter tractability and completeness II: On completeness for W[1]. *Theor. Comput. Sci.* **1995**, *141*, 109–131.
8. Alon, N.; Yuster, R.; Zwick, U. Color-coding. *J. ACM* **1995**, *42*, 844–856.
9. Fellows, M.R.; Fertin, G.; Hermelin, D.; Vialette, S. Upper and lower bounds for finding connected motifs in vertex-colored graphs. *J. Comput. Syst. Sci.* **2011**, *77*, 799–811.
10. Betzler, N.; van Bevern, R.; Fellows, M.R.; Komusiewicz, C.; Niedermeier, R. Parameterized algorithmics for finding connected motifs in biological networks. *IEEE/ACM Trans. Comput. Biol. Bioinf.* **2011**, *8*, 1296–1308.

11. Dondi, R.; Fertin, G.; Vialette, S. Complexity issues in vertex-colored graph pattern matching. *J. Discret. Algorithms* **2011**, *9*, 82–99.
12. Hüffner, F.; Wernicke, S.; Zichner, T. Algorithm engineering for color-coding with applications to signaling pathway detection. *Algorithmica* **2008**, *52*, 114–132.
13. Bonizzoni, P.; Della Vedova, G.; Dondi, R.; Pirola, Y. Variants of constrained longest common subsequence. *Inf. Process. Lett.* **2010**, *110*, 877–881.
14. Koutis, I. A faster parameterized algorithm for set packing. *Inf. Process. Lett.* **2005**, *94*, 7–9.
15. Fellows, M.R.; Knauer, C.; Nishimura, N.; Ragde, P.; Rosamond, F.A.; Stege, U.; Thilikos, D.M.; Whitesides, S. Faster fixed-parameter tractable algorithms for matching and packing problems. *Algorithmica* **2008**, *52*, 167–176.
16. Chen, J.; Lu, S.; Sze, S.H.; Zhang, F. Improved Algorithms for Path, Matching, and Packing Problems. In *SODA*; Bansal, N., Pruhs, K., Stein, C., Eds.; SIAM: Philadelphia, PA, USA, 2007; pp. 298–307.
17. Alon, N.; Gutner, S. Balanced Hashing, Color Coding and Approximate Counting. In *IWPEC*; Chen, J., Fomin, F.V., Eds.; Springer: Berlin/Heidelberg, Germany, 2009; Volume 5917, pp. 1–16.

Algorithms **2013**, *6*, 43-59; doi:10.3390/a6010043

OPEN ACCESS

algorithms

ISSN 1999-4893

www.mdpi.com/journal/algorithms

Article

Computational Study on a PTAS for Planar Dominating Set Problem

Marjan Marzban and Qian-Ping Gu *

School of Computing Science, Simon Fraser University, Burnaby BC, V5A 1S6, Canada;
E-Mail: mmarzban@cs.sfu.ca

* Author to whom correspondence should be addressed; E-Mail: qgu@cs.sfu.ca;
Tel.: +1-778-782-6705; Fax: +1-778-782-3045.

Received: 2 November 2012; in revised form: 10 January 2013 / Accepted: 13 January 2013 / Published: 21 January 2013

Abstract: The dominating set problem is a core NP-hard problem in combinatorial optimization and graph theory, and has many important applications. Baker [JACM 41,1994] introduces a k-outer planar graph decomposition-based framework for designing polynomial time approximation scheme (PTAS) for a class of NP-hard problems in planar graphs. It is mentioned that the framework can be applied to obtain an $O(2^{ck}n)$ time, c is a constant, $(1+1/k)$-approximation algorithm for the planar dominating set problem. We show that the approximation ratio achieved by the mentioned application of the framework is not bounded by any constant for the planar dominating set problem. We modify the application of the framework to give a PTAS for the planar dominating set problem. With k-outer planar graph decompositions, the modified PTAS has an approximation ratio $(1 + 2/k)$. Using $2k$-outer planar graph decompositions, the modified PTAS achieves the approximation ratio $(1+1/k)$ in $O(2^{2ck}n)$ time. We report a computational study on the modified PTAS. Our results show that the modified PTAS is practical.

Keywords: dominating set problem; PTAS; branch-decomposition based algorithms; planar graphs; computational study

---

1. Introduction

An important research area in graph theory and networks is domination; it has been energetically investigated for many years due to its large number of real-world applications, such as resource allocation [1,2] and voting [3]. Haynes *et al.* In their books, [4,5] provide a good survey on domination problems. Let G be a simple undirected graph with the set of vertices $V(G)$ and the set of edges $E(G)$. We denote $|V(G)|$ by n. The r-dominating set D of G is a subset of $V(G)$ containing r vertices, such that for every vertex v in $V(G)$, either $v \in D$ or v is adjacent to a vertex in D. The minimum integer r for which G has a r-dominating set is called the *domination number* of G and is denoted by $\gamma(G)$. The dominating set problem is to decide that given a graph G and an integer r, whether $\gamma(G) \leq r$. The optimization version of this problem is to find a minimum dominating set.

The dominating set problem is a core NP-hard problem in combinatorial optimization and graph theory [6]. There is a long history of research on the approximation and exact algorithms to tackle the intractability of the problem. A minimization problem P is $\alpha-$approximable $(\alpha \geq 1)$ if there is an algorithm which gives a solution for any instance of P in polynomial time in the instance size with solution value at most αOPT, where OPT is the value of an optimal solution for the instance of P. If P is $(1+\epsilon)-$approximable for any fixed $\epsilon > 0$ then P has a polynomial time approximation scheme (PTAS). The dominating set problem for general graphs is $(1 + \log n)-$approximable [7], however, it is not approximable within a factor $(1-\epsilon)\ln n$ for any $\epsilon > 0$ unless $NP \subseteq DTIME(n^{\log\log n})$ [8]. The dominating set problem has been widely studied on an important class of graphs, the *planar* graphs. A graph is planar if it can be drawn on the sphere with no crossing edges. The dominating set problem in planar graphs (planar dominating set problem) remains NP-hard [6] but admits a PTAS [9].

The fixed parameter algorithms have played a central role in exact algorithms for the planar dominating set problem. A minimization problem P is fixed-parameter tractable if given a parameter r, whether OPT of P is at most r can be decided in $f(r)n^{O(1)}$ time, where $f(r)$ is a computable function depending only on r [10]. Such an algorithm is called a *fixed parameter tractable* (FPT) algorithm. Readers may refer to [11] for a survey on new techniques for developing exact algorithms for NP-hard problems. It is shown in [10] that for general graphs, the dominating set problem is not fixed-parameter tractable unless some collapses occur between parametrized complexity classes. However, the planar dominating set problem is fixed-parameter tractable [10]. The planar dominating set problem also admits a linear size kernel [12].

Recent progresses in FPT algorithms result in subexponential time exact algorithms for the planar dominating set problem [13–15]. These algorithms use the tree-/branch-decomposition based approach and have running time $O(2^{c\sqrt{\gamma(G)}}n + n^{O(1)})$, c is a constant. The branch-decomposition based algorithm by Fomin and Thilikos (called FT algorithm in what follows) [14] achieves a smallest constant c in the exponent of the running time. The notion of branch-decomposition of graphs is introduced by Robertson and Seymour [16]. Informally, a branch-decomposition of a graph G is a collection of vertex cut sets of G that decomposes G into subgraphs with each edge of G a minimal subgraph. The width of a branch-decomposition is the maximum size of the vertex cuts in the collection. The branchwidth of G, denoted by $\mathrm{bw}(G)$, is the minimum width of all possible branch-decompositions of G. Given a graph G and a branch-decomposition of G with width β, FT algorithm finds an optimal solution in $O(2^{(3\log_4 3)\beta}n)$ time for the dominating set problem.

For a planar graph G, it is known that a branch-decomposition of minimum width $\mathrm{bw}(G)$ can be computed in $O(n^3)$ time [17,18] and $\mathrm{bw}(G) \leq 3\sqrt{4.5\gamma(G)}$ [14,19]. Alber *et al.* [12] give an $O(n^3)$ time algorithm which computes a subgraph H (kernel) of G such that H has $O(\gamma(G))$ vertices, $\gamma(H) \leq \gamma(G)$, and a minimum dominating set of G can be constructed from a minimum dominating set of H in linear time. Notice that for a subgraph H of G, $\text{bw}(H) \leq \text{bw}(G)$. From the above, the FT algorithm solves the planar dominating set problem in $O(2^{(3\log_4 3)\text{bw}(G)}\gamma(G) + n^3)$ and $O(2^{15.13\sqrt{\gamma(G)}}\gamma(G) + n^3)$ time (The running time of FT algorithm can be further improved to $O(2^{11.98\sqrt{\gamma(G)}}\gamma(G) + n^3)$ using fast matrix multiplication in the dynamic programming step of the algorithm [20]. However, this improvement is only of theoretical interest because the fast matrix multiplication is not practical [21]).

For graphs with small treewidth/branchwidth, an FPT algorithm may be efficient to find an optimal solution, however, for graphs with large treewidth/branchwidth, one may have to rely on approximation algorithms for the planar dominating set problem. A PTAS is highly desired if the solution values are required to be close to optimal with a guaranteed approximation ratio. Baker introduces a framework to obtain PTAS for a class of NP-hard problems [9]. This framework is based on decomposing a planar graph into k-outer planar subgraphs.

A graph G is called *outer planar* or *1-outer planar* if it has a planar embedding such that all vertices of G are incident to a same face (called outer face). For $k > 1$, G is a *k-outer planar graph*, if it has a planar embedding such that removing the vertices of G incident to the outer face will result in a $(k-1)$-outer planar graph. A k-outer planar graph G has a branchwidth of at most $2k$. Baker's PTAS framework for a problem P in a planar graph G is to decompose G into a collection of k-outer planar subgraphs, find an optimal partial solution of P in each subgraph by an exact algorithm, and take the union of the optimal partial solutions as a solution of P in G. When the framework is used for a minimization problem, G is decomposed in such a way that every two "neighbor" k-outer planar subgraphs share "one-level" vertices. Baker shows that the framework gives a $2^{O(k)}n$ time $(1+1/k)$-approximation algorithm for the vertex cover problem in planar graphs and mentions that the framework can be applied to obtain $2^{O(k)}n$ time $(1+1/k)$-approximation algorithms for many other minimization problems, including the planar dominating set problem [9]. For a maximization problem like the independent set problem in planar graphs, Baker's framework gives a $2^{O(k)}n$ time $k/(k+1)$-approximation algorithm.

We show that the approximation ratio of Baker's framework is not bounded by any constant for the planar dominating set problem when two "neighbor" k-outer planar subgraphs share only "one-level" of vertices. To get a PTAS for the planar dominating set problem, the application of the framework has to be modified. We modify the application of the framework by decomposing G into k-outer planar subgraphs such that every two "neighbor" subgraphs share "two-levels" of vertices. Let $O(2^{ck}n)$, c is a constant, be the running time of Baker's framework with "one-level" of overlapping vertices for the planar dominating set problem. We show that the modified application of the framework gives a PTAS with approximation ratio $(1+2/k)$ for the planar dominating set problem. By decomposing G into $2k$-outer planar subgraphs with "two-level" overlapping vertices, the modified PTAS achieves the approximation ratio $(1+1/k)$ in $O(2^{2ck}n)$ time.

In addition to the theoretical progresses in the algorithms for the dominating set problem, the practical performance of algorithms for the problem has received much attention. A computational study of an exact algorithm (FT algorithm) for the planar dominating set problem is reported in [21]. The study shows that the FT algorithm is practically efficient for graphs with small branchwidth. Heuristic algorithms for the dominating set problem have also been well investigated and a computational study of heuristic algorithms is reported in [22]. However, the practical performance of a PTAS is not known for the planar dominating set problem. One hurdle in evaluating the practical performance of a PTAS is the implementation of the algorithm. We conduct a computational study to evaluate the practical performance of the modified PTAS for the planar dominating set problem. In our implementation, the FT algorithm is used to compute an optimal partial solution in each k-outer planar subgraph. Our results show that the PTAS finds solutions with values very close to optimal in a practical time and much better than those given by well used heuristic algorithms. The computational study gives a concrete example on using a PTAS for solving important NP-hard problems in planar graphs and shows that the PTAS is practical for the planar dominating set problem. This work provides a tool for computing solutions close to optimal for the planar dominating set problem.

The next section gives preliminaries of the paper. In Section 3, we review Baker's framework, show that the approximation ratio of the framework is not bounded by a constant with "one-level" of overlapping vertices for the planar dominating set problem, and modify the application of the framework to give a PTAS for the problem. In Section 4, we report the computational study results. The final section concludes the paper.

2. Preliminaries

A graph G consists of a set $V(G)$ of vertices and a set $E(G)$ of edges, where each edge e of $E(G)$ is a subset of two elements from $V(G)$. For edge $e = \{u, v\} \in E(G)$, we say that vertices u and v are adjacent. The node degree of a vertex u is the number of vertices adjacent to u. Vertex u is dominated by vertex v if u and v are adjacent or $u = v$. Vertex u is dominated by a set D if u is dominated by a vertex of D. Edge e is covered by a vertex u if $u \in e$. For a subset $U \subseteq V(G)$ and a subset $A \subseteq E(G)$, we denote by $G[U]$ and $G[A]$ the subgraphs of G induced by U and A, respectively. For a subset $A \subseteq E(G)$, we denote by $E(G) \setminus A$ by $\overline{A}$ when G is clear from the context. A separation of graph G is a pair $(A, \overline{A})$ of subsets of $E(G)$. For each $A \subseteq E(G)$, we denote by $\partial(A)$ the vertex set $V(A) \cap V(\overline{A})$. The *order* of separation $(A, \overline{A})$ is $|\partial(A)| = |\partial(\overline{A})|$.

A graph G is planar if G has a planar embedding (a draw on a sphere without edge crossing). We call a planar embedding of G a plane graph. A face of a plane graph G is a connected region of the sphere bounded by edges and vertices of G and containing no edge or vertex of G in its interior. For a plane graph G and a face f of G, let $V_G(f)$ be the set of vertices in $V(G)$ incident to f. Given a plane graph G and a face f_o (called outer face) of G, let $V_1 = V_G(f_o)$. For $i \geq 1$, let $U_i = \cup_{j=1}^{i} V_j$, $G_i = G[V(G) \setminus U_i]$, f_i be the face of G_i such that $f_o \subseteq f_i$, and $V_{i+1} = V_{G_i}(f_i)$. We call the vertices of V_i *level* i vertices of G. Intuitively, G_i is the plane graph obtained from removing vertices of levels $1, 2, ..., i$ from G. V_{i+1} is the vertices of G_i incident to the outer face of G_i.

Branch-decomposition based algorithms play a central role in the PTAS studied in this paper. The notion of branch-decomposition is introduced by Robertson and Seymour [16]. A *branch-decomposition* of graph G is a pair (ϕ, T) where T is a tree each internal node of which has degree 3 and ϕ is a bijection from the set of leaves of T to $E(G)$. Consider a link e of T and let L_1 and L_2 denote the sets of leaves of T in the two respective subtrees of T obtained by removing e. We say that the separation $(\phi(L_1), \phi(L_2))$ is induced by this link e of T. We define the width of the branch-decomposition (ϕ, T) to be the largest order of the separations induced by links of T. The *branchwidth* of G, denoted by bw(G), is the minimum width of all branch-decompositions of G. In the rest of this paper, we identify a branch-decomposition (ϕ, T) with the tree T, regarding each leaf of T as an edge of G.

Given a branch-decomposition T of G, an optimization problem P in G may be solved by the dynamic programming method as follows: convert T into a rooted binary tree by replacing a link $\{x, y\}$ of T with three links $\{x, z\}, \{y, z\}, \{z, r\}$, where z and r are new nodes to T, and r is the root of T. For a link $e = \{u, v\}$ of T, assume u is the end node reachable from root r by passing through e. Let A_e be the set of leaves of T reachable from r by passing through e. Link $e = \{u, v\}$ is called a leaf link if u is a leaf node, otherwise an internal link. An internal link e has two child links e_1 and e_2 covered by u. Notice that $A_e = A_{e_1} \cup A_{e_2}$. For a leaf link e, all partial solutions of P in the subgraph $G[A_e]$ can be computed by enumeration. For an internal link e, assume that all partial solutions of P in the subgraph $G[A_{e_1}]$ and those in $G[A_{e_2}]$ have been computed. Then all partial solutions of P in the subgraph $G[A_e]$ are computed by merging the partial solutions in $G[A_{e_1}]$ and those in $G[A_{e_2}]$. The merging process is performed in a bottom-up way, from each leaf link to the link $\{z, r\}$, to find an optimal solution of P in G.

The FT algorithm is a branch-decomposition-based algorithm for the planar dominating set problem. In FT Algorithm, the number of partial solutions in $G[A_e]$ is $3^{|\partial(A_e)|}$. To compute a partial solution in $G[A_e]$, every pair (s_1, s_2) is checked, where s_1 and s_2 are partial solutions in $G[A_{e_1}]$ and $G[A_{e_2}]$, respectively. Notice that each of $|\partial(A_e)|, |\partial(A_{e_1})|, |\partial(A_{e_2})|$ is at most the width of the given branch-decomposition T. When an optimal branch-decomposition T (of width bw(G)) is given, the FT algorithm takes $O(2^{(3\log_4 3)\text{bw}(G)})$ time and $O(3^{\text{bw}(G)}\gamma(G))$ memory space to compute the partial solutions in $G[A_e]$. A planar graph G can be reduced to a kernel of size $O(\gamma(G))$ in $O(n^3)$ time and there are $O(\gamma(G))$ merging steps for the kernel. An optimal branch-decomposition of the kernel can be computed in $O((\gamma(G))^3)$ time. The FT algorithm solves the planar dominating set problem in $O(2^{(3\log_4 3)\text{bw}(G)}\gamma(G) + n^3)$ time [14]. For many other NP-hard problems, branch-decomposition-based algorithms usually have exponential time and memory space in the width of a given branch-decomposition. The exponential time and memory space are often a bottle-neck in applying branch-decomposition-based algorithms in practice.

3. PTAS for Planar Dominating Set Problem

3.1. Baker's Framework for Minimization Problem

We review Baker's PTAS framework for minimization problems. We define the terminology for describing the framework. Given a plane graph G with m levels of vertices, for integers $2 \leq k < m$ and $2 \leq s \leq k+1$, let $r = \lceil (m-s)/k \rceil$. We define $U(0, s) = \cup_{j=1}^{s} V_j$; $U(i, s) = \cup_{j=0}^{k} V_{(i-1)\times k+s+j}$ for $1 \leq i < r$; and $U(r, s) = \cup_{j=(r-1)\times k+s}^{m} V_j$. Then $G[U(0, s)]$ is the plane subgraph of G induced by the vertices of G with levels $1, ..., s$ and is s-outer planar; each $G[U(i, s)]$ is the subgraph of G induced by the vertices of G with levels $(i-1) \times k + s, ..., i \times k + s$ and is $(k+1)$-outer planar for $1 \leq i < r$; and $G[U(r, s)]$ is the subgraph of G induced by the vertices of G with levels $(r-1) \times k + s, ..., m$ and is t-outer planar, where $t = m - [(r-1) \times k + s] + 1 \leq k + 1$. Below is Baker's PTAS framework for minimization problems.

1. Let G be a plane graph with m levels of vertices for an outer face and $k \geq 2$ be an integer. Compute the vertex sets $V_1, ..., V_m$.
2. for $s = 2, ..., k+1$
   (a) Compute subgraphs $G[U(i,s)]$ for $i = 0, 1, ..., r$.
   (b) For every subgraph $G[U(i,s)]$, find an optimal solution $S(i,s)$ by an exact algorithm.
   (c) Let $S_s = \cup_{i=0}^{r} S(i,s)$.
3. Let S be a set of $S_2, ..., S_{k+1}$ with the minimum cardinality.

Baker [9] gives a proof that the above framework achieves a $(1 + 1/k)$-approximation ratio for the minimum vertex cover problem in plane graph G: find a minimum subset C of $V(G)$ such that every edge of G is covered by a vertex in C. We review Baker's proof of the approximation ratio for the vertex cover problem. This proof gives a base on our later argument for the planar dominating set problem.

Given a plane graph G, let C be a minimum vertex cover of G. Given integer k, let $S(i,s)$ be a minimum vertex cover of $G[U(i,s)]$ and let $C(i,s) = C \cap U(i,s)$, $s = 2, ..., k+1$ and $0 \leq i \leq r$. Since no vertex of G in $V(G) \setminus U(i,s)$ covers any edge of $G[U(i,s)]$, $C(i,s)$ is a vertex cover of subgraph $G[U(i,s)]$. From this and the fact that $S(i,s)$ is a minimum vertex cover of $G[U(i,s)]$, $|S(i,s)| \leq |C(i,s)|$. Therefore, $S_s = \cup_{i=0}^{r} S(i,s)$ is a vertex cover of G and

$$|S_s| \leq \sum_{i=0}^{r} |S(i,s)| \leq \sum_{i=0}^{r} |C(i,s)| \tag{1}$$

Since the vertices of $V_{i \times k+s}$ appear in both subgraphs $G[U(i,s)]$ and $G[U(i+1,s)]$, $0 \leq i < r$,

$$\sum_{i=0}^{r} |C(i,s)| = |C| + \sum_{i=0}^{r-1} |C \cap V_{i \times k+s}| \tag{2}$$

Notice that

$$\min_{s=2}^{k+1} \{\sum_{i=0}^{r-1} |C \cap V_{i \times k+s}|\} \leq \frac{|C|}{k} \tag{3}$$

Let S be a S_s with a minimum cardinality. Then from Inequalities (1), (2), and (3), we have $|S| \leq |C| + \frac{|C|}{k}$, that is, the solution produced by Baker's framework has the approximation ratio $(1 + 1/k)$ for the minimum vertex cover problem in planar graphs.

3.2. Modified Framework for Planar Dominating Set Problem

In [9], it is mentioned that the framework in the previous section can be applied to obtain a $(1+1/k)$-approximation algorithm for the planar dominating set problem. We show that this is not true. Recall that for the vertex cover problem, no vertex of G in $V(G) \setminus U(i,s)$ can cover any edge of $G[U(i,s)]$. This implies that for a minimum vertex cover C, $C(i,s) = C \cap U(i,s)$ is a vertex cover of subgraph $G[U(s,i)]$ and a minimum vertex cover $S(i,s)$ of $G[U(i,s)]$ has the property $|S(i,s)| \leq |C(i,s)|$. However, for the planar dominating set problem, the intersection of a minimum dominating set of G and $U(i,s)$ may not be a dominating set of $G[U(i,s)]$ because a vertex of G in $V(G) \setminus U(i,s)$ can dominate a vertex of $G[U(i,s)]$. More specifically, let D be a minimum dominating set of G, $D(i,s) = D \cap U(i,s)$ and $S(i,s)$

be a minimum dominating set of $G[U(i,s)]$. Then $D(i,s)$ may not be a dominating set of $G[U(i,s)]$ and $|S(i,s)| \leq |D(i,s)|$ may not hold. Below we show by an example that the approximation ratio of the mentioned application of Baker's framework is not bounded by any constant for the planar dominating set problem.

Let G be a plane graph with 4 levels of vertices shown in Figure 1. Let X_i be the set of vertices of G with labels $(i,1),...,(i,x)$, $1 \leq i \leq 6$. The subgraph $G[X_i]$ is a chain and there is a unique vertex in G dominating all vertices of X_i. For a large x, G has a unique minimum dominating set D with its six vertices shown as black squares in the figure. Let $k = 2$. For $s = 2$, the subgraphs $G[U(0,2)]$ and $G[U(1,2)]$ are shown in Figure 2 (a) and (b), respectively. Let $D(0,2) = D \cap U(0,2)$. Then $D(0,2)$ (the set of vertices denoted by black squares) is not a dominating set of $G[U(0,2)]$. On the other hand, a minimum dominating set $S(0,2)$ of $G[U(0,2)]$ contains a fraction of vertices in X_3 and $|S(0,2)| > |D(0,2)|$ for large $x = |X_3|$. Similarly, a minimum dominating set $S(1,2)$ of $G[U(1,2)]$ contains a fraction of vertices in X_2 and $|S(1,2)| > |D(1,2)|$. Let $S_2 = S(0,2) \cup S(1,2)$. Then $|S_2|/|D|$ is not bounded by any constant for non-constant x.

Figure 1. A plane graph G with four levels of vertices.

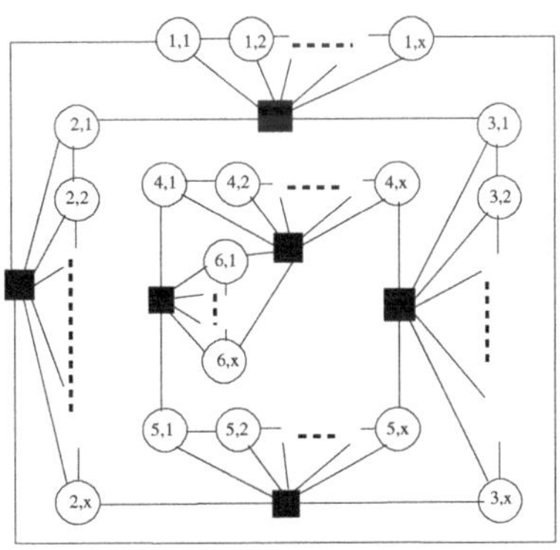

Figure 2. (**a**) Subgraph $G[U(0,2)]$ and (**b**) Subgraph $G[U(1,2)]$ of G.

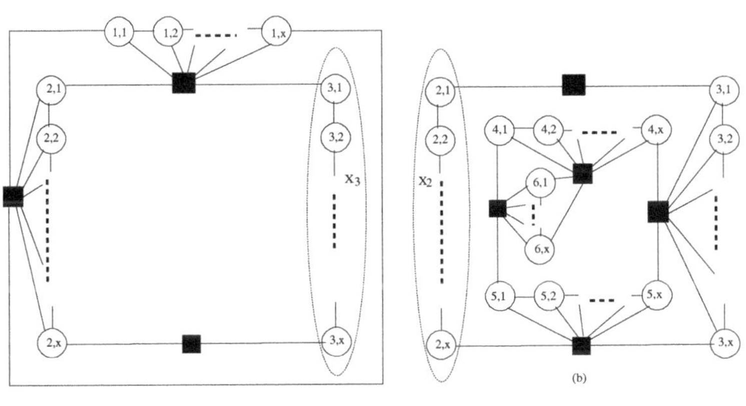

For $s = 3$, the subgraphs $G[U(0,3)]$ and $G[U(1,3)]$ are shown in Figure 3 (a) and (b), respectively. Then a minimum dominating set $S(0,3)$ of $G[U(0,3)]$ contains a fraction of vertices in X_4 and a minimum dominating set $S(1,3)$ of $G[U(1,3)]$ contains a fraction of vertices in X_5. Let $S_3 = S(0,3) \cup S(1,3)$. Then $|S_3|/|D|$ is not bounded by any constant for non-constant $x = |X_4|$. Therefore, for a set S of S_2 and S_3 with the minimum cardinality, $|S|/|D|$ is not bounded by any constant for non-constant x.

Figure 3. (**a**) Subgraph $G[U(0,3)]$ and (**b**) Subgraph $G[U(1,3)]$ of G.

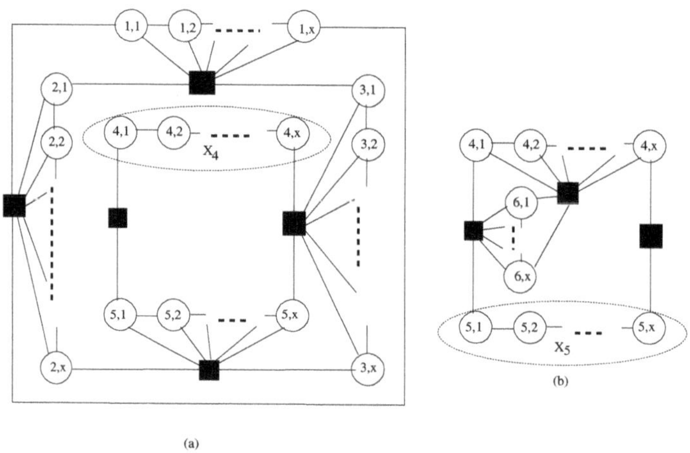

We modify the application of Baker's framework to get a PTAS for the planar dominating set problem. The idea for the modification is that instead of decomposing G into $(k+1)$-outer planar subgraphs with two neighbor subgraphs $G[U(i,s)]$ and $G[U(i+1,s)]$ overlapping on one level of vertices, we decompose G into $(k+2)$-outer planar subgraphs with two neighbor subgraphs overlapping on two levels of vertices. For each subgraph, we find a minimum set which dominates only k levels of vertices in the subgraph. The formal modification is described below.

Let G be a plane graph with m levels of vertices. For integers $2 \leq k < m$ and $2 \leq s \leq k+1$, let $r = \lceil (m-s)/k \rceil$. We define $W(0,s) = \cup_{j=1}^{s} V_j$; $W(i,s) = \cup_{j=-1}^{k} V_{(i-1)\times k+s+j}$ for $1 \leq i < r$; and $W(r,s) = \cup_{j=(r-1)\times k+s-1}^{m} V_j$. $G[W(0,s)]$ is the subgraph of G induced by the vertices of G with levels $1, ..., s$ and is s-outer planar; each $G[W(i,s)]$ is the subgraph of G induced by the vertices of G with levels $(i-1)\times k+s-1, ..., i\times k+s$ and is $(k+2)$-outer planar for $1 \leq i < r$; and $G[W(r,s)]$ is the subgraph of G induced by the vertices of G with levels $(r-1)\times k+s-1, ..., m$ and is t-outer planar, where $t = m-[(r-1)\times k+s]+2 \leq k+2$. We call the vertices of $G[W(0,s)]$ with level s, the vertices of each subgraph $G[W(i,s)]$ $(1 \leq i < r)$ with levels $(i-1)\times k+s-1$ and $i\times k+s$, and the vertices of $G[W(r,s)]$ with level $(r-1)\times k+s-1$ the *vertices on boundary*; and call the other vertices the *interior vertices*.

1. Let G be a plane graph with m levels of vertices for an outer face and $k \geq 2$ be an integer. Compute the vertex sets $V_1, ..., V_m$.
2. for $s = 2, ..., k+1$

(a) Compute subgraphs $G[W(i,s)]$ for $i = 0, 1, ..., r$.

(b) For subgraph $G[W(0,s)]$, find a minimum subset $S(0,s)$ of $W(0,s)$ that dominates every vertex of $\cup_{j=1}^{s-1} V_j$ (every interior vertex).
For every subgraph $G[W(i,s)]$, $i = 1, ..., r-1$, find a minimum subset $S(i,s)$ of $W(i,s)$ that dominates every vertex of $\cup_{j=(i-1)\times k+s}^{i\times k+s-1} V_j$ (every interior vertex).
For subgraph $G[W(r,s)]$, find a minimum subset $S(r,s)$ of $W(r,s)$ that dominates every vertex of $\cup_{j=(r-1)\times k+s}^{m} V_j$ (every interior vertex).

(c) Let $S_s = \cup_{i=0}^{r} S(i,s)$.

3. Let S be a set of $S_2, ..., S_{k+1}$ with the minimum cardinality.

Theorem 3.1 *The modified application of Baker's framework gives an $O(2^{(6\log_4 3)(k+2)}kn)$ time $(1+2/k)$-approximation algorithm for the planar dominating set problem.*

Proof: We first show the approximation ratio of the framework. Notice that $S_s = \cup_{i=0}^{r} S(i,s)$ dominates every vertex of

$$(\cup_{j=1}^{s-1} V_j) \cup [\cup_{i=1}^{r-1} (\cup_{j=(i-1)\times k+s}^{i\times k+s-1} V_j)] \cup (\cup_{j=(r-1)\times k+s}^{m} V_j) = \cup_{j=1}^{m} V_j = V(G)$$

that is, S_s is a dominating set of G. Let D be a minimum dominating set of G and let $D(i,s) = D \cap W(i,s)$, $s = 2, ..., k+1$ and $0 \le i \le r$. Since no vertex of G in $V(G) \setminus W(i,s)$ can dominate any interior vertex of $G[W(i,s)]$ and D dominates every vertex of G, $D(i,s)$ dominates every interior vertex of $G[W(i,s)]$. From this and the fact that $S(i,s)$ is a minimum subset of $W(i,s)$ dominating every interior vertex of $G[W(i,s)]$, $|S(i,s)| \le |D(i,s)|$. From this, we have

$$|S_s| \le \sum_{i=0}^{r} |S(i,s)| \le \sum_{i=0}^{r} |D(i,s)| \tag{4}$$

Since the vertices of $V_{i\times k+s-1}$ and $V_{i\times k+s}$ appear in subgraphs $G[W(i,s)]$ and $G[W(i+1,s)], 0 \le i < r$,

$$\sum_{i=0}^{r} |D(i,s)| \le |D| + \sum_{i=0}^{r-1} |D \cap V_{i\times k+s-1}| + |D \cap V_{i\times k+s}| \tag{5}$$

Notice that

$$\min_{s=2}^{k+1}\{\sum_{i=0}^{r-1} |D \cap V_{i\times k+s-1}| + |D \cap V_{i\times k+s}|\} \le \frac{2|D|}{k} \tag{6}$$

Let S be an S_s with a minimum cardinality. Then from Inequalities (4), (5), and (6), we have $|S| \le |D| + \frac{2|D|}{k}$. that is, the solution produced by the modified algorithm has the approximation ratio $(1+2/k)$ for the planar dominating set problem.

Given a planar graph G, a planar embedding of G can be computed in linear time [23]. It is obvious that Step 1 and Step 3 can be computed in linear time. Step 2 (a) and (c) can be computed in $O(kn)$ time. Recall that FT Algorithm (by Fomin and Thilikos [14]) is the most efficient known exact algorithm for the planar dominaing set problem. We use FT Algorithm for Step 2 (b). Given a graph G and a branch-decomposition of G with width β, FT Algorithm finds an optimal solution for the dominating set problem in $O(2^{(3\log_4 3)\beta}n)$ time. Each subgraph $G[W(i,s)]$ is $(k+2)$-outer planar and has branchwidth at most $2(k+2)$. A branch-decomposition of $G[W(i,s)]$ with width at most $2(k+2)$ can be computed in linear time [24]. Each vertex of G appears in at most two subgraphs for a specific value s. Therefore, Step 2 (b) takes

$$\sum_{s=2}^{k+1}\sum_{i=0}^{r} O(2^{(6\log_4 3)(k+2)}|W(i,s)|) = \sum_{s=2}^{k+1} O(2^{(6\log_4 3)(k+2)}n) = O(2^{(6\log_4 3)(k+2)}kn)$$

time which is the dominating part of the modified application's running time. []

Notice that if G is decomposed into $(2k+2)$-outer planar subgraphs, the modified PTAS achieves the approximation ratio $(1+1/k)$ and has running time $O(2^{(12\log_4 3)(k+1)}kn)$.

We conclude this section by comparing the running time of the modified PTAS with that of the application of Baker's framework in Section 3.1 for the planar dominating set problem. We assume that the most efficient FT Algorithm is used in Step 2 (b) of both algorithms. Assume that G is decomposed into $(k+1)$-outer planar subgraphs in Baker's framework in Section 3.1. Then a branch-decomposition of $G[U(i,s)]$ with width at most $2(k+1)$ can be computed in linear time and Step 2 (b) takes

$$\sum_{s=2}^{k+1}\sum_{i=0}^{r} O(2^{(6\log_4 3)(k+1)}|U(i,s)|) = O(2^{(6\log_4 3)(k+1)}kn)$$

time which is the dominating part of the framework's running time. The constant in the exponent of the running time of the modified PTAS for the approximation ratio $(1+1/k)$ is as twice as that of Baker's framework in Section 3.1.

4. Computational Study of PTAS

We study the practical performance of the PTAS for the planar dominating set problem. The PTAS is implemented in C++ and its performance is tested for four different classes of graphs including the Delaunay triangulations of point sets taken from TSPLIB [25] (Class (1)), triangulations (Class (2)) and intersection graphs (Class (3)) generated by LEDA [26] and Gabriel graphs (Class (4)) generated using the points uniformly distributed in a two-dimensional plane. Those classes of graphs are well used in previous computational studies and the branchwidth of the graphs increases in the size of graphs (for classes of graphs with small branchwidth such as the maximal random planar graphs from LEDA [26], the FT algorithm can find optimal solutions efficiently [21] and thus they are not interesting in this study). The computer used for testing has an AMD Athlon(tm) 64 X2 Dual Core Processor 4600+ (2.4 GHz) and 3 GByte of internal memory. The operating system is SUSE Linux 10.2.

We use the FT algorithm to compute an optimal solution for each $(k+2)$-outer planar subgraph. There are three major steps of FT Algorithm:

1. Compute a linear size kernel H of the subgraph using the $O(n^3)$ time kernelization algorithm by Alber *et al.* [12].
2. Compute an optimal branch-decomposition of H by the $O(n^3)$ time algorithm [17,18].
3. Find an optimal solution for H by dynamic programming based on the branch-decomposition of H and compute an optimal solution for the subgraph from the optimal solution for H.

Step 3 has exponential time complexity and memory complexity in the width of the branch-decomposition used, and is the dominating part in the running time and used memory of the FT algorithm. Thus we include the kernelization in the FT algorithm because, for a kernel H of a graph G, $\text{bw}(H) \leq \text{bw}(G)$ and it often happens that $\text{bw}(H) < \text{bw}(G)$ for a kernel computed. Also, the effort for computing an optimal branch-decomposition reduces the running time and used memory in practice. For a planar graph G, the FT algorithm implemented runs in $O(2^{(3\log_4 3)\text{bw}(H)}\gamma(G) + n^3)$ time and uses $O(3^{\text{bw}(H)}\gamma(G))$ memory space. Readers may refer to [21] for more details on the practical performance of the FT algorithm.

Table 1 shows the computational results of the PTAS for the planar dominating set problem. For every instance, we calculate the approximated solutions for two different values of k, 3 and 4, and, for every value of k, we calculate the $(k + 2)$-outer planar decomposition for every face of the instance. We choose the best value for an approximated solution. For some instances with small branchwidth, we also include the optimal solutions computed by the FT algorithm and reported in [21] in the column of "Exact Alg.". The size of a minimum dominating set of graph G, computed by the FT algorithm, is indicated by $\gamma(G)$ in Table 1, and for every value of k, D_{PTAS} is the size of dominating set computed by the PTAS. In the table, bw is the branchwidth of G, β is the branchwidth of a kernel H of G in the FT algorithm and the largest branchwidth of a kernel H of a $(k + 2)$-outer planar subgraph in PTAS. The running time is in seconds. For two large instances rand16000 and rand20000, we only compute $\gamma(G)$ but not the minimum dominating sets by the FT algorithm due to the memory constraint. These values of $\gamma(G)$ are identified by "*".

In order to compare the size of dominating sets obtained from the PTAS with the optimal solutions, we include some instances with small branchwidth for every class of graphs, such that a minimum dominating set can be computed by FT Algorithm. The Exact Alg. column shows the results of FT Algorithm reported in [21]. We use two values for k to decompose the instances into $(k+2)$-outer planar component. Notice that the branchwidth of every $(k+2)$-outer planar graph is at most $2(k+2)$. Hence, by increasing k the size of subgraphs and their branchwidth will increase. Theoretical results suggest that increasing k gives smaller approximated solutions for minimization problems. Our computing results confirm the theoretical analysis of the k-outer planar decomposition method. For example, for $k = 4$, every instance can be decomposed into subgraphs with a branchwidth of at most 12. This is the largest value of branchwidth that can be processed on our computational platform in a practical time.

Since the theory of NP-completeness has reduced hopes that NP-hard problems can be solved in polynomial time, heuristic and approximation algorithms have attracted more attentions. These algorithms compute near optimal solutions within a reasonable time for problems of practical size. We compare the performance of the PTAS with the performance of three different heuristic algorithms introduced in [22] for the planar dominating set problem. In what follows we briefly explain these heuristic algorithms (for more details please refer to [22]).

In [22], six heuristic algorithms for the dominating set problem are studied. We test the performance of these six methods, but only report three of them with better performances. The three reported heuristics are described below. Let D be a dominating set computed by these heuristics.

Table 1. Computational results (time in seconds) of PTAS for the planar dominating set problem.

	Graph	$\|E(G)\|$	bw	**Exact Alg.**			**k = 3**			**k = 4**		
	G			$\gamma(G)$	β	**time**	D_{PTAS}	β	**time**	D_{PTAS}	β	**time**
(1)	kroB150	436	10	23	10	10	28	8	2.07	-	-	-
	pr299	864	11	47	11	37	56	10	11.42	-	-	-
	tsp225	622	12	37	12	110	46	9	5.21	-	-	-
	a280	788	13	43	13	337	53	10	8.40	51	12	12.09
	rd400	1183	17	-	-	-	75	10	35.30	74	12	351.93
	pcb442	1286	17	-	-	-	79	10	10.46	78	10	10.86
	d657	1958	22	-	-	-	123	10	64.89	120	12	604.10
	pr1002	2972	21	-	-	-	190	10	115.65	182	12	1253.9
(2)	tri2000	5977	8	321	7	198	361	7	175.59	-	-	-
	tri4000	11969	9	653	7	1903	724	7	733.06	-	-	-
	tri6000	17979	9	975	8	3576	1136	8	1994.53	-	-	-
	tri8000	23975	9	1283	7	7750	1430	7	2858.63	-	-	-
	tri10000	29976	9	1606	7	16495	1804	7	4977.06	-	-	-
	tri11000	32972	14	-	-	-	1987	8	5910.8	1958	8	12341.1
	tri12000	35974	14	-	-	-	2164	7	5370.18	2132	7	6865.08
	tri14000	41974	15	-	-	-	2514	7	8220.49	2434	7	9208.72
	tri16000	47969	16	-	-	-	2920	7	10060.1	2885	7	12794.4
(3)	rand6000	10293	11	1563	9	150	1658	8	104.85	-	-	-
	rand10000	17578	13	2535	10	869	2850	8	535.87	2692	9	432.23
	rand15000	26717	14	3758	12	2769	4144	10	1313.14	-	-	-
	rand16000	28624	13	4002*	13	5917	4379	10	2443.27	4295	11	2027.7
	rand20000	35975	14	4963*	14	13993	5465	10	4241.65	5368	12	5017.02
	rand25000	40378	16	-	-	-	7101	8	6407.91	6632	12	9470
(4)	Gab500	949	13	115	12	238	136	10	18.02	129	10	18.95
	Gab600	1174	14	135	14	3074	164	10	26.05	156	10	22.10
	Gab700	1302	14	162	14	5710	187	10	22.81	183	10	24.30
	Gab800	1533	17	-	-	-	225	10	51.82	205	12	24.30
	Gab900	1758	17	-	-	-	243	10	48.39	231	12	344.50
	Gab1000	1901	18	-	-	-	260	10	49.69	259	12	781.89
	Gab1500	2870	21	-	-	-	402	10	116.37	385	12	960.71

Greedy: Initially, D is empty. In each iteration, a vertex which dominates a maximum number of vertices in $V(G) \setminus D$ is added to D.

Greedy-Rev: Initially $D = V(G)$. In each iteration, a vertex is removed from D, such that the resulting set remains a dominating set of G. A vertex is chosen to be removed, by ordering the vertices of D in increasing node degree, and removing the first vertex that does not dominate any vertex uniquely.

Greedy-Vote: Initially, D is empty. This algorithm does not include a vertex u in D only based on the number of vertices which are dominated by u. It uses a more complex voting scheme to select a vertex to be included. We omit the details of the selection scheme and readers may refer to [22] for details.

Table 2. Computational results for heuristic algorithms and PTAS for the planar dominating set problem (time in seconds).

	Graph	$\|E(G)\|$	$\gamma(G)$	Greedy Alg.		Greedy-Rev Alg.		Greedy-Vote Alg.		PTAS	
	G			D_{Gr}	time	D_{Rev}	time	D_{Vote}	time	D_{PTAS}	time
(1)	kroB150	436	23	27	0.002	31	0.01	31	0.002	28	2.08
	pr299	864	47	54	0.003	63	0.032	62	0.005	56	11.42
	tsp225	622	37	49	0.153	54	0.02	50	0.003	46	5.21
	a280	788	43	51	0.004	62	0.025	62	0.006	51	12.09
	rd400	1183	-	78	0.007	92	0.032	90	0.009	74	351.93
	pcb442	1286	-	76	0.908	90	0.063	87	0.01	78	10.86
	d657	1958	-	126	0.016	146	0.128	143	0.021	120	604.10
	pr1002	2972	-	190	0.032	236	0.328	194	0.04	182	1253.9
(2)	tri2000	5977	321	365	0.116	379	1.119	464	0.168	361	175.59
	tri4000	11969	653	729	0.183	765	1.792	787	0.544	724	733.06
	tri6000	17979	975	1118	0.418	1166	4.14	1306	0.541	1136	1994.53
	tri8000	23975	1283	1449	0.715	1522	7.003	1653	0.918	1430	2858.63
	tri10000	29976	1606	1819	1.117	1906	11.524	2302	1.572	1804	4977.06
	tri11000	32972	-	2040	1.375	2116	14.092	3431	2.561	1958	12341.1
	tri12000	35974	-	2186	1.607	2278	16.538	2741	2.243	2132	6865.08
	tri14000	41974		2576	2.462	2664	22.976	3317	3.163	2434	9208.72
	tri16000	47969	-	2917	2.839	3033	30.694	3684	4.005	2885	12794.4
(3)	rand6000	10293	1563	1932	0.748	2166	4.517	2908	1.206	1658	104.85
	rand10000	17578	2535	3197	2.06	3618	13.33	4164	2.878	2692	432.23
	rand15000	26717	3758	4698	4.861	5402	29.487	7277	7.641	4144	1313.14
	rand16000	28624	4002*	5039	5.176	5744	35.589	7552	10.327	4295	2027.7
	rand20000	35975	4963*	6273	8.053	7168	55.948	8571	11.903	5398	5017.02
	rand25000	45327	-	7772	12.467	8942	91.039	11865	20.615	6632	9470
(4)	Gab500	949	115	146	0.006	173	0.039	160	0.007	129	18.95
	Gab600	1174	135	168	0.007	199	0.051	171	0.009	156	22.10
	Gab700	1302	162	200	0.01	242	0.072	238	0.012	183	24.30
	Gab800	1533	-	227	0.012	270	0.097	307	0.019	205	24.30
	Gab900	1758	-	254	0.016	303	0.103	323	0.022	231	344.50
	Gab1000	1901	-	280	0.019	344	0.146	423	0.03	259	781.89
	Gab1500	2870	-	426	0.042	507	0.335	496	0.051	385	960.71

We study the performances of the above heuristic algorithms for the four classes of planar graphs that are used in the study of the PTAS. These heuristic algorithms are implemented in C++. Table 2 shows the computational results of these heuristic algorithms and the PTAS. In Table 2, D_{Gr}, D_{Rev}, and D_{Vote} are the sizes of dominating sets computed by the heuristic algorithm Greedy, Greedy-Rev, and Greedy-Vote, respectively. For every graph instance, if the size of the instance allows the application of the FT algorithm, we include the size of the minimum dominating set of the instance, as well. For the PTAS, we include the best result D_{PTAS} for every instance from Table 1. Time in the table is in seconds.

The results in the table show that the heuristic algorithms are always faster than the PTAS. However, the size of dominating sets computed by the heuristics are larger than those by the PTAS for most of instances.

Based on our computational results, the Greedy algorithm gives the smallest dominating sets compared to other heuristic algorithms. Table 3 shows the results of our computational study for the FT algorithm, Greedy (the best heuristic method) and PTAS for graph instances whose branchwidths are small enough to run the FT algorithm.

Table 3. Computational results for Exact, Greedy and PTAS algorithms for small instances (time in seconds).

	Graph	$\|E(G)\|$	**Exact Alg.**		**Greedy Alg.**		**PTAS**	
	G		$\gamma(G)$	**time**	D_G	**time**	D_{PTAS}	**time**
(1)	kroB150	436	23	10	27	0.002	28	2.08
	pr299	864	47	37	54	0.032	56	11.42
	tsp225	622	37	110	49	0.153	46	5.21
	a280	788	43	337	51	0.004	51	12.09
(2)	tri2000	5977	321	198	365	0.116	361	175.59
	tri4000	11969	653	1903	729	0.183	724	733.06
	tri6000	17979	975	3576	1118	0.418	1136	1994.53
	tri8000	23975	1283	7750	1449	0.715	1430	2858.63
	tri10000	29976	1606	16495	1819	1.117	1804	4977.06
(3)	rand6000	10293	1563	150	1932	0.748	1658	104.85
	rand10000	17578	2535	869	3197	2.06	2692	432.23
	rand15000	26727	3758	2769	4698	4.861	4144	1313.14
	rand16000	28624	4002*	5917	5039	5.176	4295	2027.7
	rand20000	35975	4963*	13993	6273	8.053	5398	5017.02
(4)	Gab500	949	115	238	146	0.006	129	18.95
	Gab600	1174	135*	3074	168	0.007	156	22.10
	Gab700	1302	162*	5710	200	0.01	183	24.30

Since the branchwidth of graphs in Class(1) grow quickly in the size of graphs, we have only included small instances of this class in Table 3. From the results of the table, we recommend the FT algorithm for optimal solutions if the branchwidth of a graph in Class (1) is smaller than 14. For the instances of Class (2), FT Algorithm is time consuming. If the running time is the driving factor, we suggest the Greedy algorithm for this class of graphs. For the instances of Classes (3) and (4), as the results in Table 3 suggest, the sizes of dominating sets computed by Greedy are considerably bigger than those computed by the PTAS. Moreover, the FT algorithm is time consuming, rendering the PTAS a better choice. For instance, for graph instance rand20000 with 35,975 edges, the FT algorithm takes almost four hours to compute the size of an optimal dominating set (not the set itself), while the PTAS computes a dominating set of a slightly larger size than the optimal value in less than two hours.

Table 4 shows the computational results for the instances that the FT algorithm is not able to find an optimal solution in practical time and memory space. The computational results show that for all of these instances, except one, the D_{PTAS} is smaller than D_{Gr}. In summary, for applications with running-time priority, Greedy is a better choice to compute an approximated dominating set, and if the running-time is not a big concern, the PTAS is a better option for instances whose optimal dominating set cannot be computed by the FT algorithm in a practical time.

Table 4. Computational results for Greedy and PTAS for large instances (time in seconds).

	Graph G	$\|E(G)\|$	**Greedy Alg.**		**PTAS**	
			D_{Gr}	**time**	D_{PTAS}	**time**
(1)	rd400	1183	78	0.007	74	351.93
	pcb442	1286	76	0.908	78	10.86
	d657	1958	126	0.016	120	604.10
	pr1002	2972	190	0.032	182	1253.9
(2)	tri11000	32972	2040	1.375	1958	12341.1
	tri12000	35974	2186	1.607	2132	6865.08
	tri14000	41974	2576	2.462	2434	9208.72
	tri16000	47969	2917	2.839	2885	12794.4
(3)	rand25000	45327	7772	12.467	6632	9470
(4)	Gab800	1533	227	0.012	205	24.30
	Gab900	1758	254	0.016	231	344.50
	Gab1000	1901	280	0.019	259	781.89
	Gab1500	2870	426	0.042	385	960.71

5. Concluding Remarks

It is mentioned that Baker's k-outer planar graph decomposition framework can be applied to obtain a PTAS for the planar dominating set problem. We show that, in order to get a PTAS for the planar dominating set problem, the mentioned application needs some modification. We modify the application and give a PTAS for the planar dominating set problem. We also report a computational study on the modified PTAS. Computational studies on exact algorithms and heuristic algorithms for the planar dominating set problem have already been conducted, but no report on PTAS has yet been given. Our study on the PTAS makes the computational study of planar dominating set problem more comprehensive. For larger k, the PTAS gives better solutions, but is more time/memory consuming. Due to the computation platform limitation, we only evaluated the PTAS for small k. It would be interesting to test the practical performances of the PTAS for larger k on more powerful computation platforms. The practical performances of PTASes for other optimization problems in planar graphs are worth investigation.

Acknowledgements

The authors thank the anonymous reviewers for their constructive comments.

References

1. Berge, C. *Graphs and Hypergraphs*; American Elsevier: New York, NY, USA, 1973.
2. Liu, C. *Introduction to Combinatorial Mathematics*; McGraw-Hill: New York, NY, USA, 1963.
3. Norman, R.; Harary, F.; Cartwright, D. *Structural Models: An Introduction to the Theory of Directed Graphs*; Wiley: Weinheim, Germany, 1966.
4. Haynes, T.W.; Hedetniemi, S.T.; Slater, P.J. Domination in Graphs. In *Monographs and Textbooks in Pure and Applied Mathematics*; Marcel Dekker: New York, NY, USA, 1998.
5. Haynes, T.W.; Hedetniemi, S.T.; Slater, P.J. Fundamentals of Domination in Graphs. In *Monographs and Textbooks in Pure and Applied Mathematics*; Marcel Dekker: New York, NY, USA, 1998.
6. Garey, M.R.; Johnson, D.S. *Computers and Intractability, a Guide to the Theory of NP-Completeness*; Freeman: New York, NY, USA, 1979.
7. Johnson, D.S. Approximation algorithms for combinatorial problems. *J. Comput. Syst. Sci* **1974**, *9*, 256–278.
8. Fiege, U. A threshold of $\ln n$ for approximating set cover. *J. ACM* **1998**, *45*, 634–652.
9. Baker, B.S. Approximation algorithms for NP-complete problems on planar graphs. *J. ACM* **1994**, *41*, 153–180.
10. Downey, R.G.; Fellows, M.R. Parameterized Complexity. In *Monographs in Computer Science*; Springer-Verlag: Berlin/Heidelberg, Germany, 1999.
11. Fomin, F.V.; Grandoni, F.; Kratch, D. Some new techniques in design and analysis of exact (exponential) algorithms. *Bull. EATCS* **2005**, *87*, 47–77.
12. Alber, J.; Fellows, M.R.; Niedermeier, R. Polynomial time data reduction for dominating set. *J. ACM* **2004**, *51*, 363–384.
13. Alber, J.; Bodlaender, H.L.; Fernau, H.; Kloks, T.; Niedermeier, R. Fixed parameter algorithms for dominating set and related problems on planar graphs. *Algorithmica* **2002**, *33*, 461–493.
14. Fomin, F.V.; Thilikos, D.M. Dominating sets in planar graphs: Branch-width and exponential speed-up. *SIAM J. Comput.* **2006**, *36*, 281–309.
15. Kanj, I.A.; Perkovic, L. Improved Parameterized Algorithms for Planar Dominating Set. In *Proceedings of the 27th Mathematical Foundations of Computer Science. LNCS 2420*, Warsaw, Poland, Augaust, 2002; pp. 399–410.
16. Robertson, N.; Seymour, P.D. Graph minors X. Obstructions to tree decomposition. *J. Comb. Theory Ser. B* **1991**, *52*, 153–190.
17. Gu, Q.; Tamaki, H. Optimal branch-decomposition of planar graphs in $O(n^3)$ time. *ACM Trans. Algorithm* **2008**, *4*, 30:1–30:13.
18. Seymour, P.D.; Thomas, R. Call routing and the ratcatcher. *Combinatorica* **1994**, *14*, 217–241.
19. Fomin, F.V.; Thilikos, D.M. New upper bounds on the decomposability of planar graphs. *J. Graph Theory* **2006**, *51*, 53–81.
20. Dorn, F. Dynamic Programming and Fast Matrix Multiplication. In *Proceedings of the 14th Annual European Symposium on Algorithms (ESA2006) LNCS 4168*, Zurich, Switerland, September, 2006; pp. 280–291.

21. Marzban, M.; Gu, Q.; Jia, X. Computational study on planar dominating set problem. *Theor. Comput. Sci.* **2009**, *410*, 5455–5466.
22. Sanchis, L.A. Experimental analysis of heuristic algorithms for the dominating set problem. *Algorithmica* **2002**, *33*, 3–18.
23. Hopcroft, J.; Tarjan, R. Efficient planarity testing. *J. ACM* **1974**, *21*, 549–568.
24. Tamaki, H. A linear Time Heuristic for the Branch-decomposition of Planar Graphs. In *Proceedings of the 11th Annual European Symposium*, Budapest, Hungary, 16–19 September 2003; pp. 765–775.
25. Reinelt, G. TSPLIB-A traveling salesman library. *ORSA J. Comput.* **1991**, *3*, 376–384.
26. Library of Efficient Data Types and Algorithms, Version 5.2. Available online: http://www.algorithmic-solutions.com/leda/index.html (accessed on 1 July 2007).

Algorithms **2013**, *6*, 60-83; doi:10.3390/a6010060

OPEN ACCESS

algorithms

ISSN 1999-4893

www.mdpi.com/journal/algorithms

Article

Tractabilities and Intractabilities on Geometric Intersection Graphs *

Ryuhei Uehara

School of Information Science, Japan Advanced Institute of Science and Technology, Asahidai 1-1, Nomi, Ishikawa 923-1292, Japan; E-Mail: uehara@jaist.ac.jp

* Parts of Results were Presented at ISAAC 2008 and WALCOM 2008.

Received: 23 October 2012; in revised form: 10 January 2013 / Accepted: 14 January 2013 / Published: 25 January 2013

Abstract: A graph is said to be an intersection graph if there is a set of objects such that each vertex corresponds to an object and two vertices are adjacent if and only if the corresponding objects have a nonempty intersection. There are several natural graph classes that have geometric intersection representations. The geometric representations sometimes help to prove tractability/intractability of problems on graph classes. In this paper, we show some results proved by using geometric representations.

Keywords: bandwidth; chain graphs; graph isomorphism; Hamiltonian path problem; interval graphs; threshold graphs; unit grid intersection graphs

1. Introduction

A graph $G = (V, E)$ is said to be an intersection graph if and only if there is a set of objects such that each vertex v in V corresponds to an object O_v and $\{u, v\} \in E$ if and only if O_v and O_u have a nonempty intersection. Interval graphs are a typical intersection graph class, and widely investigated. One reason is that interval graphs have wide applications including scheduling and bioinformatics [1]. Another reason is that an interval graph has a simple structure, and hence we can solve many problems efficiently, whereas the problems are hard in general [1,2]. Some natural generalizations and/or restrictions on interval graphs have been investigated (see, e.g., [2–4]). One of the reasons why these intersection graphs are investigated is that their geometric representations sometimes give intuitive simple proof of the tractable/intractable results. On the tractable results, we can solve a problem by using their geometric representations. The geometric representation of a graph gives us an intuitive expression of how to solve a problem using the representation. On the other hand, on the intractable representation, we can express the difficulty of a problem using the geometric representation of a graph. This gives us an intuition of why the problem is difficult to solve. That is, the property of the graph representation also represents the intractableness of the problem. This extracts the essence of the difficulty of the problem and helps us to understand not only the property of the class of graphs, but also the difficulty of the problem.

In this paper, the author reorganizes and shows some related results about graph classes with geometric representations presented at two conferences [5,6] with recent progress. We will mainly consider threshold graphs, chain graphs, and grid intersection graphs. A threshold graph is a graph such that each vertex has a weight, and two vertices are adjacent if and only if their total weight is greater than a given threshold value. The vertex set of a threshold graph is partitioned into two groups such that "light" vertices induce an independent set while "heavy" vertices induce a clique. The threshold graphs form a proper subclass of interval graphs, and can be represented in a compact representation of $O(n)$ space. A chain graph is a bipartite analogy of the notion of threshold graphs. From a threshold graph, we can obtain a chain graph by removing edges between heavy vertices. In a sense, a chain graph can be seen as a two dimensional extension of a threshold graph. From this viewpoint, a grid intersection graph is a two dimensional extension of an interval graph. More precisely, a bipartite graph $G = (X, Y, E)$ is a grid intersection graph if and only if each vertex $x \in X$ (and $y \in Y$) corresponds to a vertical line (a horizontal line, resp.) such that two vertices are adjacent when they are crossing.

We first focus on a tractable problem on a graph that has a geometric representation. The bandwidth problem is one of the classic problems defined below. A layout of a graph $G = (V, E)$ is a bijection π between the vertices in V and the set $\{1, 2, \ldots, |V|\}$. The bandwidth of a layout π equals $\max\{|\pi(u) - \pi(v)| \mid \{u, v\} \in E\}$. The bandwidth of G is the minimum bandwidth of all layouts of G. The bandwidth has been studied since the 1950s; it has applications in sparse matrix computations (see [7,8] for survey). From the graph theoretical point of view, the bandwidth of G is strongly related to the proper interval completion problem [9]. The proper interval completion problem is motivated by research in molecular biology, and hence it attracts much attention (see, e.g., [10]). However, computing the bandwidth of a graph G is one of the basic and classic $\mathcal{NP}$-complete problems [11] (see also [12, GT40]). Especially, it is $\mathcal{NP}$-complete even if G is restricted to a caterpillar with hair length 3 [13]. The bandwidth problem is $\mathcal{NP}$-complete not only for trees, but also for split graphs [14] and convex bipartite graphs [15]. From the viewpoint of exact algorithms, the problem seems to be a difficult one; Feige developed an $O(10^n)$ time exact algorithm for the bandwidth problem of general graphs in 2000 [16], and recently, Cygan and Pilipczuk improved it to $O(4.383^n)$ time (see [17–19] for further details). Therefore approximation algorithms for several graph classes have been developed (see, e.g., [15,20–23]). Only a few graph classes have been known for which the bandwidth problem can be solved in polynomial time. These include chain graphs [24], cographs and related classes (see [25] for the details), interval graphs [26–28], and bipartite permutation graphs [6,29] (see [25] for a comprehensive survey).

One of the interesting graph classes for which the bandwidth problem can be solved efficiently is the class of interval graphs. In 1987, Kratsch proposed a polynomial time algorithm of the bandwidth problem for interval graphs [30]. Unfortunately, the algorithm has a flaw, which has been fixed by Mahesh *et al.* [27]. Kleitman and Vohra also show a polynomial time algorithm [26], and Sprague improves the time complexity to $O(n \log n)$ by sophisticated implementation of the algorithm [28]. All the algorithms above solve the decision problem that asks if an interval graph G has bandwidth at most k for given G and k. Thus, using binary search for k, we can compute the bandwidth $\mathsf{bw}(G)$ of an interval graph G in $O(M(n) \cdot \log \mathsf{bw}(G))$ time, where $M(n) = O(n \log n)$ is the time complexity to solve the decision problem [28]. In the literature, it is mentioned that there are two unsolved problems for interval graphs. The first one is direct computation of the bandwidth of an interval graph. All the known algorithms are strongly dependent on the given upper bound k to construct a desired layout. To find a best layout directly, we need deeper insight into the problem and/or the graph class. The second one is to improve the time complexity to linear time. Since interval graphs have a relatively simple representation, many $\mathcal{NP}$-hard problems can be solved in linear time including early results of recognition [31] and graph isomorphism [32].

Another interesting class consists of chain graphs. Chain graphs form a compact subclass of bipartite permutation graphs that plays an important role in developing efficient algorithms for the class of bipartite permutation graphs [33,34]. The algorithm by Kloks, Kratsch, and Müller computes the bandwidth of a chain graph in $O(n^2 \log n)$ time [24]. Their algorithm uses the algorithm for an interval graph as a subroutine, and the factor $O(n \log n)$ comes from the time complexity to solve the bandwidth problem for the interval graph in [28].

In this paper, we propose simple algorithms for the bandwidth problem for the classes of threshold graphs and chain graphs.

The first algorithm computes the bandwidth of a threshold graph G in $O(n)$ time and space. We note that threshold graphs form a proper subclass of interval graphs, and can be represented in a compact representation of $O(n)$ space. The algorithm directly constructs an optimal layout, that is, we give a partial answer to the open problem for interval graphs, and improve the previously known upper bound $O(n \log n \log \mathsf{bw}(G))$ to optimal.

Extending the first algorithm for threshold graphs, we next show an algorithm that computes the bandwidth of a chain graph in $O(n)$ time and space. This algorithm also directly constructs an optimal layout, and improves the previously known bound $O(n^2 \log n)$ in [24] to optimal.

More precisely, we first give a simple interval representation for a given threshold graph, and simplify the previously known algorithm for interval graphs. (We also show a new property of a previously known algorithm to show correctness.) Next, the simplified interval representation of a threshold graph is extended to the one of a chain graph in a nontrivial way.

Next we turn to the intractable problems on a graph that has a geometric representation. We focus on the class of grid intersection graphs that is a natural bipartite analogy and 2D generalization of the class of interval graphs; a bipartite graph $G = (X, Y, E)$ is a grid intersection graph if and only if G is an intersection graph of X and Y, where X corresponds to a set of horizontal line segments, and Y corresponds to a set of vertical line segments. It is easy to see that the class of chain graphs is a proper subset of the class. Otachi, Okamoto, and Yamazaki investigate relationships between the class of grid intersection graphs and other bipartite graph classes [35]. In this paper, we show that grid intersection graphs have a rich structure. More precisely, we show two hardness results. First, the Hamiltonian cycle problem is still $\mathcal{NP}$-complete even if graphs are restricted to unit length grid intersection graphs. The Hamiltonian cycle problem is one of the classic and basic $\mathcal{NP}$-complete problems [12]. Second, the graph isomorphism problem is still GI-complete even if graphs are restricted to grid intersection graphs. (We say the graph isomorphism problem is GI-complete if the problem is as hard as to solve the problem on general graphs.) The results imply that (unit length) grid intersection graphs have so rich structure that many other hard problems may still be hard even on (unit length) grid intersection graphs.

We note that they are solvable in linear time on an interval graph [32,36]. Hence we can observe that the generalized interval graphs have so rich structure that some problems become hard on the graphs. Intuitively speaking, the linear (or one dimensional) structure of an interval graph makes these problems tractable, and this two dimensional extension makes them intractable. Such results for intractability also can be found in the literature; the Hamiltonian cycle problem is $\mathcal{NP}$-complete on chordal bipartite graphs [37], and the graph isomorphism problem is GI-complete on chordal bipartite graphs and strongly chordal graphs [38].

It is worth mentioning that, recently, the computational complexity of the graph isomorphism problem for circular arc graphs became open again. (A circular arc graph is the intersection graph of circular arcs, which is another natural generalization of an interval graph.) The first "polynomial" time algorithm was given by Wu [39], but Eschen pointed out a flaw [40]. Hsu claimed an $O(nm)$ time algorithm for the graph isomorphism problem on circular-arc graphs [41]. However, recently, a counterexample to the correctness of the algorithm was found [42].

2. Preliminaries

The *neighborhood* of a vertex v in a graph $G = (V, E)$ is the set $N_G(v) = \{u \in V \mid \{u, v\} \in E\}$, and the *degree* of a vertex v is $|N_G(v)|$ denoted by $d_G(v)$. If no confusion can arise we will omit the index G. For a subset U of V, the subgraph of G induced by U is denoted by $G[U]$. Given a graph $G = (V, E)$, its *complement* $\bar{G} = (V, \bar{E})$ is defined by $\bar{E} = \{\{u, v\} \mid \{u, v\} \notin E\}$. A vertex set I is an *independent set* if and only if $G[I]$ contains no edges, and then the graph $\bar{G}[I]$ is said to be a *clique*. Two vertices u and v are called *twins* if and only if $N(u) \cup \{u\} = N(v) \cup \{v\}$.

For a graph $G = (V, E)$, a sequence of distinct vertices $v_0, v_1, \ldots, v_l$ is a *path*, denoted by $(v_0, v_1, \ldots, v_l)$, if $\{v_j, v_{j+1}\} \in E$ for each $0 \le j < l$. The *length* of a path is the number of edges on the path. For two vertices u and v, the *distance* of the vertices, denoted by $dist(u, v)$, is the minimum length of the paths joining u and v. A *cycle* consists of a path $(v_0, v_1, \ldots, v_l)$ of length at least 2 with an edge $\{v_0, v_l\}$, and is denoted by $(v_0, v_1, \ldots, v_l, v_0)$. The *length* of a cycle is the number of edges on the cycle (equal to the number of vertices). A path P in G is said to be *Hamiltonian* if P visits every vertex in G exactly once. The *Hamiltonian path problem* is to determine if a given graph has a Hamiltonian path. The *Hamiltonian cycle problem* is defined similarly for a cycle. The problems are well known $\mathcal{NP}$-complete problem (see, e.g., [12]).

An edge that joins two vertices of a cycle but is not itself an edge of the cycle is a *chord* of that cycle. A graph is *chordal* if every cycle of length at least 4 has a chord. In this paper, we will discuss about intersection graphs of geometrical objects. Interval graphs are characterized by intersection graphs of intervals, and it is well known that chordal graphs are intersection graphs of subtrees of a tree (see, e.g., [2]). A graph $G = (V, E)$ is *bipartite* if and only if V can be partitioned into two sets X and Y such that every edge joins a vertex in X and the other vertex in Y. We sometimes denote a bipartite graph by

$G = (X, Y, E)$ to specify the two vertex sets. A bipartite graph is *chordal bipartite* if every cycle of length at least 6 has a chord.

A graph (V, E) with $V = \{v_1, v_2, \ldots, v_n\}$ is an *interval graph* if there is a finite set of intervals $\mathcal{I} = \{I_{v_1}, I_{v_2}, \ldots, I_{v_n}\}$ on the real line such that $\{v_i, v_j\} \in E$ if and only if $I_{v_i} \cap I_{v_j} \neq \emptyset$ for each i and j with $0 < i, j \leq n$. We call the set $\mathcal{I}$ of intervals an *interval representation* of the graph. For each interval I, we denote by $R(I)$ and $L(I)$ the right and left endpoints of the interval, respectively (therefore we have $L(I) \leq R(I)$ and $I = [L(I), R(I)]$). An interval representation is called *proper* if and only if $L(I) \leq L(J)$ and $R(I) \leq R(J)$ for every pair of intervals I and J or vice versa. An interval graph is *proper* if and only if it has a proper interval representation. It is known that the class of proper interval graphs coincides with the class of unit interval graphs [43]. That is, any proper interval graph has a proper interval representation that consists of intervals of unit length (explicit and simple construction is given in [44]). Moreover, each connected proper interval graph has essentially unique proper (or unit) interval representation up to reversal in the following sense (see, e.g., [45, Corollary 2.5]):

Proposition 1 *For any connected proper interval graph $G = (V, E)$ without twins, there is a unique ordering (up to reversal) $v_1, v_2, \ldots, v_n$ of n vertices such that G has a unique proper interval representation $\mathcal{I}(G)$ such that $L(I_{v_1}) < L(I_{v_2}) < \cdots < L(I_{v_n})$ (and hence $R(I_{v_1}) < R(I_{v_2}) < \cdots < R(I_{v_n})$). In other words, for a connected proper interval graph $G = (V, E)$ without twins, there exists a vertex ordering $v_1, v_2, \ldots, v_n$ such that every interval representation of G satisfies either $L(I_{v_1}) < L(I_{v_2}) < \cdots < L(I_{v_n})$ or $L(I_{v_n}) < \cdots < L(I_{v_2}) < L(I_{v_1})$.*

We note that when G contains twins u and v, they correspond to the congruent intervals with $L(I_v) = L(I_u)$ and $R(I_v) = R(I_u)$. In a sense, the ordering is still unique even if G contains twins up to isomorphism if the graph is unlabeled.

For any interval representation $\mathcal{I}$ and a point p, $N[p]$ denotes the set of intervals that contain the point p.

A graph $G = (V, E)$ is called a *threshold graph* when there exist nonnegative weights $w(v)$ for all $v \in V$ and a threshold value t such that $\{u, v\} \in E$ if and only if $w(u) + w(v) \geq t$.

Let $G = (X, Y, E)$ be a bipartite graph with $X = \{x_1, x_2, \ldots, x_n\}$ and $Y = \{y_1, y_2, \ldots, y_{n'}\}$. The ordering of X has the *adjacency property* if and only if, for each vertex $y \in Y$, $N(y)$ consists of vertices that are consecutive in the ordering of X. A bipartite graph $G = (X, Y, E)$ is said to be a *chain graph* if and only if there are orderings of X and Y that fulfill the adjacency property, and the ordering of X satisfies that $N(x_n) \subseteq N(x_{n-1}) \subseteq \cdots \subseteq N(x_1)$. (The last property implies that the ordering of Y also satisfy $N(y_1) \subseteq N(y_2) \subseteq \cdots \subseteq N(y_{n'})$; see, e.g., [46].)

A graph $G = (V, E)$ with $V = \{v_1, v_2, \ldots, v_n\}$ is said to be a *permutation graph* if and only if there is a permutation σ over V such that $\{v_i, v_j\} \in E$ if and only if $(i - j)(\sigma(v_i) - \sigma(v_j)) < 0$. Intuitively, each vertex v in a permutation graph corresponds to a line segment ℓ_v joining two points on two parallel line segments L_1 and L_2. Then two vertices v and u are adjacent if and only if the corresponding line segments ℓ_v and ℓ_u intersect. The ordering of vertices gives the ordering of the points on L_1, and the permutation of the ordering gives the ordering of the points on L_2. We call the intersection model a *line representation* of the permutation graph. When a permutation graph is bipartite, it is said to be a *bipartite permutation graph*. Although a permutation graph has (exponentially) many line representations, a connected bipartite graph essentially has a unique line representation up to isomorphism (see [47, Lemma 3] for further details):

Lemma 2 *Let $G = (V, E)$ be a connected bipartite permutation graph without twins. Then the line representation of G is unique up to isomorphism.*

The following proper inclusions are known (see, e.g., [46,48]):

Lemma 3 *(1) Threshold graphs $\subset$ interval graphs; (2) chain graphs $\subset$ bipartite permutation graphs.*

A natural bipartite analogy of interval graphs are called *interval bigraphs* which are intersection graphs of two-colored intervals so that we do not join two vertices if they have the same color. Based on the definition, Müller showed that the recognition problem for interval bigraphs can be solved in polynomial time [49]. Later, Hell and Huang show an interesting characterization of interval bigraphs, which is based on the idea to characterize the complements of the graphs [50]. Recently, efficient recognition algorithm based on forbidden graph patterns is developed by Rafiey [51].

A bipartite graph $G = (X, Y, E)$ is a *grid intersection graph* if every vertex $x \in X$ and $y \in Y$ can be assigned line segments I_x and J_y in the plane, parallel to the horizontal and vertical axis so that for all $x \in X$ and $y \in Y$, $\{x, y\} \in E$ if and only if I_x and J_y cross each other. We call $(\mathcal{I}, \mathcal{J})$ a *grid representation* of G, where $\mathcal{I} = \{I_x \mid x \in X\}$ and $\mathcal{J} = \{J_y \mid y \in Y\}$. A grid representation is *unit* if all line segments in the representation have the same (unit) length. A bipartite graph is a *unit grid intersection graph* if it has a unit grid representation.

Otachi, Okamoto, and Yamazaki show some relationship between (unit) grid intersection graphs and other graph classes [35]; for example, interval bigraph is included in the intersection of unit grid intersection graphs and chordal bipartite graphs. It is worth mentioning that it is open whether chordal bipartite graphs are included in grid intersection graphs or not.

Two graphs $G = (V, E)$ and $G' = (V', E')$ are *isomorphic* if and only if there is a one-to-one mapping $\phi : V \rightarrow V'$ such that $\{u, v\} \in E$ if and only if $\{\phi(u), \phi(v)\} \in E'$ for every pair of vertices $u, v \in V$. We denote by $G \sim G'$ if G and G' are isomorphic. The *graph isomorphism (GI) problem* is to determine if $G \sim G'$ for given graphs G and G'. A graph class $\mathcal{C}$ is said to be *GI-complete* if there is a polynomial time reduction from the graph isomorphism problem for general graphs to the graph isomorphism problem for $\mathcal{C}$. Intuitively, the graph isomorphism problem for the class $\mathcal{C}$ is as hard as the problem for general graphs if $\mathcal{C}$ is GI-complete. The graph isomorphism problem is GI-complete for several graph classes; for example, chordal bipartite graphs, and strongly chordal graphs [38]. On the other hand, the graph isomorphism problem can be solved efficiently for many graph classes; for example, interval graphs [32], probe interval graphs [52], permutation graphs [53], directed path graphs [54], and distance hereditary graphs [55].

3. Polynomial Time Algorithms for the Bandwidth Problem

A *layout* of a graph $G = (V, E)$ on n vertices is a bijection π between the vertices in V and the set $\{1, 2, \ldots, n\}$. The *bandwidth of a layout* π equals $\max\{|\pi(u) - \pi(v)| \mid \{u, v\} \in E\}$. The *bandwidth of G*, denoted by $\mathsf{bw}(G)$, is the minimum bandwidth of all layouts of G. A layout achieving $\mathsf{bw}(G)$ is called an *optimal layout.* On a layout π, we denote by $S < S'$ for two vertex sets S, S' if and only if $\pi(u) < \pi(v)$ holds for every pair of $u \in S$ and $v \in S'$.

For given graph $G = (V, E)$, a *proper interval completion of* G is a superset E' of E such that $G' = (V, E')$ is a proper interval graph. Hereafter, we will omit the "proper interval" since we always consider proper interval completions. We say a completion E' is *minimum* if and only if $|C'| \leq |C''|$ for maximum cliques C' in $G' = (V, E')$ and C'' in $G'' = (V, E'')$ for any other completion E''.

For a minimum completion E', it is known that $\mathsf{bw}(G) = |C'| - 1$, where C' is a maximum clique in $G' = (V, E')$ [9]. Let $G = (V, E)$ be an interval graph with an interval representation $\mathcal{I} = \{I_{v_1}, I_{v_2}, \ldots, I_{v_n}\}$. For each maximal clique C, there is a point p such that $N[p]$ induces the clique C by Helly property. Thus, for any given graph G, we can compute $\mathsf{bw}(G)$ by Algorithm 1.

Algorithm 1: Bandwidth of a general graph

Input : Graph $G = (V, E)$
Output: $\mathsf{bw}(G)$
generate a proper interval graph $G' = (V, E')$ that gives a minimum completion of G;
make the unique proper interval representation $\mathcal{I}(G')$ of G';
find a point p such that $|N[p]| \geq |N[p']|$ for any other point p' on $\mathcal{I}(G')$;
return $(|N[p]| - 1)$.

In Algorithm 1, the key point is how to find the minimum completion of G in the first step. The following observation may not be explicitly given in literature, but it can be obtained from the results in [9] straightforwardly (for example, the proof of Theorem 3.2 in [9], this fact is implicitly used):

Observation 4 *For a minimum completion $G' = (V, E')$ of $G = (V, E)$, let $\mathcal{I}(G') = (I'_{v_1}, I'_{v_2}, \ldots, I'_{v_n})$ be the unique proper interval representation of G' stated in Proposition 1. Then the ordering $v_1, v_2, \ldots, v_n$ gives an optimal layout of G, and vice versa.*

Here we show a technical lemma for the proper interval subgraph of an interval graph that will play an important role of our results.

Lemma 5 *Let $G = (V, E)$ be an interval graph with $V = \{v_1, v_2, \ldots, v_n\}$, and $\mathcal{I} = \{I_{v_1}, I_{v_2}, \ldots, I_{v_n}\}$ an interval representation of G. Let $\mathcal{J} = \{J_{u_1}, J_{u_2}, \ldots, J_{u_k}\}$ be a subset of $\mathcal{I}$ such that $\mathcal{J}$ forms a proper interval representation. That is, we have $U = \{u_1, \ldots, u_k\} \subseteq V$, and we can order $\mathcal{J}$ as $L(J_{u_i}) \leq L(J_{u_{i+1}})$ and $R(J_{u_i}) \leq R(J_{u_{i+1}})$ for each $1 \leq i < k$. Let ρ be the injection from $\mathcal{J}$ to $\mathcal{I}$ with $J_{u_i} = I_{v_{\rho(i)}}$ for each $1 \leq i \leq k \leq n$. Then, G has an optimal layout π such that each interval J_{u_i} appears according to the ordering in $\mathcal{J}$. More precisely, for each i with $1 \leq i < k$, we have $\pi(v_{\rho(i)}) < \pi(v_{\rho(i+1)})$.*

Proof. The proof is strongly related to the algorithm, which we call Algorithm KV, developed by Kleitman and Vohra in [26]. To be self-contained, we give a description of Algorithm KV in Appendix A. We recall that for given an interval representation of an interval graph $G = (V, E)$ and a positive integer k, Algorithm KV constructs a layout π of V that achieves the bandwidth at most k if $\mathsf{bw}(G) \leq k$. The main idea is as follows. We assume that we give the interval representation $\mathcal{I}$ and $\mathsf{bw}(G)$ as an input to Algorithm KV. Through the construction of the optimal layout π, indeed, Algorithm KV does not change the ordering in $\mathcal{J}$. We note that Algorithm KV itself does not mind the set $\mathcal{J}$. That is, for an interval graph $G = (V, E)$, Algorithm KV does not change the ordering of any subset $\mathcal{J}$ if $\mathcal{J}$ induces a proper interval graph.

Basically, Algorithm KV greedily labels each interval from 1 to n, from left to right. Unlabeled intervals are divided into two groups; the intervals incident to labeled intervals and others. The former group is again divided into sets S_j^q. A set S_j^q contains unlabeled intervals that should have labels up to $(j + q)$, where q is the largest label so far. In the first saturated S_j^q with respect to $(j + q)$, the interval having the smallest left endpoint is chosen as the next interval (ties are broken by the right endpoints).

To prove the lemma, we have to show the leftmost unlabeled interval J_{u_i} in $\mathcal{J}$ has to be chosen before $J_{u_{i+1}}$ when Algorithm KV chooses an interval in $\mathcal{J}$. When Algorithm KV picks up the first saturated S_j^q in Step 7, we have $S_1^q \subseteq S_2^q \subseteq \cdots \subseteq S_j^q$. Hence, by a simple property of proper intervals, S_j^q contains all unlabeled J_{u_i} with $i' < i \leq i''$ such that $J_{u_{i'}}$ is the rightmost labeled interval in $\mathcal{J}$ and $J_{u_{i''}}$ is the rightmost unlabeled interval in $\mathcal{J}$ that is adjacent to a labeled interval. Among them, Algorithm KV picks up the interval that has the smallest left endpoint (in Step 2 or 8). Thus, with appropriate tie-breaking, the next labeled interval can be $J_{u_{i'+1}}$ before $J_{u_{i'+2}}$. Therefore, Algorithm KV labels all intervals in $\mathcal{J}$ from left to right, and we have the lemma. ∎

3.1. Linear Time Algorithm for a Threshold Graph

We first show a linear time algorithm for computing $\mathsf{bw}(G)$ of a connected threshold graph G. For a threshold graph $G = (V, E)$, there exist nonnegative weights $w(v)$ for $v \in V$ and t such that $\{u, v\} \in E$ if and only if $w(u) + w(v) \geq t$. We assume that a threshold graph is given in the standard adjacency list manner. That is, each vertex has its own neighbor list and it knows its degree and weight. We assume that G is connected and V is already ordered as $\{v_1, v_2, \ldots, v_n\}$ with $w(v_i) \leq w(v_{i+1})$ for $1 \leq i < n$ (this sort can be done in $O(n)$ time by a standard bucket sort [56, Section 5.2.5] according to the degrees of vertices; ties may occur by twins, and are broken in any way). We can find ℓ such that $w(v_{\ell-1}) + w(v_\ell) < t$ and $w(v_\ell) + w(v_{\ell+1}) \geq t$ in $O(n)$ time. Then G has the following interval representation $\mathcal{I}(G)$:

- For $1 \leq i \leq \ell$, v_i corresponds to the point i, that is, $I_{v_i} = [i, i]$.
- For $\ell < i \leq n$, v_i corresponds to the interval $[j, \ell]$, where j is the minimum index with $w(v_i) + w(v_j) \geq t$.

For example, Figure 1(a) is a threshold graph; each number in a circle is its weight, and threshold value is 5. We have $\ell = 5$ and its interval representation is given in Figure 1(b).

Figure 1. (**a**) Threshold graph and (**b**) its interval representation.

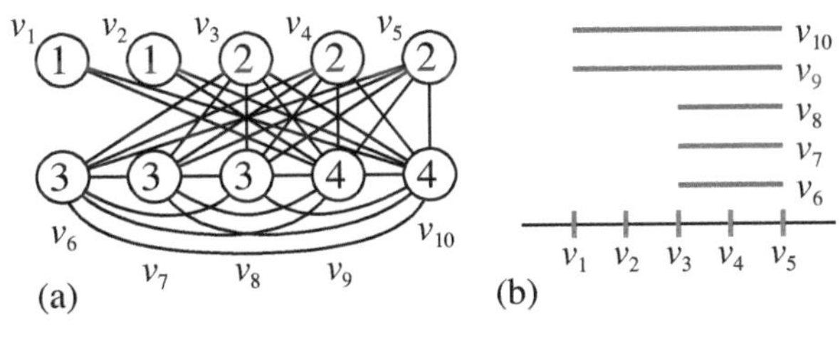

Theorem 6 *We assume that a connected threshold graph $G = (V, E)$ is given in the interval representation $\mathcal{I}(G)$ stated above. Then we can compute* $\mathsf{bw}(G)$ *in $O(n)$ time and space.*

Proof. We first observe that $L(I_{v_i}) < L(I_{v_{i+1}})$ and $R(I_{v_i}) < R(I_{v_{i+1}})$ for each v_i with $1 \leq i < \ell$, and $L(I_{v_i}) \geq L(I_{v_{i+1}})$ and $R(I_{v_i}) = R(I_{v_{i+1}}) = \ell$ for each i with $\ell < i < n$. That is, G consists of two proper interval graphs induced by $\{v_1, v_2, \ldots, v_\ell\}$ and $\{v_\ell, v_{\ell+1}, \ldots, v_n\}$ (note that v_ℓ is shared). Their proper interval representations also appear in $\mathcal{I}(G)$. Hence, by Lemma 5, there exists an optimal layout π of $V = \{v_1, \ldots, v_n\}$ such that $\pi(v_1) < \pi(v_2) < \cdots < \pi(v_\ell)$ and $\pi(v_\ell) > \pi(v_{\ell+1}) > \pi(v_{\ell+2}) > \cdots > \pi(v_n)$. Thus we can obtain an optimal layout by merging two sequences of vertices.

To obtain an optimal layout, by Observation 4, we construct a minimum completion of G from two sequences. The longest interval is given by v_n; since G is connected, $[L(I_{v_n}), R(I_{v_n})] = [1, \ell]$. Hence, we extend all intervals (except I_{v_n}) to length $\ell - 1$ and construct a minimum completion. We denote the extended interval I_{v_i} by I'_{v_i}. That is, the length of $I'_{v_i} = \ell - 1$ for all i with $1 \leq i \leq n$. The extension is illustrated in Figure 2. The extension of intervals I_{v_i} for $i > \ell$ is straightforward; just extend them to the right, which does not increase the size of a maximum clique. Thus we focus on the points $I_{v_i} = [i, i]$ with $i \leq \ell$, which are extended to I'_{v_i} with length $\ell - 1$.

Figure 2. Construction of a minimum completion.

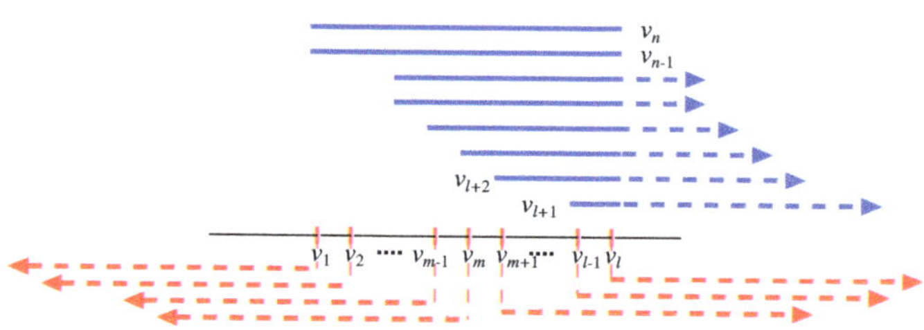

If I'_{v_i} does not contain the point 1, I'_{v_i} has to contain the point ℓ since it has to have length $\ell - 1$. On the other hand, once I'_{v_i} contains the point ℓ, we can set $I'_{v_i} = [i..\ell + i - 1]$ without loss of generality. Otherwise, the size of a maximum clique at the left side of the point i may increase. Similarly, once I'_{v_i} does not contain the point ℓ, we can set $I'_{v_i} = [-\ell + i + 1..i]$ without loss of generality. That is, we can assume that $L(I'_{v_i}) = i$ or $R(I'_{v_i}) = i$ for each $1 \leq i \leq \ell$. If two intervals I'_{v_i} and I'_{v_j} satisfy $i < j \leq \ell$, $L(I'_{v_i}) = i$, and $R(I'_{v_j}) = j$, we can make $R(I'_{v_i}) = i$, and $L(I'_{v_j}) = j$ without increasing the size of a maximum clique. Specifically, we can take $R(I'_{v_1}) = 1$ and $L(I'_{v_\ell}) = \ell$.

From the above observation, a minimum completion is given by the following proper interval representation of n intervals of length $\ell - 1$ for some m with $1 \leq m < \ell$: (0) for each $i > \ell$, $L[I_{v_i}] = j$, where j is the minimum index with $w(v_i) + w(v_j) \geq t$; (1) for each $1 \leq i \leq m$, $R[I_{v_i}] = i$, and (2) for each $m < i \leq \ell$, $L[I_{v_i}] = i$ (Figure 2). Thus, to construct a minimum completion, we search the index m that minimizes a maximum clique in the proper interval graph represented by above proper interval representation determined by m.

In the minimum completion, there are ℓ distinct cliques $C_i = N[i]$, one induced at each point i with $1 \leq i \leq \ell$. Now we consider a maximum clique of the corresponding proper interval graph for a fixed $m \in [1..\ell]$.

At points in $[m+1..\ell]$, it is easy to see that $N[m+1] \subseteq \cdots \subseteq N[\ell]$ and hence the point ℓ induces maximum clique of size $(n-(\ell+1)+1)+(\ell-(m+1)+1)=(n-m)$.

We next consider each point i in $[1..m]$. At the point i, $N[i]$ induces a clique that consists of $\{v_i, v_{i+1}, \ldots, v_m\}$ and $\{v_j, v_{j+1}, \ldots, v_n\}$, where j is the minimum index with $w(v_i)+w(v_j) \geq t$. Hence we have a clique of size $(m-i+1)+(n-j+1)$ at point i. Thus we have to find i in $[1..m]$ that gives a maximum one.

Therefore, for a fixed m, we compute these two candidates for a maximum clique from $[1..m]$ and $[m+1..\ell]$, compare them, and obtain a maximum one. For every m, we have to find a minimum one of the maximum cliques, whose size gives $\mathsf{bw}(G)+1$. Thus we can compute $\mathsf{bw}(G)$ by Algorithm 2.

Algorithm 2: Bandwidth of a threshold graph

Input : Threshold graph $G=(V,E)$ with $w(v_1) \leq w(v_2) \leq \cdots \leq w(v_n)$ and t
Output: $\mathsf{bw}(G)$
let ℓ be the minimum index with $w(v_\ell)+w(v_{\ell+1}) \geq t$;
set $bw := \infty$;
for $m = 1, 2, \ldots, \ell-1$ **do**
  set $lc := 0$; `// size of a maximum clique at points in` $[1..m]$
  for $i = 1, 2, \ldots, m$ **do**
    let j be the minimum index with $w(v_i)+w(v_j) \geq t$;
    if $lc < (m-i+1)+(n-j+1)$ **then** set $lc := (m-i+1)+(n-j+1)$;
    ;
  if $\max\{lc, n-m\} < bw$ **then** $bw := \max\{lc, n-m\}$;
  ;
return $(bw-1)$.

The correctness of Algorithm 2 follows from Observation 4, Lemma 5 and the above discussions.

Algorithm 2 runs in $O(n^2)$ time and $O(n)$ space by a straightforward implementation. However, careful implementation achieves $O(n)$ time and space as follows. When the algorithm updates m in step 3, the proper interval representation does not change except for one vertex v_{m+1}. We assume that the value of the variable m is changed from m' to $m''=m'+1$. Then, the interval $I'_{v_{m''}}$ is "flipped" from right to left centered at m''. More precisely, changing from m' to $m''=m'+1$ means changing $I'_{v_{m''}}$ from $[m''..\ell+m''-1]$ to $[-\ell+m''+1..m'']$, or equivalently, from $L(I'_{v_{m''}})=m''$ to $R(I'_{v_{m''}})=m''$. This flip has two influences: First, the variable lc, which was the size of a maximum clique in $[1..m']$, will be updated by either (1) current $lc+1$ (added by $v_{m''}$ since it is flipped from $L(I_{v_{m''}})=m''$ to $R(I_{v_{m''}})=m''$) or (2) $n-j+2$, which is the size of clique induced at the new point m'', where j is the minimum index with $w(v_{m''})+w(v_j) \geq t$. Second, the maximum clique in the range $[m''+1..\ell]$ is updated from $(n-m')$ to $(n-m'')$. Thus, to find a maximum clique in the range $[1..m'']$, the algorithm does not need to check all indices in $[1..m'']$ by the for-loop in steps 5 to 8. Precisely, we move step 4 to between steps 2 and 3, and replace the for-loop in steps from 5 to 8 by the following steps;

let j be the minimum index with $w(v_m)+w(v_j) \geq t$;
set $lc := \max\{lc+1, n-j+2\}$;

We can precompute a table that gives the minimum index j with $w(v_i) + w(v_j) \geq t$ for each i in $O(n)$ time. Using the table, the modified algorithm runs in $O(n)$ time and space. ∎

We assume that a connected threshold graph $G = (V, E)$ is given in the interval representation $\mathcal{I}(G)$ stated above. Let V_0 and V_1 be the sets of light and heavy vertices v_i with $i \leq \ell$ and $i > \ell$, respectively. Then, for a connected threshold graph $G = (V, E)$, we have an optimal layout that satisfies $V_0^0 < V_1 < V_0^1$, where V_0^0 and V_0^1 are a partition of V_0 such that $w(v) < w(u)$ for each $v \in V_0^0$ and $u \in V_0^1$. Moreover, the optimal layout gives a maximum clique $G'[V_1 \cup V_0^1]$ of the graph $G' = (V, E')$ where E' is the completion. We can also partition V_1 into $V_1^0 = \{v_n, v_{n-1}, \ldots, v_{m'}\}$ and $V_1^1 = \{v_{m'-1}, \ldots, v_{\ell+1}\}$ such that $N(v_m) = \{v_n, \ldots, v_{m'}\}$ on $G = (V, E)$. Then we can observe that any arrangement of vertices in $V_0^1 \cup V_1^1$ gives us an optimal layout. The following corollary will give us an important property in a chain graph.

Corollary 7 *For a connected threshold graph $G = (V, E)$, we have an optimal layout with indices m and m' such that $V_0^0 < V_1^0 < (V_0^1 \cup V_1^1)$ and any arrangement of vertices in $V_0^1 \cup V_1^1$ gives an optimal layout. Moreover, there is no edge between $u \in V_0^0$ and $v \in V_0^1 \cup V_1^1$ on the completion.*

3.2. Linear Time Algorithm for a Chain Graph

We next show a linear time algorithm for computing $\mathsf{bw}(G)$ of a connected chain graph $G = (X, Y, E)$. We assume that $X = \{x_1, x_2, \ldots, x_n\}$ and $Y = \{y_1, y_2, \ldots, y_{n'}\}$ are already ordered by inclusion of neighbors; $N(x_n) \subseteq N(x_{n-1}) \subseteq \cdots \subseteq N(x_1)$ and $N(y_1) \subseteq N(y_2) \subseteq \cdots \subseteq N(y_{n'})$. Since G is connected, we have $N(x_1) = Y$ and $N(y_{n'}) = X$. We assume that a chain graph $G = (X, Y, E)$ with $|X| = n$ and $|Y| = n'$ is given in $O(n + n')$ space; each vertex $y \in Y$ stores one endpoint $d(y)$ such that $N(y) = \{x_1, x_2, \ldots, x_{d(y)}\}$, and each vertex $x \in X$ stores one endpoint $n' - d(x) + 1$ such that $N(x) = \{y_{n'}, y_{n'-1}, \ldots, y_{n'-d(x)+1}\}$. (We abuse the degree $d(\cdot)$ as a maximum index of the neighbors.) A chain graph has an intersection model of horizontal and vertical line segments (an example in Figure 3(a) has an intersection model in Figure 3(c)); X corresponds to a set of horizontal line segments such that all left endpoints have the same x-coordinate, and Y corresponds to a set of vertical line segments such that all top endpoints have the same y-coordinate. By the property of the inclusions of neighbors, on the intersection model, vertices in X can be placed from top to bottom and vertices in Y can be placed from right to left such that the lengths of their line segments are monotone. This also can be transformed to the line representation of a bipartite permutation graph in a natural way (Figure 3(b)). Then the endpoints on L_1 are sorted as $x_n, \ldots, x_1, y_{n'}, \ldots, y_1$ from left to right.

Figure 3. Chain graph (**a**) and its corresponding representations (**b**)–(**e**).

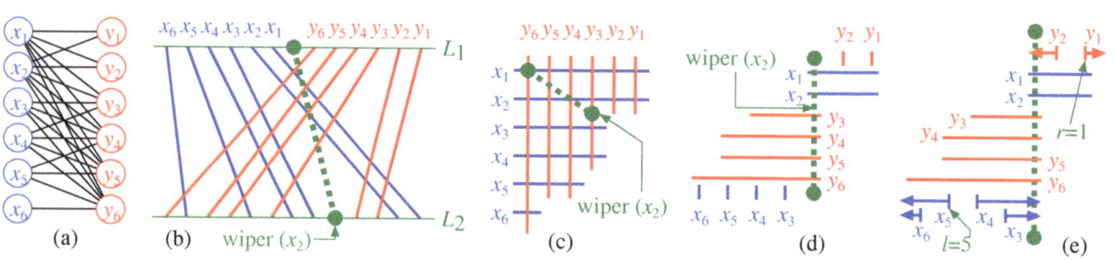

For a chain graph $G = (X, Y, E)$, a graph $H_i = (X \cup Y, E_i)$ is defined as follows [24]: We first define $H_0 = (X \cup Y, E_0)$ to be a graph obtained from G by making a clique of X; that is, $E_0 = E \cup \{\{x, x'\} \mid x, x' \in X \text{ and } x \neq x'\}$. For $1 \leq i \leq n-1$, let C_i be the set $\{x_1, x_2, \ldots, x_i\} \cup N(x_{i+1})$. Then the graph H_i is obtained from G by making a clique of C_i. More precisely, $E_i := E \cup \{\{x_{i'}, x_{i''}\} \mid 1 \leq i', i'' \leq i\} \cup \{\{y_{j'}, y_{j''}\} \mid (n' - d(x_{i+1}) + 1) \leq j', j'' \leq n'\}$. Then, the following lemma plays an important role in the algorithm in [24], which computes the $\mathsf{bw}(G)$ for a chain graph G by finding the minimum value of $\mathsf{bw}(H_i)$ for each i.

Lemma 8 ([24]) *(1) H_i is an interval graph for each i; (2)* $\mathsf{bw}(G) = \min_i \mathsf{bw}(H_i)$.

We first observe that H_0 is a threshold graph that has an interval representation in the form shown in Figure 3(c); that is, we project the representation in Figure 3(c) onto a horizontal line. The length of each x_i does not change, and each y_j degenerates to a point on the line. Intuitively, we can regard each $y \in Y$ as a point and each $x \in X$ as an interval. More precisely, we assign the weights of the vertices as follows. For each $y_j \in Y$, $w(y_j) = j$. For each $x_i \in X$, $w(x_i) = 2|X| + |Y| - j$, where j is the minimum index of $N(x)$. Letting $t = 2|X| + |Y|$, we can obtain the desired threshold graph with interval representation obtained from the projection of one in Figure 3(c). Thus, by Theorem 6, $\mathsf{bw}(H_0)$ can be computed in $O(n + n')$ time and space. Hereafter, we construct all minimum completions of H_i directly for $1 \leq i \leq n-1$.

We introduce a $\mathsf{wiper}(x_i)$ which is a line segment joining two points p_1 and p_2 on L_1 and L_2, respectively, on the line representation of a chain graph $G = (X, Y, E)$ as follows (Figure 3(b)); p_1 is a fixed point on L_1 between x_1 and $y_{n'}$, and p_2 is a point on L_2 between x_{i+1} and q, where q is the right neighbor point of x_{i+1} on L_2. More precisely, q is either (1) x_i if $N(x_i) = N(x_{i+1})$, or (2) the maximum vertex y_j in $N(x_i) \setminus N(x_{i+1})$ if $N(x_i) \setminus N(x_{i+1}) \neq \emptyset$. Using the wiper, H_i can be obtained from G by making a clique C_i which consists of the vertices corresponding to line segments intersecting $\mathsf{wiper}(x_i)$ on the line representation.

Intuitively, the interval representation of H_i can be obtained as follows; first, we construct a line representation of G and put the $\mathsf{wiper}(x_i)$ (Figure 3(b)), second, we modify it to the intersection model of horizontal and vertical line segments with $\mathsf{wiper}(x_i)$ placed between x_i and x_{i+1} or y_j, where y_j is the minimum vertex in $N(x_{i+1})$ (Figure 3(c)), and finally, we stretch the $\mathsf{wiper}(x_i)$ to vertical line segment, or just a point 0 on an interval representation, and arrange the line segments corresponding to the vertices in X and Y (Figure 3(d)). We note that the interval representation of H_i in Figure 3(d) is a combination of two interval representations (Figure 1(b)) of two threshold graphs that are separated by the $\mathsf{wiper}(x_i)$. More precise and formal construction of the interval representation of H_i is as follows. By Helly's property, the intervals in the clique C_i share a common point, say 0 (which corresponds to $\mathsf{wiper}(x_i)$). Then, centering the point 0, we can construct a symmetric interval representation as follows (Figure 3(d)); (1) each $x_{i'} \in X$ with $i' \leq i$ corresponds to an interval $[0, (d(x_{i'}) - d(x_i))]$, (2) each $x_{i'} \in X$ with $i' > i$ corresponds to the point $-(i'-i) = i-i'(< 0)$, (3) each $y_j \in Y$ with $j > n' - d(x_{i+1})$ corresponds to an interval $[-(d(y_j) - i), 0] = [(i - d(y_j)), 0]$, and (4) each $y_j \in Y$ with $j \leq n' - d(x_{i+1})$ corresponds to the point $i - j + 1$. We let $X_i^R := \{x_{i'} \in X \mid i' \leq i\}$, $X_i^L := \{x_{i'} \in X \mid i' > i\}$, $Y_i^L := \{y_j \in Y \mid j > n' - d(x_{i+1})\}$, and $Y_i^R := \{y_j \in Y \mid j \leq n' - d(x_{i+1})\}$. Then, two induced subgraphs $H_i[X_i^R \cup Y_i^R]$ and $H_i[X_i^L \cup Y_i^L]$ of H_i are threshold graphs, which allows us to apply the algorithm in Section 3.1. (In Figure 3(d), $H_i[X_i^R \cup Y_i^R]$ is induced by $\{x_1, x_2, y_1, y_2\}$ and $H_i[X_i^L \cup Y_i^L]$ is induced by $\{x_3, x_4, x_5, x_6, y_3, y_4, y_5, y_6\}$.) Now we are ready to prove the main theorem in this section.

Theorem 9 *We assume that a chain graph $G = (X, Y, E)$ is given in $O(n + n')$ space as stated above. Then we can compute* $\mathsf{bw}(G)$ *in $O(n + n')$ time and space.*

Proof. By Lemma 8, we can compute $\mathsf{bw}(G)$ by computing the minimum $\mathsf{bw}(H_i)$ for $i = 0, 1, 2, \ldots, n-1$. By the fact that H_0 is a threshold graph and Theorem 6, we can compute $\mathsf{bw}(H_0)$ in linear time and space. We only consider the case that $1 \le i \le n-1$. We separate the proof into three phases.

Algorithm: Consider a fixed index i. The basic idea is similar to the algorithm for a threshold graph. We directly construct a minimum completion of H_i. When G is a threshold graph, we put a midpoint m such that each point $[j, j]$ less than or equal to m is extended to an interval I_v with $R[I_v] = j$, and each point $[j, j]$ greater than m is extended to an interval I_v with $L[I_v] = j$, where v is the vertex corresponding to the point $[j, j]$. Similarly, we put two midpoints ℓ in $H_i[X_i^L \cup Y_i^L]$ and r in $H_i[X_i^R \cup Y_i^R]$. Now we make a proper interval representation instead of a unit interval representation to simplify the proof. (We note that any proper interval representation can be extended to a unit interval representation in a natural way [44]. Hence we can use a proper interval representation instead of a unit interval representation.) For two midpoints ℓ and r, we make a proper interval representation as follows; (1) for each $x_{i'} \in X_i^L$ with $i' \ge \ell$, $I'_{x_{i'}} = [i - n..i - i']$, (2) for each $x_{i'} \in X_i^L$ with $\ell < i'$, $I'_{x_{i'}} = [i - i'..0]$, (3) for each $y_j \in Y_i^R$ with $r < j (\le n' - d(x_{i+1}))$, $I'_{y_j} = [0..i - j + 1]$, and (4) for each $y_j \in Y_i^R$ with $j \le r$, $I'_{y_j} = [i - j + 1..i]$. In Figure 3(e), we give an example with $\ell = 5$ and $r = 1$. For each possible pair (ℓ, r) of ℓ and r with $i + 2 \le \ell \le n$ and $1 \le r \le n' - d(x_{i+1}) - 1$, we compute the size of a maximum clique in the proper interval representation. At this time, we have three candidates for a maximum clique at the left, the center, and the right parts of the proper interval representation. More precisely, for each fixed i, ℓ, and r, we define three maximum cliques $\mathsf{RC}_i(\ell, r)$, $\mathsf{CC}_i(\ell, r)$, and $\mathsf{LC}_i(\ell, r)$ in three proper interval graphs induced by $\{x_\ell, x_{\ell+1}, \ldots, x_n\} \cup \{y_j, y_{j+1}, \ldots, y_{n'}\}$, where y_j is the minimum vertex in $N(x_\ell)$, $\{x_1, x_2, \ldots, x_{\ell-1}\} \cup \{y_{r+1}, y_{r+2}, \ldots, y_{n'}\}$, and $\{x_1, x_2, \ldots, x_{i'}\} \cup \{y_1, y_2, \ldots, y_r\}$, where $x_{i'}$ is the maximum vertex in $N(y_r)$, respectively. For example, in Figure 3(e), three sets are $\{x_5, x_6, y_4, y_5, y_6\}$, $\{x_1, x_2, x_3, x_4, y_2, y_3, y_4, y_5, y_6\}$, and $\{x_1, x_2, y_1\}$, and hence $\mathsf{RC}_i(5, 1) = \{x_5, y_4, y_5, y_6\}$ at point -3 (or $R(x_5)$), $\mathsf{CC}_i(5, 1) = \{x_1, x_2, x_3, x_4, y_2, y_3, y_4, y_5, y_6\}$ at point 0, and $\mathsf{LC}_i(5, 1) = \{x_1, x_2, y_1\}$ at point 2. Thus for $(\ell, r) = (5, 1)$, we have a maximum clique $\mathsf{CC}_i(5, 1)$ of size 9. For each pair (ℓ, r), we compute $\max\{|\mathsf{RC}_i(\ell, r)|, |\mathsf{CC}_i(\ell, r)|, |\mathsf{LC}_i(\ell, r)|\}$, and then we take the minimum value of $\max\{|\mathsf{RC}_i(\ell, r)|, |\mathsf{CC}_i(\ell, r)|, |\mathsf{LC}_i(\ell, r)|\}$ for all pairs, which is equal to $\mathsf{bw}(H_i) + 1$ for the fixed i. In the case in Figure 3(d) ($i = 2$), $(\ell, r) = (3, 2)$ gives the minimum value $6 (= \mathsf{RC}_2(3, 2) = \mathsf{CC}_2(3, 2))$. We next compute the minimum one for all i, which gives $\mathsf{bw}(G) + 1$. Summarizing, we have Algorithm 3.

Correctness: By Lemma 8, each graph H_i is an interval graph and $\min_i \mathsf{bw}(H_i) = \mathsf{bw}(G)$. For the interval representation of H_i, we consider two proper interval subgraphs. The first induced subgraph $H_i[X_i^R \cup Y_i^L]$, which consists of positive length intervals in H_i, is a proper interval graph, and the second induced subgraph $H_i[X_i^L \cup Y_i^R]$, which consists of intervals of length 0 (or points), is also a proper interval graph. Hence, by Lemma 5, there is an optimal layout that keeps their natural orderings over

$X_i^R \cup Y_i^L$ and $X_i^L \cup Y_i^R$. Therefore, by Observation 4, we can compute $\mathsf{bw}(H_i)$ by extending intervals in them together to be proper. Using the same argument as in the proof of Theorem 6, we can use the set $X_i^R \cup Y_i^L$ of intervals as a proper interval representation as is, and we must extend each interval in $X_i^L \cup Y_i^R$ to be proper with respect to $X_i^R \cup Y_i^L$. Using the same argument twice, we can see that using the idea of two midpoints ℓ and r achieves an optimal layout.

Algorithm 3: Bandwidth of a chain graph

Input : Chain graph $G = (X, Y, E)$ with $N(x_n) \subseteq \cdots \subseteq N(x_1)$ and $N(y_1) \subseteq \cdots \subseteq N(y_{n'})$
Output: $\mathsf{bw}(G)$

```
bw := bw(H_0) // by Algorithm 2
for i = 1, 2, ..., n − 1 do
    construct the interval representation I(H_i) of the graph H_i with wiper(x_i);
    for ℓ = n, n − 1, ..., i + 1 do
        for r = 1, 2, ..., n' − d(x_{i+1}) do
            if max{|RC_i(ℓ, r)|, |CC_i(ℓ, r)|, |LC_i(ℓ, r)|} < bw then
                bw = max{|RC_i(ℓ, r)|, |CC_i(ℓ, r)|, |LC_i(ℓ, r)|};;
return (bw − 1).
```

Linear time implementation: A straightforward implementation gives $O((n+n')^3)$ time and $O(n+n')$ space algorithm. We here show how to improve the time complexity to linear time. Intuitively, we maintain the differences of three maximum cliques LC_i, CC_i, and RC_i efficiently, and we use the same idea as in the proof of Theorem 6 twice.

We first fix $i = 1$. In this case, we can compute LC_1, CC_1, and RC_1 in $O(n + n')$ time; the algorithm first starts $\mathsf{RC}_1{}' := \{x_1, y_1, \ldots, y_{n'-d(x_2)}\}$, $\mathsf{CC}_1{}' := \{x_1, y_{n'-d(x_2)+1}, \ldots, y_{n'}\}$, and $\mathsf{LC}_1{}' := \{x_2, \ldots, x_n, y_{n'-d(x_2)+1}, \ldots, y_{n'}\}$. That is, all points in $X_2^R (= \{x_2, \ldots, x_n\})$ are extended to the left, and all points in $Y_2^L (= Y \setminus N(x_2))$ are extended to the right. If $\max\{|\mathsf{LC}_1{}'|, |\mathsf{RC}_1{}'|\} > |\mathsf{CC}_1{}'|$, the algorithm flips the interval (or updates ℓ or r) into $\mathsf{CC}_1{}'$, decreases $|\mathsf{LC}_1{}'|$ or $|\mathsf{RC}_1{}'|$, and increases $|\mathsf{CC}_1{}'|$. Repeating this process, in $O(n+n')$ time, when the algorithm meets $\max\{|\mathsf{LC}_1|, |\mathsf{RC}_1|\} = |\mathsf{CC}_1|$ or $\max\{|\mathsf{LC}_1|, |\mathsf{RC}_1|\} = |\mathsf{CC}_1| - 1$, the value gives the minimum size of the maximum cliques in three parts, or equivalently, gives a minimum completion of H_1. When we have a minimum completion of H_1, we say this pair (ℓ, r) is the *best pair* for H_1.

Now, we compute LC_2, CC_2, and RC_2 from LC_1, CC_1, and RC_1 with the best pair for H_1 in $O(d(x_1) - d(x_3))$ time. Intuitively, H_2 is obtained from H_1 by the following steps; (1) remove $I_{x_2} = [1, 1]$ from the point 1, and put it as an interval $[0, d(x_1)]$; (2) shift all positive points I_{y_j} at $d(x_1) - j + 1$ with $y_j \in N(x_1) \setminus N(x_2)$ to $d(x_2) - j + 1$; and (3) remove all intervals $I_{y_j} = [-1, 0]$ with $y_j \in N(x_2) \setminus N(x_3)$ and put them at $d(x_2) - j + 1$ as points. The movements have influences on LC_1, CC_1, and RC_1, and from them, we construct LC_2, CC_2, and RC_2, and obtain the best pair for H_2 in a similar way to that used in the proof of Theorem 6. Then, since $N(x_3) \subseteq N(x_2) \subseteq N(x_1)$, the total difference (or the total number of flipped intervals) can be bounded above by $|\{x_2\} \cup (N(x_1) \setminus N(x_2)) \cup (N(x_2) \setminus N(x_3))| = |\{x_2\} \cup (N(x_1) \setminus N(x_3))| = d(x_1) - d(x_3) + 1$. Hence the computation of LC_2, CC_2, and RC_2 from LC_1, CC_1, and RC_1 requires $O(d(x_1) - d(x_3))$ time.

Repeating this process, the computation of LC_i, CC_i, RC_i, and the best pair of H_i from LC_{i-1}, CC_{i-1}, and RC_{i-1} with the best pair for H_{i-1} requires $O(d(x_{i-1}) - d(x_{i+1}))$ time for each $1 < i \leq n$. Hence, by maintaining the differences, the total computation time of Algorithm 3 is the sum of the computations of (1) $\mathsf{bw}(H_0)$, (2) LC_1, CC_1, RC_1, and the best pair of H_1, and (3) LC_i, CC_i, and RC_i with the best pair of H_i from LC_{i-1}, CC_{i-1}, RC_{i-1}, and the best pair of H_{i-1} for $i = 2, 3, \ldots, n-1$, which is equal to $O(n + n') + \sum_{i=2}^{n-1} O(d(x_{i-1}) - d(x_{i+1})) = O(n + n')$. ∎

Here we extend Corollary 7 to a chain graph.

Corollary 10 *For a connected chain graph $G = (X, Y, E)$, we assume that $X = \{x_1, x_2, \ldots, x_n\}$ and $Y = \{y_1, y_2, \ldots, y_{n'}\}$ are already ordered by inclusion of neighbors. Then we have an optimal layout that satisfies $X_0 < Y_0 < X_1 \cup Y_1 < X_2 < Y_2$ such that (1) $X_0 = \{x_1, \ldots, x_i\}$, $X_1 = \{x_{i+1}, \ldots, x_j\}$, and $X_2 = \{x_{j+1}, \ldots, x_n\}$ for some $1 \leq i \leq j \leq n$, and (2) $Y_2 = \{y_1, \ldots, y_k\}$, $Y_1 = \{y_{k+1}, \ldots, y_\ell\}$, and $Y_0 = \{y_{\ell+1}, \ldots, y_{n'}\}$ for some $1 \leq k \leq \ell \leq n$. Any arrangement of vertices in $X_1 \cup Y_1$ gives us an optimal layout. Moreover, the bandwidth is determined by an edge between (1) X_0 and Y_0, (2) $(X_1 \cup X_2)$ and $(Y_0 \cup Y_1)$, or (3) X_2 and Y_2.*

Proof. For an optimal layout, we have a corresponding wiper. Then the set X_0 is determined by $x_i \in X$ which is the maximum vertex in X not crossing the wiper. Then Y_0 is determined by the maximum vertex y_k in $N(x_i)$. Similarly, the set Y_2 is determined by the minimum vertex y_ℓ not crossing the wiper, and X_2 is determined by the minimum vertex in $N(y_\ell)$. Considering the maximum cliques which can give the bandwidth, the corollary follows. ∎

4. Intractable Problems on a (Unit) Grid Intersection Graph

In this section, we turn to the grid intersection graphs and intractable problems for the class.

4.1. The Hamiltonian Cycle Problem

We give two hardness results for grid intersection graphs in this section.

Theorem 11 *The Hamiltonian cycle problem is $\mathcal{NP}$-complete for unit grid intersection graphs.*

Proof. It is clear that the problem is in $\mathcal{NP}$. Hence we show $\mathcal{NP}$-hardness. We show a similar reduction in [57]. We start from the Hamiltonian cycle problem in planar directed graph with degree bound two, which is still $\mathcal{NP}$-hard [58]. Let $G_0 = (V_0, A)$ be a planar directed graph with degree bound two. (We deal with directed graphs only in this proof; we will use (u, v) as a directed edge, called *arc*, which is distinguished from $\{u, v\}$.) As shown in [57,58], we can assume that G_0 consists of two types of vertices: (type $\triangle$) with indegree two and outdegree one, and (type $\bigtriangledown$) with indegree one and outdegree two. Hence, the set V_0 of vertices can be partitioned into two sets $V_\triangle$ and $V_\bigtriangledown$ that consist of the vertices in type $\triangle$ and $\bigtriangledown$, respectively.

Moreover, we have two more claims; (1) the unique arc from a type $\triangle$ vertex has to be the unique arc to a type $\bigtriangledown$ vertex; and (2) each of two arcs from a type $\bigtriangledown$ vertex has to be one of two arcs to a type $\triangle$ vertex. If the unique arc from a type $\triangle$ vertex v is into one of a type $\triangle$ vertex u, the vertex u has to be visited from v to make a Hamiltonian cycle. Hence the vertex u can be replaced by an arc from

v to the vertex w which is pointed from u. On the other hand, if one of two arcs from a type $\bigtriangledown$ vertex v reaches another type $\bigtriangledown$ vertex u, the vertex u should be visited from v. Hence the other arc a from v can be removed from G_0. Then the vertex w incident to a has degree 2. Hence we have two cases; w can be replaced by an arc, or we can conclude G_0 does not have a Hamiltonian cycle. Repeating these processes, we have the claims (1) and (2), which imply that we have $|V_\triangle| = |V_\bigtriangledown|$, the underlying graph of G_0 is bipartite (with two sets $V_\triangle$ and $V_\bigtriangledown$), and any cycle contains two types of vertices alternately.

By the claims, we can partition arcs into two groups; (1) arcs from a type $\triangle$ vertex to a type $\bigtriangledown$ vertex called *thick arcs*, and (2) arcs from a type $\bigtriangledown$ vertex to a type $\triangle$ vertex called *thin arcs*. By above discussion, we can observe that any Hamiltonian cycle has to contain all thick arcs (Moreover, contracting thick arcs, we can show $\mathcal{NP}$-completeness of the Hamiltonian cycle problem even if we restrict ourselves to the directed planar graphs that only consist of vertices of two outdegrees and two indegrees.)

Now, we construct a unit grid intersection graph $G_1 = (V_1, E_1)$ from $G_0 = (V_0, A)$ which satisfies the above conditions. One type $\bigtriangledown$ vertex is represented by five vertical lines and two horizontal lines, and one type $\triangle$ vertex is represented by three vertical lines and one horizontal line in Figure 4 (each corresponding line segments are in gray area). Each thick arc is represented by alternations of one parallel vertical line and one parallel horizontal line in Figure 4, and each thin arc is represented by alternations of two parallel vertical lines and two parallel horizontal lines in Figure 5. The vertices are joined by the arcs in a natural way. An example is illustrated in Figure 6.

Figure 4. Reduction of thick arcs.

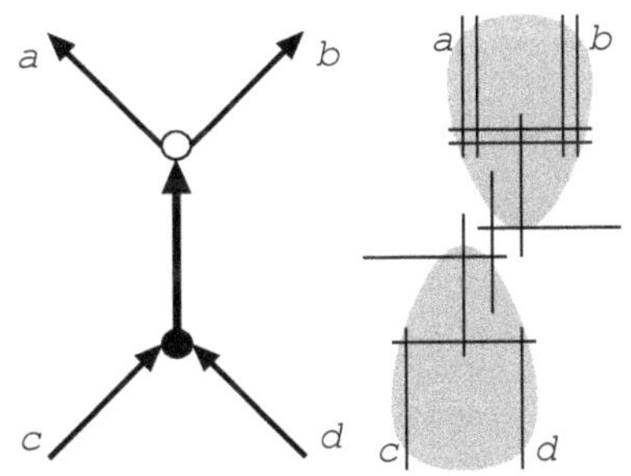

Figure 5. Reduction of thin arcs.

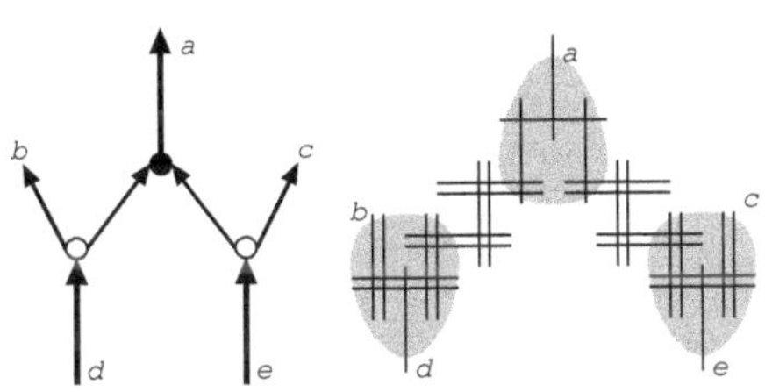

Figure 6. Reduction of a graph G_0.

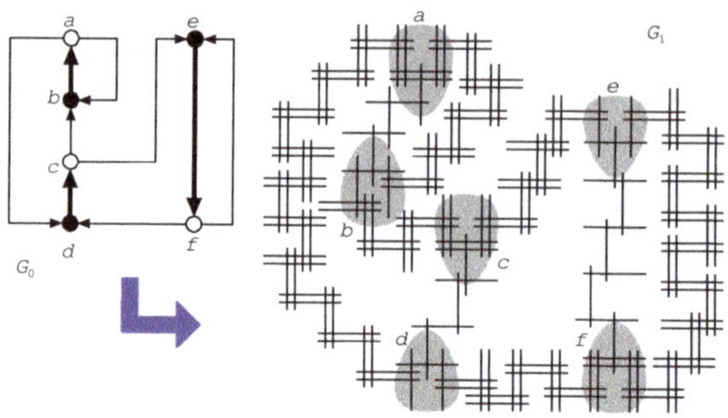

For the resultant graph G_1, it is obvious that the reduction can be done in a polynomial time, and G_1 is a unit grid intersection graph. Hence we show G_0 has a Hamiltonian cycle if and only if G_1 has a Hamiltonian cycle. First, we assume that G_0 has a Hamiltonian cycle C_0, and show that G_1 also has a Hamiltonian cycle C_1. C_1 visits the vertices (or line segments) in G_1 along C_0 as follows. For each thick arc in G_0, the corresponding segments in G_1 are visited straightforwardly. We show how to visit the segments corresponding to thin arcs (Figure 7). For each thin arc not on C_0, they are visited by C_1 as shown in the left side of Figure 7 (between u and v); a pair of parallel lines are used to sweep the arc twice, and the endpoints are joined by one line segment in the gadget of a type $\triangle$ vertex (v). On the other hand, for each thin arc on C_0, they are visited by C_1 as shown in the right side of Figure 7 (between w and v); a pair of parallel lines are used to sweep the arc once, and the path goes from e to a. Hence from a given Hamiltonian cycle C_0 on G_0, we can construct a Hamiltonian cycle C_1 on G_1.

Figure 7. How to sweep thin arcs.

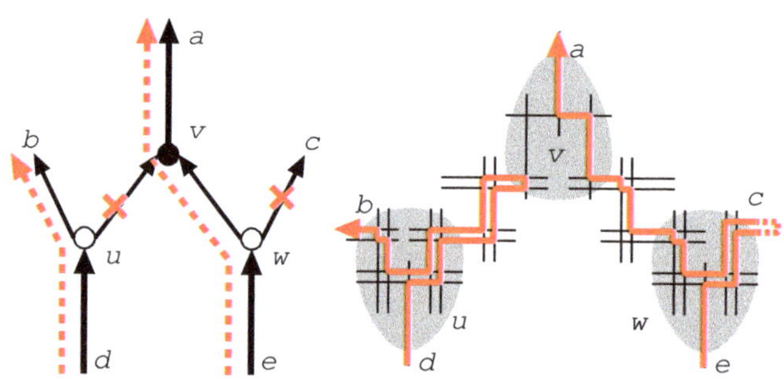

Now we assume that G_1 has a Hamiltonian cycle C_1, and show that G_0 also has a Hamiltonian cycle C_0. By observing that there are no ways for C_1 to visit lines corresponding to thick arcs described above, and the unique center horizontal line of a type $\triangle$ vertex can be used exactly once, we can see that C_1 forms a Hamiltonian cycle of G_1 as in the same manner represented above. Hence C_0 can be constructed from C_1 in the same way. ∎

∎

Corollary 12 *The Hamiltonian path problem is $\mathcal{NP}$-complete for unit grid intersection graphs.*

Proof. We reduce the graph G_1 in the proof of Theorem 11 to G_1' as follows; pick up any line segment in a thick arc, and add one more line segment as in Figure 8. Then, it is easy to see that G_1 has a Hamiltonian cycle if and only if G_1' has a Hamiltonian path (with an endpoint corresponding to the additional line segment). Hence we have the corollary. ∎ ∎

Figure 8. Hamiltonian path problem.

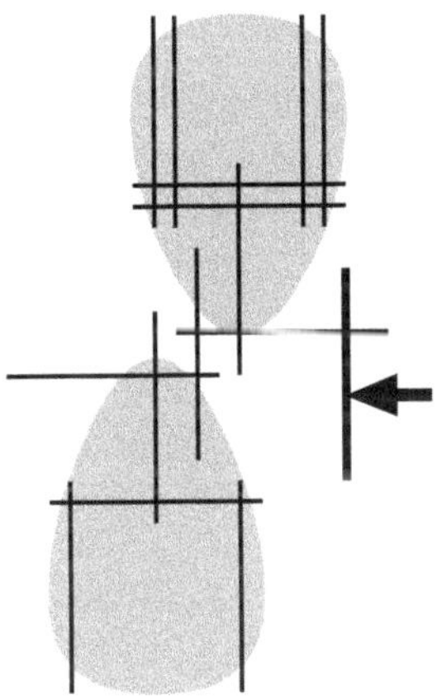

4.2. The Graph Isomorphism Problem

Theorem 13 *The graph isomorphism problem is GI-complete for grid intersection graphs.*

Proof. We show a similar reduction in [38,54]. We start by considering the graph isomorphism problem for general graphs. Let $G_0 = (V_0, E_0)$ and $G_0' = (V_0', E_0')$ with $|V_0| = |V_0'| = n$ and $|E_0| = |E_0'| = m$ be an instance of the graph isomorphism problem. (We will refer the graph G_0 in Figure 9(1) as an example). Without loss of generality, we assume that G_0 is connected. From G_0, we define a bipartite graph $G_1 = (V_0, E_0, E_1)$ with two vertex sets V_0 and E_0 by $E_1 := \{\{v, e\} \mid v \text{ is one endpoint of } e\}$. (Intuitively, each edge is divided into two edges joined by a new vertex; see Figure 9(2)). Then, $e \in E_0$ have degree 2 by its two endpoints in V_0. It is easy to see that $G_0 \sim G_0'$ if and only if $G_1 \sim G_1'$ for any graphs G_0 and G_0' with resultant graphs G_1 and G_1'.

Figure 9. Reduction for GI-completeness.

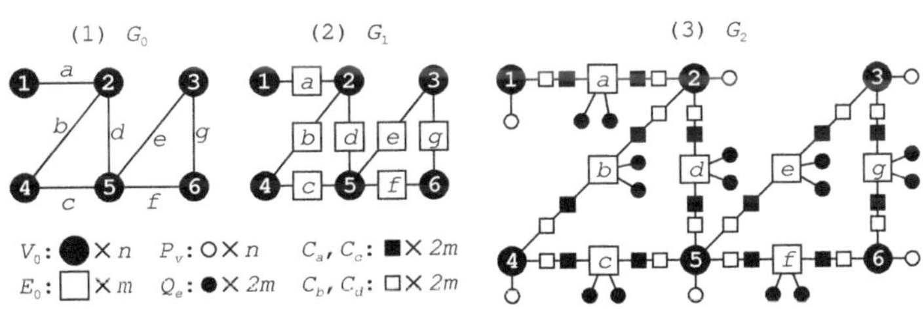

Now, we construct a grid intersection graph $G_2 = (V_2, E_2)$ from the bipartite graph $G_1 = (V_0, E_0, E_1)$ such that $G_1 \sim G_1'$ if and only if $G_2 \sim G_2'$ in the same manner. The vertex set V_2 consists of the following sets (see Figure 9(3)):

V_0, E_0; we let $V_0 = \{v_1, v_2, \ldots, v_n\}$, $E_0 = \{e_1, e_2, \ldots, e_m\}$, where $e_i = \{v_i, v_j\}$ for some $1 \leq i, j \leq n$.

P_v, Q_e; each vertex in $P_v \cup Q_e$ is called *pendant* and $P_v := \{p_1, p_2, \ldots, p_n\}$, $Q_e := \{q_1, q_2, \ldots, q_m, q_1', q_2', \ldots, q_m'\}$. That is, we have $|P_v| = n$ and $|Q_e| = 2m$.

C_a, C_b, C_c, C_d; each vertex in $C_a \cup C_b \cup C_c \cup C_d$ is called *connector*, and $C_a := \{a_1, a_2, \ldots, a_m\}$, $C_b := \{b_1, b_2, \ldots, b_m\}$, $C_c := \{c_1, c_2, \ldots, c_m\}$, and $C_d := \{d_1, d_2, \ldots, d_m\}$.

The edge set E_2 contains the following edges (Figure 9(3)):

1. For each i with $1 \leq i \leq n$, each pendant p_i is joined to v_i. That is, $\{p_i, v_i\} \in E_2$ for each i with $1 \leq i \leq n$.
2. For each j with $1 \leq j \leq m$, two pendants q_j and q_j' are joined to e_j. That is, $\{q_j, e_j\}, \{q_j', e_j\} \in E_2$ for each j with $1 \leq j \leq m$.
3. For each e_j with $1 \leq j \leq m$, we have two vertices v_i and $v_{i'}$ with $\{v_i, e_j\}, \{v_{i'}, e_j\} \in E_1$. For the three vertices $e_j, v_i, v_{i'}$, we add $\{e_j, a_j\}$, $\{v_i, b_j\}$, $\{a_j, b_j\}$, $\{e_j, c_j\}$, $\{v_{i'}, d_j\}$, $\{c_j, d_j\}$ into E_2. Intuitively, each edge in G_1 is replaced by a path of length 3 that consists of one vertex in $C_a \cup C_c$ and the other one in $C_b \cup C_d$.

The edge set E_2 also contains the edges $\{v_i, e_j\}$ for each i, j with $1 \leq i \leq n$ and $1 \leq j \leq m$. In other words, every vertex in V_0 is connected to all vertices in E_0 (the edges are omitted in Figure 9(3) to simplify).

Let G_0 and G_0' be any two graphs. Then, it is easy to see that $G_0 \sim G_0'$ implies $G_2 \sim G_2'$. Hence, we have to show that G_2 is a grid intersection graph, and G_0 can be reconstructed from G_2 uniquely up to isomorphism.

We can represent the vertices in $V_0 \cup Q_e \cup C_a \cup C_c$ (white vertices in Figure 9(3)) as horizontal segments and the vertices in $E_0 \cup P_v \cup C_b \cup C_d$ (black vertices in Figure 9(3)) as vertical segments as follows (Figure 10): First, all vertices in V_0 correspond to unit length horizontal segments that are placed in parallel. All vertices in E_0 correspond to unit length vertical segments placed in parallel, and the segments corresponding to vertices in V_0 and E_0 make a mesh structure (as in Figure 10). Each pendant vertex in P_v and Q_e corresponds to a short segment, and is attached to its neighbor in an arbitrary way, for example, as in Figure 10. Each pair of connectors in C_a and C_b (or C_c and C_d) joins corresponding vertices in V_0 and E_0 as in Figure 10. Then it is easy to see that the resultant grid representation gives G_2.

Next, we show that G_0 can be reconstructed from G_2 uniquely up to isomorphism. First, any vertex of degree 1 is a pendant in G_2. Hence we can distinguish $P_v \cup Q_e$ from the other vertices. Then, for each vertex $v \in V_2 \setminus (P_v \cup Q_e)$, $|N(v) \cap (P_v \cup Q_e)| = 1$ if and only if $v \in V_0$, and $|N(v) \cap (P_v \cup Q_e)| = 2$ if and only if $v \in E_0$. Hence two sets V_0 and E_0 are distinguished, and then $P_v \cup Q_e$ can be divided into P_v and Q_e. Moreover, we have $C_a \cup C_b \cup C_c \cup C_d = V_2 \setminus (P_v \cup Q_e \cup V_0 \cup E_0)$. Thus, tracing the paths induced by $C_a \cup C_b \cup C_c \cup C_d$, we can reconstruct each edge $e_j = (v_i, v_{i'})$ with $e_j \in E_0$ and $v_i, v_{i'} \in V_0$. Therefore, we can reconstruct G_0 from G_2 uniquely up to isomorphism.

Hence the graph isomorphism problem for grid intersection graphs is as hard as the graph isomorphism problem for general graphs. Thus the graph isomorphism problem is GI-complete for grid intersection graphs. ∎ ∎

Figure 10. Grid representation of G_2.

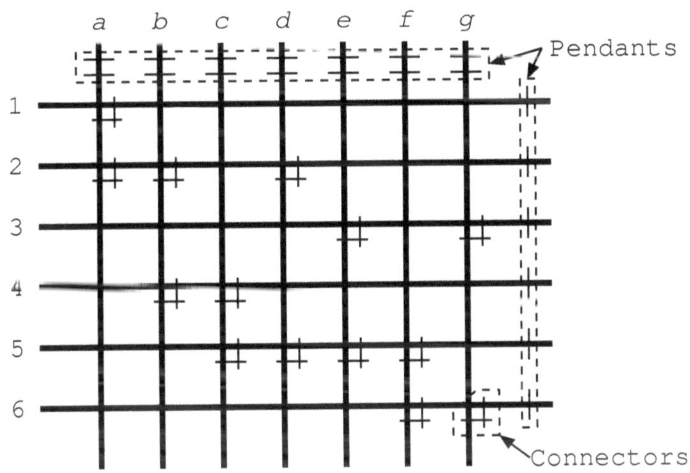

5. Conclusions

In this paper, we focus on geometrical intersection graphs. From the viewpoint of the parameterized complexity (see Downey and Fellow [59]), it is interesting to investigate efficient algorithms for these graph classes with some constraints. What if the number of vertical lines (or the possible positions on the coordinate of vertical lines) is bounded by a constant? In this case, we can use the dynamic programming technique for the graphs. Do the restrictions make some intractable problems solvable in polynomial time? From the graph theoretical point of view, a geometric model for chordal bipartite graphs is open. It is pointed out by Spinrad in [60], but it is not solved yet. The graph isomorphism problem for unit grid intersection graphs is also interesting. By Theorem 13, the graph isomorphism problem is GI-complete for grid intersection graphs. In the proof, we only need two kinds of lengths—long line segments and short line segments, but the difference of these two lengths is essential in the proof, and we cannot make all line segments unit length in the reduction.

Appendix

A. Algorithm by Kleitman and Vohra

In [26], Kleitman and Vohra developed an algorithm for determining whether an interval graph $G = (V, E)$ has a bandwidth less than or equal to a given integer k. Their algorithm plays an important role in the proof of Lemma 5. To be self-contained, we give the details of their algorithm below:

Algorithm 4: Algorithm KV

Input : An interval graph $G = (V, E)$ and a positive integer k.
Output: A layout realizing $\mathsf{bw}(G) \leq k$ if it exists.
Set $Label(i) = 0$ and $Mark(i) = n$ for all $i \in V$ where $n = |V|$. Set $U = \{i \in V \mid Label(i) = 0\}$ and $q = 0$;
Select $i \in U$ with smallest $L(i)$ (break ties by selecting the interval with smallest $R(i)$) and set $q = q + 1$;
Set $Label(i) = q$ and $U = U \setminus \{i\}$. If $U = \emptyset$, stop, all vertices have been labeled;
If $r \in U$ overlaps i and $Mark(r) = n$ set $Mark(r) = \min\{Label(i) + k, n\}$;
Let $S_j^q = \{r \in U \mid Mark(r) \leq q + j\}$. If $|S_j^q| \leq j$ for all $j \geq k - q + 1$, go to step 7;
There is a j such that $|S_j^q| > j$. Stop, for the bandwidth of the graph is $> k$;
Find the smallest value j_0, such that $|S_{j_0}^q| = j_0$;
Select $i \in S_{j_0}^q$ with smallest $L(i)$ (break ties as in Step 2). Set $q = q + 1$ and go to Step 3.

References

1. Golumbic, M. *Algorithmic Graph Theory and Perfect Graphs*, 2nd ed.; Elsevier: Amsterdam, The Netherlands, 2004.
2. Spinrad, J. *Efficient Graph Representations*; American Mathematical Society: Providence, RI, USA, 2003.
3. Fishburn, P.C. *Interval Orders and Interval Graphs*; Wiley & Sons, Inc.: Hoboken, NJ, USA, 1985.
4. McKee, T.; McMorris, F. *Topics in Intersection Graph Theory*; SIAM: Philadelphia, PA, USA, 1999.
5. Uehara, R. Simple Geometrical Intersection Graphs. In *Proceedings of the Workshop on Algorithms and Computation (WALCOM 2008)*; Springer-Verlag: Berlin/Heidelberg, Germany, 2008; pp. 25–33.
6. Uehara, R. Bandwidth of Bipartite Permutation Graphs. In *Proceedings of the Annual International Symposium on Algorithms and Computation (ISAAC 2008)*; Springer-Verlag: Berlin/Heidelberg, Germany, 2008; pp. 824–835.
7. Lai, Y.L.; Williams, K. A survey of solved problems and applications on bandwidth, edgesum, and profile of graphs. *J. Graph Theory* **1999**, *31*, 75–94.
8. Chinn, P.Z.; Chvátalová, J.; Dewdney, A.K.; Gibbs, N.E. The bandwidth problem for graphs and matrices—A survey. *J. Graph Theory* **1982**, *6*, 223–254.

9. Kaplan, H.; Shamir, R. Pathwidth, bandwidth, and completion problems to proper interval graphs with small cliques. *SIAM J. Comput.* **1996**, *25*, 540–561.
10. Kaplan, H.; Shamir, R.; Tarjan, R. Tractability of parameterized completion problems on chordal, strongly chordal, and proper interval graphs. *SIAM J. Comput.* **1999**, *28*, 1906–1922.
11. Papadimitriou, C.H. The NP-completeness of the bandwidth minimization problem. *Computing* **1976**, *16*, 263–270.
12. Garey, M.; Johnson, D. *Computers and Intractability—A Guide to the Theory of NP-Completeness*; Freeman: Gordonsville, VA, USA, 1979.
13. Monien, B. The bandwidth minimization problem for caterpillars with hair length 3 is NP-complete. *SIAM J. Alg. Disc. Meth.* **1986**, *7*, 505–512.
14. Kloks, T.; Kratsch, D.; Borgne, Y.L.; Müller, H. Bandwidth of Split and Circular Permutation Graphs. In *Proceedings of the WG 2000*; Springer-Verlag: Berlin/Heidelberg, Germany, 2000; pp. 243–254.
15. Shrestha, A.M.S.; Tayu, S.; Ueno, S. Bandwidth of Convex Bipartite Graphs and Related Graphs. In *Proceedings of the COCOON 2011*; Springer-Verlag: Berlin/Heidelberg, Germany, 2011; pp. 307–318.
16. Feige, U. Coping with the NP-Hardness of the Graph Bandwidth Problem. In *Proceedings of the 7th Scandinavian Workshop on Algorithm Theory (SWAT 2000)*; Springer-Verlag: Berlin/Heidelberg, Germany, 2000; pp. 10–19.
17. Cygan, M.; Pilipczuk, M. Exact and approximate bandwidth. *Theor. Comput. Sci.* **2010**, *411*, 3701–3713.
18. Cygan, M.; Pilipczuk, M. Even faster exact bandwidth. *ACM Trans. Algorithm* **2012**, *8*, 1–14.
19. Cygan, M.; Pilipczuk, M. Bandwidth and distortion revisited. *Discrete Appl. Math.* **2012**, *160*, 494–504.
20. Haralambides, J.; Makedon, F.; Monien, B. Bandwidth minimization: An approximation algorithm for caterpillars. *Theory Comput. Syst.* **1991**, *24*, 169–177.
21. Kloks, T.; Kratsch, D.; Müller, H. Approximating the bandwidth for asteroidal triple-free graphs. *J. Algorithm* **1999**, *32*, 41–57.
22. Karpinski, M.; Wirtgen, J.; Zelikovsky, A. *An Approximation Algorithm for the Bandwidth Problem on Dense Graphs*; TR-97-017, Electronic Colloquium on Computational Complexity (ECCC), 1997. Available online: http://eccc.hpi-web.de/report/1997/017/ (accessed on 24 January 2013).
23. Gupta, A. Improved bandwidth approximation for trees and chordal graphs. *J. Algorithm* **2001**, *40*, 24–36.
24. Kloks, T.; Kratsch, D.; Müller, H. Bandwidth of chain graphs. *Inf. Process. Lett.* **1998**, *68*, 313–315.
25. Kloks, T.; Tan, R.B. Bandwidth and topological bandwidth of graphs with few P_4's. *Discrete Appl. Math.* **2001**, *115*, 117–133.
26. Kleitman, D.; Vohra, R. Computing the Bandwidth of Interval Graphs. *SIAM J. Disc. Math.* **1990**, *3*, 373–375.
27. Mahesh, R.; Rangan, C.P.; Srinivasan, A. On finding the minimum bandwidth of interval graphs. *Inf. Comput.* **1991**, *95*, 218–224.

28. Sprague, A. An $O(n \log n)$ algorithm for bandwidth of interval graphs. *SIAM J. Discrete Math.* **1994**, *7*, 213–220.
29. Heggernes, P.; Kratsch, D.; Meister, D. Bandwidth of bipartite permutation graphs in polynomial time. *J. Discret. Algorithm* **2009**, *7*, 533–544.
30. Kratsch, D. Finding the minimum bandwidth of an interval graph. *Inf. Comput.* **1987**, *74*, 140–158.
31. Booth, K.; Lueker, G. Testing for the consecutive ones property, interval graphs, and graph planarity using PQ-tree algorithms. *J. Comput. Syst. Sci.* **1976**, *13*, 335–379.
32. Lueker, G.; Booth, K. A linear time algorithm for deciding interval graph isomorphism. *J. ACM* **1979**, *26*, 183–195.
33. Brandstädt, A.; Lozin, V. On the linear structure and clique-width of bipartite permutation graphs. *Ars Comb.* **2003**, *67*, 273–281.
34. Uehara, R.; Valiente, G. Linear structure of bipartite permutation graphs with an application. *Inf. Process. Lett.* **2007**, *103*, 71–77.
35. Otachi, Y.; Okamoto, Y.; Yamazaki, K. Relationships between the class of unit grid intersection graphs and other classes of bipartite graphs. *Discrete Appl. Math.* **2007**, *155*, 2383–2390.
36. Keil, J. Finding hamiltonian circuits in interval graphs. *Inf. Process. Lett.* **1985**, *20*, 201–206.
37. Müller, H. Hamiltonian circuit in chordal bipartite graphs. *Discret. Math.* **1996**, *156*, 291–298.
38. Uehara, R.; Toda, S.; Nagoya, T. Graph isomorphism completeness for chordal bipartite graphs and strongly chordal graphs. *Discret. Appl. Math.* **2004**, *145*, 479–482.
39. Wu, T.H. An $O(n^3)$ isomorphism test for circular-arc graphs. Ph.D. Thesis, Applied Mathematics and Statistics, SUNY-Stonybrook, New York, NY, USA, 1983.
40. Eschen, E.M. Circular-arc graph recognition and related problems. Ph.D. Thesis, Department of Computer Science, Vanderbilt University, Nashville, TE, USA, 1997.
41. Hsu, W.L. $O(M \cdot N)$ Algorithms for the recognition and isomorphism problem on circular-arc graphs. *SIAM J. Comput.* **1995**, *24*, 411–439.
42. Curtis, A.R.; Lin, M.C.; McConnell, R.M.; Nussbaum, Y.; Soulignac, F.J.; Spinrad, J.P.; Szwarcfiter, J.L. Isomorphism of graph classes related to the circular-ones property. arXiv:1203.4822v1.
43. Roberts, F.S. Indifference Graphs. In *Proof Techniques in Graph Theory*; Harary, F., Ed.; Academic Press: Waltham, MA, USA, 1969; pp. 139–146.
44. Bogart, K.P.; West, D.B. A short proof that "proper=unit". *Discret. Math.* **1999**, *201*, 21–23.
45. Deng, X.; Hell, P.; Huang, J. Linear-time representation algorithms for proper circular-arc graphs and proper interval graphs. *SIAM J. Comput.* **1996**, *25*, 390–403.
46. Uehara, R.; Uno, Y. On computing longest paths in small graph classes. *Int. J. Found. Comput. Sci.* **2007**, *18*, 911–930.
47. Saitoh, T.; Otachi, Y.; Yamanaka, K.; Uehara, R. Random Generation and Enumeration of Bipartite Permutation Graphs. In *Proceedings of the 20th International Symposium on Algorithms and Computation (ISAAC 2009)*; Springer-Verlag: Berlin/Heidelberg, Germany, 2009; pp. 1104–1113.
48. Brandstädt, A.; Le, V.; Spinrad, J. *Graph Classes: A Survey*; SIAM: Philadelphia, PA, USA, 1999.

49. Müller, H. Recognizing interval digraphs and interval bigraphs in polynomial time. *Disc. Appl. Math.* **1997**, *78*, 189–205. Available online: http://www.comp.leeds.ac.uk/hm/pub/node1.html (accessed on 22 January 2013).
50. Hell, P.; Huang, J. Interval bigraphs and circular Arc graphs. *J. Graph Theory* **2004**, *46*, 313–327.
51. Rafiey, A. Recognizing interval bigraphs using forbidden patterns. Unpublished work, 2012.
52. Uehara, R. Canonical Data Structure for Interval Probe Graphs. In *Proceedings of the 15th Annual International Symposium on Algorithms and Computation (ISAAC 2004)*; Lecture Notes in Computer Science Volume 3341, Springer-Verlag: Berlin/Heidelberg, Germany, 2004; pp. 859–870.
53. Colbourn, C. On testing isomorphism of permutation graphs. *Networks* **1981**, *11*, 13–21.
54. Babel, L.; Ponomarenko, I.; Tinhofer, G. The isomorphism problem for directed path graphs and for rooted directed path graphs. *J. Algorithm* **1996**, *21*, 542–564.
55. Nakano, S.-I.; Uehara, R.; Uno, T. A New Approach to Graph Recognition and Applications to Distance Hereditary Graphs. In *Proceedings of the 4th Annual Conference on Theory and Applications of Models of Computation (TAMC 07)*; Springer-Verlag: Berlin/Heidelberg, Germany, 2007; pp. 115–127.
56. Knuth, D. Sorting and Searching. In *The Art of Computer Programming*; 2nd ed.; Addison-Wesley Publishing Company: Boston, MA, USA, 1998.
57. Uehara, R.; Iwata, S. Generalized Hi-Q is NP-Complete. *Trans. IEICE* **1990**, *E73*, 270–273. Available online: http://www.jaist.ac.jp/~uehara/pdf/phd7.ps.gz (accessed on 22 January 2013).
58. Plesník, J. The NP-completeness of the hamiltonian cycle problem in planar digraphs with degree bound two. *Inf. Process. Lett.* **1979**, *8*, 199–201.
59. Downey, R.; Fellows, M. *Parameterized Complexity*; Springer: Berlin/Heidelberg, Germany, 1999.
60. Spinrad, J. Open Problem List, 1995. Available online: http://www.vuse.vanderbilt.edu/~spin/open.html (accessed on 22 January 2013).

Algorithms **2013**, *6*, 84-99; doi:10.3390/a6010084

OPEN ACCESS

algorithms

ISSN 1999-4893

www.mdpi.com/journal/algorithms

Article

Dubins Traveling Salesman Problem with Neighborhoods: A Graph-Based Approach

Jason T. Isaacs * and João P. Hespanha

Department of Electrical and Computer Engineering, University of California, Santa Barbara, CA 93106-9560, USA; E-Mail: hespanha@ece.ucsb.edu

* Author to whom correspondence should be addressed; E-Mail: jtisaacs@ece.ucsb.edu; Tel.: +1-805-893-7785; Fax: +1-805-893-3262.

Received: 31 October 2012; in revised form: 17 January 2013 / Accepted: 18 January 2013 / Published: 4 February 2013

Abstract: We study the problem of finding the minimum-length curvature constrained closed path through a set of regions in the plane. This problem is referred to as the Dubins Traveling Salesperson Problem with Neighborhoods (DTSPN). An algorithm is presented that uses sampling to cast this infinite dimensional combinatorial optimization problem as a Generalized Traveling Salesperson Problem (GTSP) with intersecting node sets. The GTSP is then converted to an Asymmetric Traveling Salesperson Problem (ATSP) through a series of graph transformations, thus allowing the use of existing approximation algorithms. This algorithm is shown to perform no worse than the best existing DTSPN algorithm and is shown to perform significantly better when the regions overlap. We report on the application of this algorithm to route an Unmanned Aerial Vehicle (UAV) equipped with a radio to collect data from sparsely deployed ground sensors in a field demonstration of autonomous detection, localization, and verification of multiple acoustic events.

Keywords: traveling salesman problem; graph transformation; nonholonomic vehicles

1. Introduction

Research in the area of unmanned aerial vehicles (UAV) has evolved in recent years. There is rich literature covering various areas of autonomy including path planning, trajectory planning, task allocation, cooperation, sensing, and communications. As the mission objectives of UAVs have increased in complexity and importance, problems are starting to arise at the intersection of these disciplines. The Dubins Traveling Salesman Problem with Neighborhoods (DTSPN) combines the problem of path planning with trajectory planning while using neighborhoods to represent communication ranges or sensor footprints. In this problem the UAV simply needs to enter a region surrounding each objective waypoint.

1.1. Relevant Literature

The path planning problem seeks to determine the optimal sequence of waypoints to visit in order to meet certain mission objectives while minimizing costs, such as the total length of the mission [1,2]. Path planning problems typically rely on approximating the cost of the mission by the length of the solution to a Euclidean Traveling Salesman Problem (ETSP), where the cost to travel from one waypoint to the next is approximated by the Euclidean distance between the two waypoints. This approximation simplifies the overall optimization but may lead to UAV routes that are far from optimal because the aircraft kinematic constraints are not considered.

Another area of UAV research is trajectory planning, in which the goal given an initial and final waypoint pair is to determine the optimal control inputs to reach the final waypoint in minimum time given kinematic constraints of the aircraft. In 1957, Dubins showed that for an approximate model of aircraft dynamics, the optimal motion between a pair of waypoints can be chosen among six possible paths [3]. Similar results were proven later in [4] using tools from optimal control theory. In [5], the authors propose a means of choosing the optimal Dubins path without computing all six possible Dubins optimal paths.

A significant amount of research has gone into combining the problems of motion planning and path planning [6–10]. In these works, the dynamics of the UAV are taken into consideration by using the Dubins model when determining the optimal sequence of waypoints. This problem is typically referred to as the Dubins Traveling Salesman Problem (DTSP).

A third area of UAV related research is a version of path planning that takes into account the communication range of the aircraft or the sensor footprint of the aircraft. This problem is best described as a Traveling Salesman Problem with Neighborhoods (TSPN). Now, not only does one determine a sequence of regions but also an entry point at each region. Many researchers have addressed this problem with various regions, but most have used the Euclidean distance as the cost function [11–13]. Obermeyer was the first to tackle the TSPN with the Dubins vehicle model in [14] using a genetic algorithm approach, then later in [15] by using a sampling-based roadmap method, which we will call RCM, that is proven to be resolution complete. In the latter method, the DTSPN is transformed into a General Traveling Salesman Problem (GTSP) with non-overlapping node sets, and then to an Asymmetric Traveling Salesmen Problem (ATSP) through a version of the Noon and Bean transformation [16].

1.2. Contributions

We propose an algorithm to approximate the DTSPN via a sampling-based roadmap method similar to that of [15] but use a more general version of the Noon and Bean transformation [17] in which the GTSP can contain intersecting node sets. We show that for the same set of samples this method will produce a tour that is no longer than that of RCM from [15] and performs significantly better when the regions intersect frequently. Finally, we report on the application of this algorithm to guide a UAV in collecting data from a sparsely deployed sensor network.

The proposed method converts the DTSPN into a GTSP by sampling, and the Noon and Bean transformation is used to convert the resulting problem into an ATSP, a problem with numerous exact and approximate solvers. The optimal solution of the GTSP can then be recovered from the optimal solution to the resulting ATSP. It should be noted that the Noon and Bean transformations [16,17] only preserve the optimal solution. There is no guarantee that suboptimal solutions to the ATSP will result in good solutions or even feasible solutions to the GTSP [18]. However, experimental results exist that show that the Noon and Bean transformation works well for small to moderate instances of the GTSP [19]. In our experience, the Noon and Bean transformation was suitable for solving GTSP instances of several hundred nodes without any feasibility issues. For very large instances it may be appropriate to avoid the transformation to an ATSP by using a direct GTSP solver such as the memetic algorithm due to Gutin and Karapetyan [18].

1.3. Organization

The remainder of this article is organized as follows. In Section 2, the Dubins Traveling Salesman Problem with Neighborhoods is formally introduced. Section 3 describes the proposed approximation algorithm for the DTSPN. In Section 4, we present a numerical study comparing our algorithm with an existing algorithm for various sized regions and various amounts of overlap. The results from a field demonstration are reported in Section 5 along with a summary of modifications necessary for operational deployment. Conclusions and future work are discussed in Section 6.

2. Problem Statement

The kinematics of the UAV can be approximated by the Dubins vehicle in the plane. The pose of the Dubins vehicle X can be represented by the triplet $(x, y, \theta) \in SE(2)$, where $(x, y) \in \mathbb{R}^2$ define the position of the vehicle in the plane and $\theta \in \mathbb{S}^1$ defines the heading of the vehicle. The vehicle kinematics are then written as,

$$\begin{bmatrix} \dot{x} \\ \dot{y} \\ \dot{\theta} \end{bmatrix} = \begin{bmatrix} \nu\cos(\theta) \\ \nu\sin(\theta) \\ \frac{\nu}{\rho}u \end{bmatrix} \tag{1}$$

where ν is the forward speed of the vehicle, ρ is the minimum turning radius, and $u \in [-1, 1]$ is the bounded control input. Let $\mathcal{L}_\rho : SE(2) \times SE(2) \to \mathbb{R}_+$ associate the length $\mathcal{L}_\rho(X_1, X_2)$ of the minimum length path from an initial pose X_1 of the Dubins vehicle to a final pose X_2, subject to the kinematic constraints in Equation (1). Notice that this length depends implicitly on the forward speed of the vehicle and the minimum turning radius through the kinematic constraints in Equation (1). This length, which we will refer to as the Dubins distance from X_1 to X_2, can be computed in constant time [5].

Let $\mathcal{R} = \{\mathcal{R}_1, \mathcal{R}_2, ..., \mathcal{R}_n\}$ be set of n compact regions in a compact region $\mathcal{Q} \subset \mathbb{R}^2$, and let $\Sigma = (\sigma_1, \sigma_2, \ldots, \sigma_n)$ be an ordered permutation of $\{1, \ldots, n\}$. Define a projection from $SE(2)$ to

$\mathbb{R}^2$ as $\mathcal{P} : SE(2) \rightarrow \mathbb{R}^2$, *i.e.*, $\mathcal{P}(X) = [x\ y]^T$, and let P_i be an element of $SE(2)$ whose projection lies in $\mathcal{R}_i$. We denote the vector created by stacking a vehicle configuration P_i for each of the n regions as $P \in SE(2)^n$.

The DTSPN involves finding the minimum length tour in which the Dubins vehicle visits each region in $\mathcal{R}$ while obeying the kinematic constraints of Equation (1). This is an optimization over all possible permutations Σ and configurations P. Stated more formally:

Problem 2.1 (DTSPN).

$$\begin{aligned} \underset{\Sigma,P}{\textit{minimize}} \quad & \mathcal{L}_\rho(P_{\sigma_n}, P_{\sigma_1}) + \sum_{i=1}^{n-1} \mathcal{L}_\rho(P_{\sigma_i}, P_{\sigma_{i+1}}) \\ \textit{subject to} \quad & \mathcal{P}(P_i) \in \mathcal{R}_i,\ i = 1, \ldots, n \end{aligned}$$

The problem presented in Problem 2.1 is combinatorial in Σ, the sequence of regions to visit and infinite dimensional in P, the poses of the vehicle. We present an algorithm to convert this problem to a finite dimensional combinatorial optimization on a graph by first generating a set of $m \geq n$ sample configurations $S_i \in SE(2)$, $\mathcal{S} := \{\mathbf{S}_1, \ldots, \mathbf{S}_m\}$ such that

$$\mathcal{P}(\mathbf{S}_k) \in \bigcup_{i=1}^{n} \mathcal{R}_i,\ k = 1, \ldots, m \tag{2}$$

and $\forall i\ \exists k$ s.t. $\mathcal{P}(\mathbf{S}_k) \in \mathcal{R}_i$. The algorithm then approximates Problem 2.1 by finding the best sample configurations $P \subseteq \mathcal{S}$ and the order Σ in which to visit them.

Problem 2.2 (Sampled DTSPN).

$$\begin{aligned} \underset{\Sigma,P}{\textit{minimize}} \quad & \mathcal{L}_\rho(P_{\sigma_n}, P_{\sigma_1}) + \sum_{i=1}^{n-1} \mathcal{L}_\rho(P_{\sigma_i}, P_{\sigma_{i+1}}) \\ \textit{subject to} \quad & \mathbf{P}_i \in \mathcal{S} \\ & \mathcal{P}(P_i) \in \mathcal{R}_i,\ i = 1, \ldots, n \end{aligned}$$

3. DTSPN Intersecting Regions Algorithm

Problem 2.2 can now be formulated as a Generalized Traveling Salesman Problem (GTSP) with intersecting node sets in the following manner. The GTSP can be described with a directed graph $\mathcal{G} := (\mathcal{N}, \mathcal{A}, \mathcal{V})$, with nodes $\mathcal{N}$ and arcs $\mathcal{A}$ where the nodes are members of predefined node sets $\mathcal{V}_i, i = 1, 2, \ldots, n$. Here each node represents sample vehicle pose $S_i, i = 1, 2, \ldots, m$, and the arc connecting node S_i to node S_j represents the length of the minimum length path for a Dubins vehicle $c_{i,j} = \mathcal{L}_\rho(S_i, S_j)$ from configuration S_i to configuration S_j. The node set $\mathcal{V}_k$ corresponding to region $\mathcal{R}_k$ contains all samples whose projection lies in $\mathcal{R}_k$, $\mathcal{V}_k := \{S_i \mid \mathcal{P}(S_i) \in \mathcal{R}_k\}$ for $i \in \{1, 2, \ldots, m\}$ and $k \in \{1, 2, \ldots, n\}$. The objective of the GTSP is to find a minimum cost cycle passing through each node set exactly one time. An example instance of Problem 2.2 can be seen in Figure 1(a).

Next, the GTSP can be converted to an Asymmetric TSP through a series of graph transformations due to Noon and Bean [17]. What follows is a brief summary of the Noon–Bean transformation from [17] as it is used in this work. The transformation is best described in three stages. The first stage converts the asymmetric GTSP to a GTSP with mutually exclusive node sets. The second stage converts the GTSP to the canonical form by eliminating intra-set arcs. Finally the third stage converts the canonical form to a clustered TSP and then to an Asymmetric TSP.

Figure 1. Example DTSPN with the corresponding "GTSP with intersecting node sets". (**a**) Example instance of DTSPN with three circular regions $\mathcal{R}_1, \mathcal{R}_2$, and $\mathcal{R}_3$ and samples $S_1, S_2, \ldots, S_8$. The circuit through samples S_2, and , S_8 is the optimal tour; (**b**) Problem (P0): A GTSP with intersecting node sets representation of the DTSPN example. Note: only an essential subset of arcs is shown for clarity of illustration.

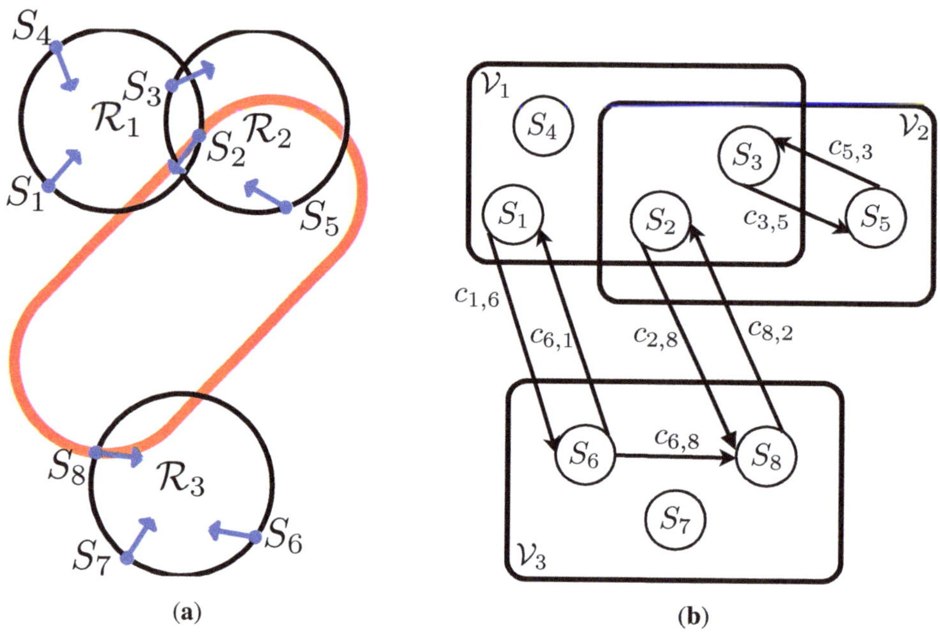

3.1. Stage 1

We begin by restating the problem above in a compact manor to facilitate the discussion. Problem $(P0)$ is a GTSP defined by the graph $\mathcal{G}^0 := (\mathcal{N}^0, \mathcal{A}^0, \mathcal{V}^0)$ with the corresponding cost vector c^0. An example of Problem (P0) is shown in Figure 1(b). The first stage converts the GTSP $(P0)$ to a new problem $(P1)$ which is a GTSP with mutually exclusive node sets. This is done by first eliminating any arcs from $\mathcal{A}^0$ that do not enter at least one new node set.

Problem $(P1)$ is a GTSP defined by the graph $\mathcal{G}^1 := (\mathcal{N}^1, \mathcal{A}^1, \mathcal{V}^1)$ with the corresponding cost vector c^1. Where $\mathcal{N}^1 = \mathcal{N}^0$, and $\mathcal{V}^1 = \mathcal{V}^0$. The arc set $\mathcal{A}^1$ is formed by first setting $\mathcal{A}^1 = \mathcal{A}^0$, and then removing any edges that do not enter at least one new node set. Let $\mathcal{M}(i)$ denote the set of node sets of which node i is a member, *i.e.*, if $i \in \mathcal{V}_k$, then $k \in \mathcal{M}(i)$. For every $(i, j) \in \mathcal{A}^0$, if $\mathcal{M}(j) \subset \mathcal{M}(i)$, then remove the arc (i, j) from set $\mathcal{A}^1$, see Figure 2(a).

Figure 2. Example of Problem (P1) and Problem (P2) from Stage 1 of transformation. (**a**) Problem (P1): Any arcs that do not enter at least one new node set $\{(3,5)$ and $(6,8)\}$ have been removed from the graph in Problem (P0); (**b**) Problem (P2): A large finite cost α is added to each edge. Here $\hat{c}_{i,j} = c^2_{i,j}$, where $c^2_{i,j}$ is defined in Equation (4).

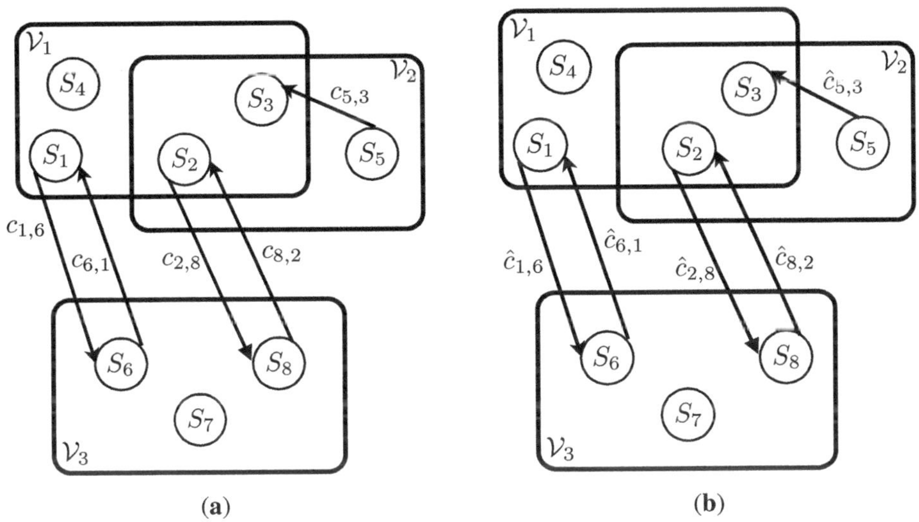

Next, a constant is added to the cost of each arc entering a new node set. Problem $(P2)$ is a GTSP defined by the graph $\mathcal{G}^2 := (\mathcal{N}^2, \mathcal{A}^2, \mathcal{V}^2)$ with the corresponding cost vector c^2. Where $\mathcal{N}^2 = \mathcal{N}^1$, $\mathcal{A}^2 = \mathcal{A}^1$, and $\mathcal{V}^1 = \mathcal{V}^0$. Notice that all arc costs are nonnegative. We now define a finite, positive constant α as,

$$\infty > \alpha \geq \sum_{(i,j)\in\mathcal{A}^1} c^1_{i,j} \tag{3}$$

For every arc $(i,j) \in \mathcal{A}^1$, set the cost of the arc $(i,j) \in \mathcal{A}^2$ in the following manner,

$$c^2_{i,j} = (|\mathcal{M}(j) - \{\mathcal{M}(i) \cap \mathcal{M}(j)\}|)\alpha + c^1_{i,j} \tag{4}$$

Here $|Z|$, represents the cardinality of the set Z. Notice that Equation (4) adds to the original arc cost an additional cost of α for each new node set entered by arc (i,j). An example of Problem (P2) can be seen in Figure 2(b), where $\hat{c}_{i,j}$ represents $c^2_{i,j}$.

Next, any nodes that belong to more than one node set are duplicated and placed in different node sets so as to allow each node to have membership in only one node set. Problem $(P3)$ is a GTSP over the graph $\mathcal{G}^3 := (\mathcal{N}^3, \mathcal{A}^3, \mathcal{V}^3)$ with the corresponding cost vector c^3. The set of nodes $\mathcal{N}^3$ will be populated with the same set of nodes in $\mathcal{N}^2$ plus the additional nodes created to account for the nodes that fall into multiple node sets. For every $i \in \mathcal{N}^2$, create $|\mathcal{M}(i)|$ nodes and assign each to a different node set. For all $k \in \mathcal{M}(i)$, add the node i_k to $\mathcal{N}^3$, and to the node set $\mathcal{V}^3_k$. This insures that $|\mathcal{M}(i_k)| = 1$. Any arcs to and from the original nodes are duplicated as well. For every arc $(i,j) \in \mathcal{A}^2$, create the arc $(i^p, j^q) \in \mathcal{A}^3$ with the corresponding cost $c^3_{i^p,j^q} = c^2_{i,j}$ for every $p \in \mathcal{M}(i)$ and $q \in \mathcal{M}(j)$. In addition, zero cost arcs are added between all the spawned nodes of each multiple membership node. For each node $i \in \mathcal{N}^2$ with multiple node set membership $|\mathcal{M}(i)| > 1$, create arcs $(i^p, i^q) \in \mathcal{A}^3$ with associated costs $c^3_{i^p,i^q} = 0$ for all $p \in \mathcal{M}(i), q \in \mathcal{M}(i)$, such that $p \neq q$. See Figure 3(a) for an example of Problem (P3).

Figure 3. Example of Problem (P3) and Problem (P4) from Stage 1 and Stage 2 of transformation. (**a**) Problem (P3): Nodes S_2 and S_3 from (P2) lie in multiple node sets. These nodes are duplicated and the spawned nodes $S_{2'}$ and $S_{3'}$ are placed in node set $\mathcal{V}_2$. Zero cost arcs (dashed arrows) are added connecting S_2 to $S_{2'}$ and S_3 to $S_{3'}$; (**b**) Problem (P4): The intra-set arc $(5, 3')$ from Problem (P3) is removed.

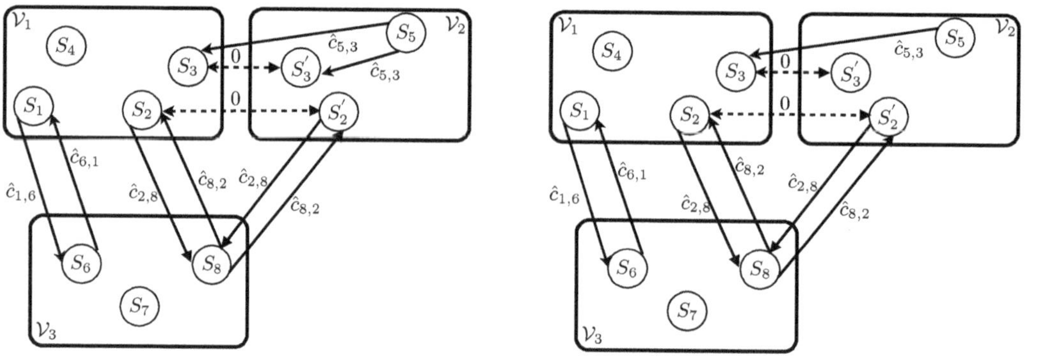

(**a**) (**b**)

To summarize, Stage 1 of the Noon–Bean transformation takes GTSP with intersecting node sets and transforms it into a GTSP with mutually exclusive node sets. The following theorem from [17] summarizes the relationships between problems $(P0)$, $(P1)$, $(P2)$, and $(P3)$.

Theorem 3.1 (Noon and Bean [17])**.** *Given a GTSP in the form of* $(P0)$, *we can transform the problem to a problem of the form of* $(P3)$. *Given an optimal solution to* $(P3)$ *with cost less than* $(m+1)\alpha$, *we can construct an optimal solution to* $(P0)$. *If an optimal solution to* $(P3)$ *has a cost greater than or equal to* $(m+1)\alpha$, *the problem* $(P0)$ *is infeasible.*

3.2. Stage 2

The second stage takes the GTSP with mutually exclusive node sets and eliminates any intra-set arcs, leaving a GTSP in "canonical form." Define a problem $(P4)$ that differs from problem $(P3)$ only by the arcs and arc costs. Problem $(P4)$ is a GTSP over the graph $\mathcal{G}^4 := (\mathcal{N}^4, \mathcal{A}^4, \mathcal{V}^4)$ with the corresponding cost vector c^4 where $\mathcal{N}^4 = \mathcal{N}^3$ and $\mathcal{V}^4 = \mathcal{V}^3$. The arc set $\mathcal{A}^4$ is populated in the following manner. For every i, j pair of nodes in $\mathcal{N}^3$ for which $\mathcal{M}(i) \neq \mathcal{M}(j)$, calculate the lowest cost path from i to j over the arc set $\mathcal{A}_{i,j} \subseteq \mathcal{A}^3$. An arc $(k, l) \in \mathcal{A}_{i,j}$ if the following four conditions hold,

1. $\mathcal{M}(k) \subseteq \mathcal{M}(i) \cup \mathcal{M}(j)$,
2. $\mathcal{M}(l) \subseteq \mathcal{M}(i) \cup \mathcal{M}(j)$,
3. if $\mathcal{M}(l) = \mathcal{M}(i)$ then $\mathcal{M}(k)$ must also equal $\mathcal{M}(i)$,

4. if $\mathcal{M}(k) = \mathcal{M}(j)$ then $\mathcal{M}(l)$ must also equal $\mathcal{M}(j)$.

If the shortest path has finite cost, add the arc (i, j) to the arc set $\mathcal{A}^4$, and set the corresponding arc cost $c^4_{i,j}$ equal to the shortest path cost. If no feasible path exists, then the arc (i, j) will not be part of $\mathcal{A}^4$. The problem defined on $\mathcal{G}^4$ is now in the GTSP canonical form with mutually exclusive node sets and no intra-set arcs. See Figure 3(b) for an example of Problem (P4). The following theorem from [17] establishes the correctness of the transformation in Stage 2.

Theorem 3.2 (Noon and Bean [17])**.** *Given an optimal solution, y^*, to $(P4)$, we can construct the optimal solution, x^*, to $(P3)$.*

3.3. Stage 3

The third stage of the transformation converts the canonical GTSP to a "clustered" TSP. Problem $(P5)$ is a clustered TSP over the graph $\mathcal{G}^5 := (\mathcal{N}^5, \mathcal{A}^5)$ with the corresponding cost vector c^5 where $\mathcal{N}^5 = \mathcal{N}^4$. For every node set $\mathcal{V}_i$ corresponding to nodes in $\mathcal{N}^4$, define a cluster $\mathcal{C}_i$ corresponding to the nodes in $\mathcal{N}^5$. The nodes in each cluster are first enumerated. Let $i^1, i^2, \ldots, i^r$ denote the ordered nodes of $\mathcal{C}_i$ where r represents the cardinality of the cluster, $r = |\mathcal{C}_i|$. Next, a zero cost cycle is created for each cluster by adding zero cost edges between consecutive nodes in each cluster and connecting the first node to the last. For each cluster i with $r > 1$, add the arcs $(i^1, i^2), (i^2, i^3), \ldots, (i^{r-1}, i^r), (i^r, i^1)$ to $\mathcal{A}^5$, and for each of these intra-cluster arcs assign a zero cost, *i.e.*, $c^5_{i^1,i^2} = \cdots = c^5_{i^r,i^1} = 0$. The inter-set edges are then shifted so they emanate from the previous node in its cycle. For every inter-set arc $(i^k, j^l) \in \mathcal{A}^4$, with $k > 0$, create the arc $(i^{k-1}, j^l) \in \mathcal{A}^5$ with the corresponding cost, $c^5_{i^{k-1},j^l} = c^4_{i^k,j^l}$. For each interest arc $(i^1, j^l) \in \mathcal{A}^4$, create the arc $(i^r, j^l) \in \mathcal{A}^5$ with the corresponding cost, $c^5_{i^r,j^l} = c^4_{i^1,j^l}$, where $r = |\mathcal{C}_i|$. See Figure 4(a) for an example of Problem (P5).

Finally, the clustered TSP is converted to an ATSP by adding a large finite cost to each inter-cluster arc cost.

Problem $(P6)$ is a ATSP over the graph $\mathcal{G}^6 := (\mathcal{N}^6, \mathcal{A}^6)$ with the corresponding cost vector c^6 where $\mathcal{N}^6 = \mathcal{N}^5$ and $\mathcal{A}^6 = \mathcal{A}^5$. The arc costs are differ from $(P5)$ in the following way. For every arc $(i, j) \in \mathcal{A}^6$, if i and j belong to the same clusters in $(P5)$, then $c^6_{i,j} = c^5_{i,j}$. If i and j belong to different clusters in $(P5)$, then

$$c^6_{i,j} = c^5_{i,j} + \beta \tag{5}$$

where

$$\infty > \beta > \sum_{(i,j)\in\mathcal{A}^5} c^5_{i,j} \tag{6}$$

An example can be seen in Figure 4(b), where $\bar{c}_{i,j}$ depicts $c^6_{i,j}$. The optimal tour is shown in red.

The following theorem from [17] establishes the correctness of the transformation in Stage 3.

Theorem 3.3 (Noon and Bean [17])**.** *Given a canonical GTSP in the form of $(P4)$ with n node sets, we can transform the problem into a standard TSP in the form of $(P6)$. Given an optimal solution y^* to $(P6)$ with $c^6y^* < (n+1)\beta$, we can construct an optimal solution x^* to $(P4)$.*

Figure 4. Example of Problem (P5) and Problem (P6) from Stage 3 of transformation. (**a**) Problem (P5): The clustered TSP is created by forming zero cost intra-set cycles and adjusting the originating node in each inter-set arc; (**b**) Problem (P6): A large finite cost β is added to each inter-set edge. Here $\bar{c}_{i,j} = c^6_{i,j}$, where $c^6_{i,j}$ is defined in Equation (5). The optimal tour is shown in red with a cost of $\hat{c}_{8,2} + \beta + \hat{c}_{2,8}$.

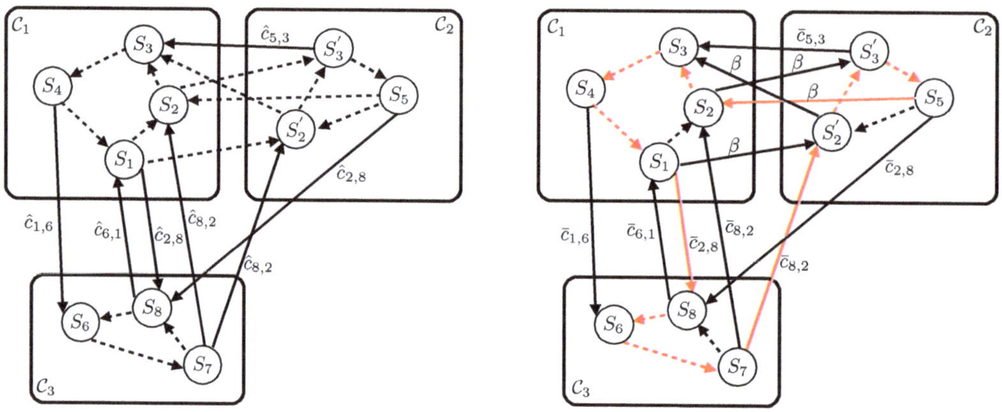

(**a**) (**b**)

3.4. Performance Comparison

The Intersecting Regions Algorithm (IRA) proposed here is similar to the Resolution Complete Method (RCM) proposed in [15] with the key exception that we use the fact that visiting one of the samples in the intersection of multiple regions achieves the goal of visiting all the regions in the intersection. Figure 5 illustrate this key difference. The RCM requires mutually exclusive node sets for the conversion from DTSPN to a GTSP with disjoint node sets. To meet this requirement, samples are assigned directly to the node set of the region from whose boundary they are drawn, as depicted in Figure 5(b). If multiple regions overlap and a sample lies in the intersection, IRA assigns this sample to all the node sets corresponding to the intersecting regions, as depicted in Figure 5(a), while RCM does not. The IRA then uses this additional information in the optimization.

Theorem 3.4 (IRA Performance). *Given $\rho > 0$, the set of $n \geq 2$ possibly intersecting regions, $\mathcal{R}$, and the set of m sample configurations, $\mathcal{S}$, let T_{IRA} and T_{RCM} denote the tours produced by IRA and the RCM [15], respectively. Then the length of T_{IRA} is no greater than that of T_{RCM},*

$$\text{length}(T_{IRA}) \leq \text{length}(T_{RCM}) \tag{7}$$

Proof. [Proof of Theorem 3.4] Let $T = \{S_1, S_2, \ldots, S_n\}$ be a feasible tour, and note that both IRA and RCM minimize the tour length plus an additive constant while ensuring that all regions are visited. The difference is that IRA may produce tours visiting fewer than n unique samples, should some samples lie in the multiple regions. In particular, the IRA ensures that each leg of the tour enters at least one new region, by construction. Therefore, in performing the optimization IRA will either consider T, or subset of T, in which samples at the end of legs not entering an unvisited region have been removed. Due to the Dubins distance function satisfying the triangle inequality [20], a tour that visits a redundant sample will be longer than a tour that visits a subset of the samples. The optimal tour T_{IRA} cannot be longer than T_{RCM}, because both optimize over the same set of feasible tours except for the tours in which IRA bypasses these unneeded samples. □

The property *resolution complete method* as used in [15], dictates that the method converges to a solution at least as good as any nonisolated optimum solution as the number of sample configurations goes to infinity.

Corollary 3.5 (IRA is Resolution Complete)**.** *Given $\rho > 0$, the set of $n \geq 2$ possibly intersecting regions, $\mathcal{R}$, and the set of m sample configurations, $\mathcal{S}$ drawn from a Halton quasi-random sequence[21] as in RCM, then IRA is Resolution Complete.*

Proof. [Proof of Corollary 3.5] From [15], the RCM is a resolution complete method and converges as the number of samples goes to infinity, and from Theorem 3.4, we have shown that for the same set of sample configurations IRA will produce a tour that is no longer than RCM. □

Figure 5. A comparison of IRA and RCM on an example DTSPN instance with three regions and three sample poses. (**a**) Example Tour: IRA, Tour Length $= 7.7$; (**b**) Example Tour: RCM, Tour Length $= 15.4$.

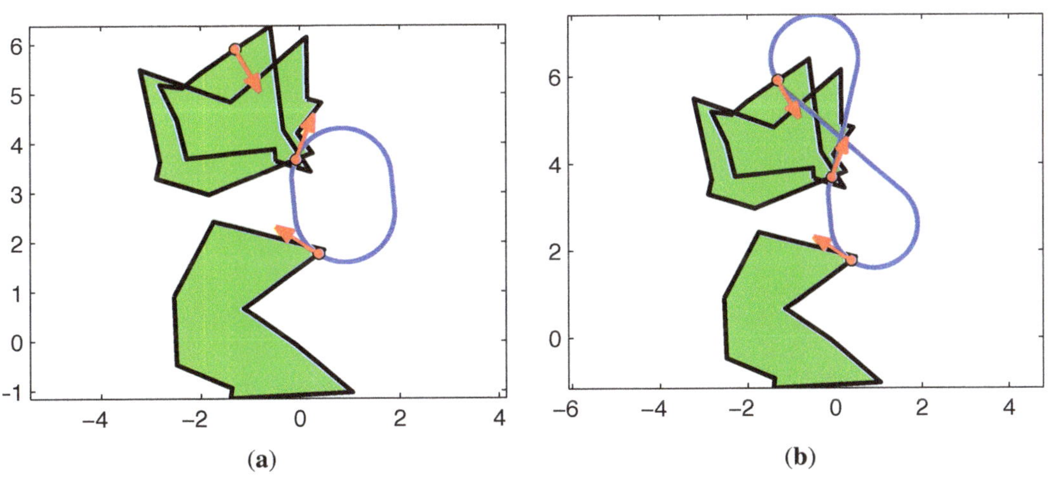

3.5. Complexity of Intersecting Regions Algorithm

We have provided an algorithm that takes advantage of sample configurations that lie in overlapping regions, and we have shown that this algorithm produces a tour that is no longer than the previous best algorithms in the literature. However, the size of the ATSP is increased by the number of multiple node set duplicate nodes. Given m samples from n regions, this algorithm will compute the ATSP over at most mn nodes. The worst case computational complexity of the Noon and Bean transformation [17] is $O(m^2n^4)$. Then the worst case complexity for solving the ATSP using the modified version of Christofides' algorithm provided in [22] is $O(m^3n^3)$.

4. Numerical Results

In Theorem 3.4 we have shown that for the same sample set, IRA will perform no worse than the resolution complete method from [15], but at the cost of solving a larger ATSP problem when there exist samples that are contained in multiple regions. In this section, we use Monte Carlo simulation to investigate the level of performance improvement that can be gained as well as the degree of increase in the size of the resulting ATSP by using IRA compared with the RCM.

Figure 6. Simulation results for 100 Monte Carlo trials where both IRA and RCM optimized over the same 50 sample poses. (**a**) The color represents the average of the ratio of the tour length under IRA to the tour length under the RCM planning algorithm. Here the red regions indicate near parity in performance while the blue regions indicate that IRA produced tours that are approximately half the length of tours produced by the RCM algorithm; (**b**) The color represents the average of the ratio of the size of the ATSP solved under IRA to the size of the ATSP solved under the RCM planning algorithm. Here the blue regions indicate near parity in size while the red regions indicate that IRA increased the size of the ATSP by as much as four times.

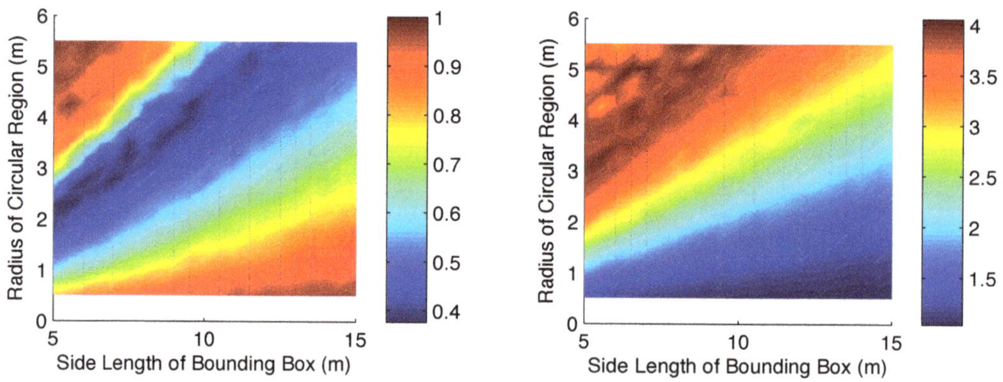

(**a**) (**b**)

The centers of circular regions of variable but homogeneous diameters are randomly placed in a square of variable side length. By varying both the size of regions and the area in which the centers of the regions are confined we are able to vary the degree of overlap. The turning radius of the UAV ρ is set to unit radius. To solve for the tours we used the symmetric TSP solver *linkern* available at [23], which uses the Chained Lin–Kernighan Heuristic from [24]. The radii of the circular regions were varied over $\{0.5, 0.75, 1.00, \ldots, 5.5\}$, and the length of the sides of the square were varied over $\{5, 5.5, \ldots, 15\}$.

For the first test, we ran 100 trials where 10 regions were randomly placed in the bounding box and 50 samples were drawn from the boundaries of the regions. The results can be seen in Figure 6, where the average ratio of the length of the tours found by the IRA to those found by RCM are displayed for each test configuration (Figure 6(a)) as well as the average ratio of the size of the resulting ATSP (Figure 6(b)). In a second test, we repeated the same test parameters where IRA optimized over 50 sample poses, but allowed the RCM to optimize over the same 50 samples plus an additional sample for each duplicated node in the IRA. These extra samples ensured that both algorithms solved the same size ATSP. The results can be seen in Figure 7, where the average ratio of the length of the tours found by the IRA to those found by RCM are displayed for each test configuration. In both instances, it is clear that for small regions and large bounding box (bottom right of plots), there is little to no overlap, and the two algorithms perform equivalently. The tests of interest are when the regions grow, and the bounding area shrinks (moving from bottom right to top left). For these cases we see that on average, IRA finds tours that are nearly half the length of RCM. It should be noted that as the density increases, there becomes a point where a single sample will be contained in all regions (the top left corner). In this case, RCM would still visit n samples (one from each region) while IRA would only visit the single sample contained in all regions. In practice there is no need for planning once it is recognized that a single loiter circle will visit all the regions, thus both algorithms were assigned the length of one loiter radius. It should also be noted that the size of the resulting ATSP is increased by only as much as $4\times$, which is significantly less than the worst case analysis would predict $(10\times)$.

Figure 7. Simulation results for the where IRA optimized over 50 sample poses and RCM optimized over the same 50 samples plus an additional sample for each duplicated node in the IRA. These extra samples ensured that both algorithms solved the same size ATSP.

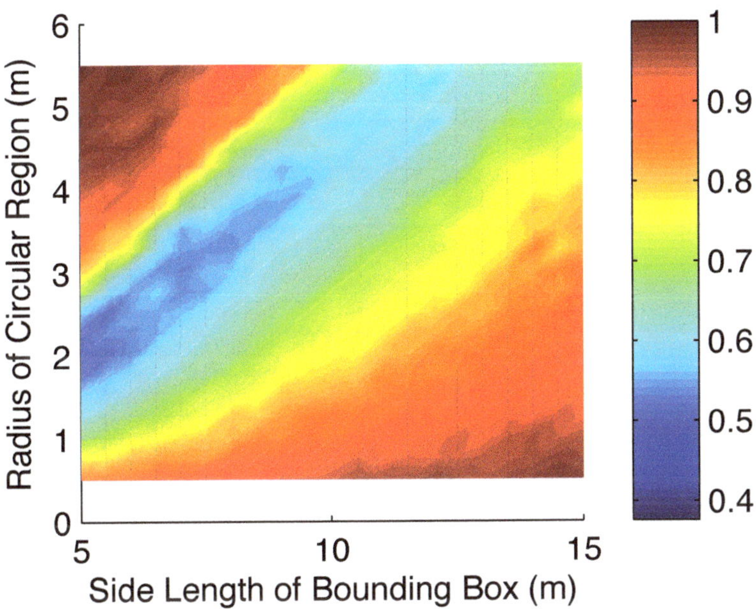

5. Demonstration

The algorithm presented here was demonstrated as part of a large field test conducted in June 2011 at Camp Roberts, CA by a team consisting of Teledyne Scientific Company, the University of California,

Santa Barbara, the U.S. Army Research Laboratory, the U.S. Army Engineer Research and Development Center, and IBM UK. The goal of the field test included the integration of multiple autonomously controlled UAVs to gather information regarding the detection and localization of multiple acoustic events by sparsely deployed ground sensors, and the use of the International Technology Alliance (ITA) Sensor Network Fabric [25].

A schematic of the system used in the deployment is shown in Figure 8(a). We deployed six ToA sensors over a region that was roughly 1.3 km $\times$ 0.5 km in size. We used GPS receivers at each sensor to estimate their locations and synchronize them in time. Two propane cannons that have acoustic characteristics similar to artillery were fired randomly and potentially close to one another in time. A UAV traveled along a DTSPN tour produced by IRA, gathering ToAs and inferring possible event locations. When the inference algorithm had sufficient confidence in a candidate event, it dispatched a second UAV, fitted with a gimbaled camera, to fly over the estimated location and image the source. The data gathering and event imaging was done continuously, with the events being imaged on a first come first served basis.

Figure 8. The configuration of sensors and UAV trajectory during the field demonstration at Camp Roberts, CA. (**a**) Field Demonstration Description. The acoustic sensors visited by the data collecting UAV are shown as yellow dots; (**b**) The blue lines represent the GPS logs of the path taken by data collecting UAV during the test. The desired path was sent to the autopilot via the square waypoints. The sensors and communication regions are represented by green and blue circles respectively.

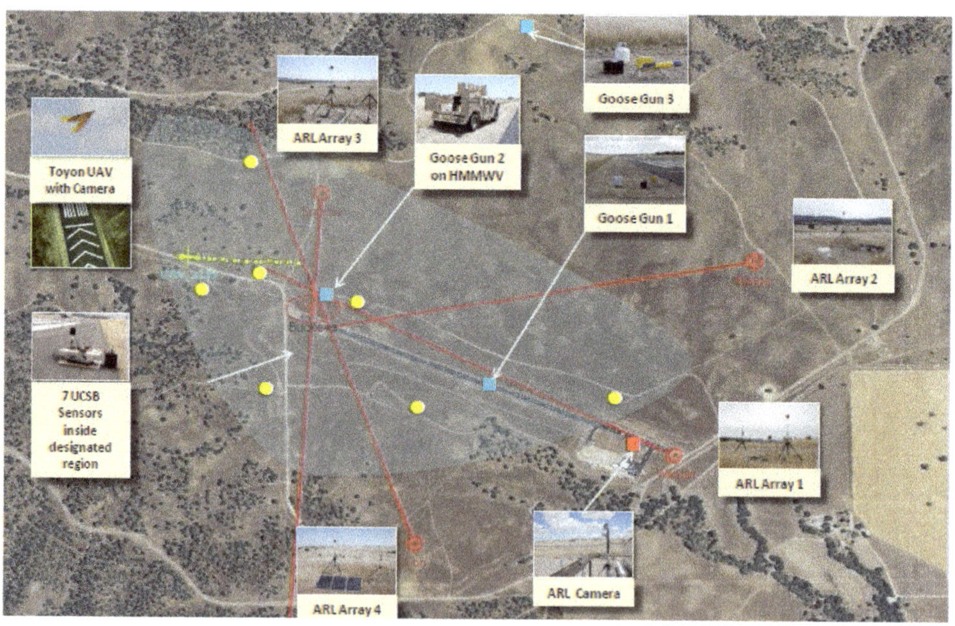

(**a**)

Figure 8. *Cont.*

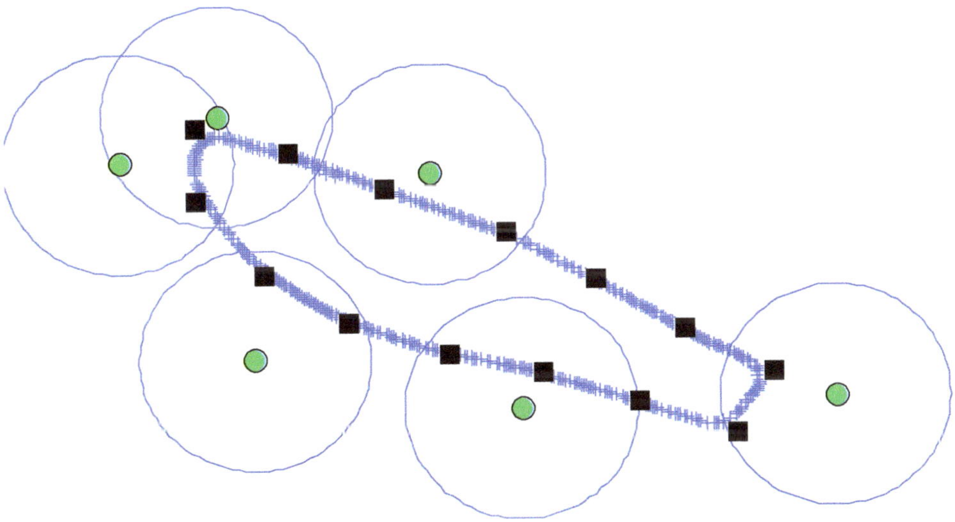

(b)

5.1. Modifications for the Demonstration

The Intersecting Regions Algorithm from above is designed as a path planning algorithm. If the planned path is followed in an open-loop fashion, the system is susceptible to disturbances such as wind and modeling errors. As such the IRS was modified slightly to be more robust to disturbances such as wind as well as allow for waypoint control of the UAV. The first modification of the routing algorithm reduced the size of the communication regions in the optimization to ensure that the resulting path would penetrate the original communication region even under the influence of small disturbances. The second modification involved sampling the desired path to obtain a finite sequence of waypoints to command to the UAV autopilot.

The route flown by the mule-UAV and the communication regions used in the DTSPN path planning algorithm are shown in Figure 9(b). It took on average two minutes and fifty seconds for the mule-UAV to complete the circuit and collect measurements from all ground sensors. This time is conservative due to the modifications to the algorithm that ensure that the UAV enters into each communication region (radius = 200 m).

6. Conclusions

We have introduced an algorithm addressing the Dubins Traveling Salesman Problem with Neighborhoods. This algorithm samples the regions and then utilizes the Noon and Bean transformation [17] for intersecting node sets to transform the problem to an ATSP. We show that for the same set of samples this method will produce a tour that is no longer than that of [15] and presented numerical results that show performance improvement when there is overlap in the regions of interest.

There are many directions in which this work may be extended. Although we have focused on the Dubins model for a fixed wing UAV, the IRA could be applied to any nonholonomic vehicle whose node to node cost is well defined. Also, it is of interest to understand if a deterministic way to sample the configurations would be of benefit in possibly reducing the number samples needed to achieve a certain level of performance. For instance, if there is significant overlap, would it be beneficial to ensure that at least one sample is taken from each subregion. Finally, for large instances of the DTSPN, we are interested in comparing the performance of this method with direct GTSP solvers such as the memetic algorithm due to Gutin and Karapetyan [18].

Acknowledgements

This work was supported by the Institute for Collaborative Biotechnologies through grant W911NF-09-0001 from the U.S. Army Research Office. The content of the information does not necessarily reflect the position or the policy of the Government, and no official endorsement should be inferred.

References

1. Klein, D.J.; Schweikl, J.; Isaacs, J.T.; Hespanha, J.P. On UAV Routing Protocols for Sparse Sensor Data Exfiltration. In *Proceedings of the American Control Conference*, Baltimore, Maryland, USA, 30 June–2 July 2010; pp. 6494–6500.
2. Bopardikar, S.D.; Smith, S.L.; Bullo, F.; Hespanha, J.P. Dynamic vehicle routing for translating demands: Stability analysis and receding-horizon policies. *IEEE Trans. Autom. Control* **2010**, *55*, 2554–2569.
3. Dubins, L.E. On curves of minimal length with a constraint on average curvature, and with prescribed initial and terminal positions and tangents. *Am. J. Math.* **1957**, *79*, 497–516.
4. Boissonnat, J.D.; Cérézo, A.; Leblond, J. Shortest paths of bounded curvature in the plane. *J. Intell. Robot. Syst.* **1994**, *11*, 5–20.
5. Shkel, A.M.; Lumelsky, V. Classification of the Dubins set. *Robot. Auton. Syst.* **2001**, *34*, 179–202.
6. Le Ny, J.; Frazzoli, E.; Feron, E. The Curvature-constrained Traveling Salesman Problem for High Point Densities. In *Proceedings of the IEEE Conference on Decision and Control*, New Orleans, Louisiana, USA, 12–14 December 2007; pp. 5985–5990.
7. Le Ny, J.; Feron, E.; Frazzoli, E. On the curvature-constrained traveling salesman problem. *IEEE Trans. Autom. Control*, in press.
8. Savla, K.; Frazzoli, E.; Bullo, F. Traveling salesperson problems for the Dubins vehicle. *IEEE Trans. Autom. Control* **2008**, *53*, 1378–1391.
9. Ma, X.; Castanon, D. Receding Horizon Planning for Dubins Traveling Salesman Problems. In *Proceedings of the IEEE Conference on Decision and Control*, San Diego, California, USA, 13–15 December 2006; pp. 5453–5458.
10. Rathinam, S.; Sengupta, R.; Darbha, S. A resource allocation algorithm for multiple vehicle systems with non-holnomic constraints. *IEEE Trans. Autom. Sci. Eng.* **2007**, *4*, 98–104.

11. Dumitrescu, A.; Mitchell, J.S.B. Approximation algorithms for TSP with neighborhoods in the plane. *J. Algorithm.* **2003**, *48*, 135–159.
12. Elbassioni, K.; Fishkin, A.V.; Mustafa, N.H.; Sitters, R. Approximation Algorithms for Euclidean Group TSP. In *Proceedings of the International Colloquim on Automata, Languages and Programming*, Lisbon, Portugal, 11–15 July 2005; pp. 1115–1126.
13. Yuan, B.; Orlowska, M.; Sadiq, S. On the optimal robot routing problem in wireless sensor networks. *IEEE Trans. Knowl. Data Eng.* **2007**, *19*, 1252–1261.
14. Obermeyer, K.J. Path Planning for a UAV Performing Reconnaissance of Static Ground Targets in Terrain. In *Proceedings of the AIAA Conference on Guidance, Navigation, and Control*, Chicago, Illinois, USA, 10–13 August 2009.
15. Obermeyer, K.J.; Oberlin, P.; Darbha, S. Sampling-Based Roadmap Methods for a Visual Reconnaissance UAV. In *Proceedings of the AIAA Conference on Guidance, Navigation, and Control*, Toronto, Ontario, Canada, 2–5 August 2010.
16. Noon, C.E.; Bean, J.C. *An Efficient Transformation of the Generalized Traveling Salesman Problem*; Technical Report 91–26; Department of Industrial and Operations Engineering, University of Michigan: Ann Arbor, MI, USA, 1991.
17. Noon, C.E.; Bean, J.C. *An Efficient Transformation of the Generalized Traveling Salesman Problem*; Technical Report 89–36; Department of Industrial and Operations Engineering, University of Michigan: Ann Arbor, MI, USA, 1989.
18. Gutin, G.; Karapetyan, D. A memetic algorithm for the generalized traveling salesman problem. *Nat. Comput.* **2010**, *9*, 47–60.
19. Ben-Arieh, D.; Gutin, G.; Penn, M.; Yeo, A.; Zverovitch, A. Transformations of generalized ATSP into ATSP. *Oper. Res. Lett.* **2003**, *31*, 357–365.
20. Yadlapalli, S.; Malik, W.A.; Rathinam, S.; Darbha, S. A Lagrangian-based Algorithm for a Combinatorial Motion Planning Problems. In *Proceedings of the IEEE Conference on Decision and Control*, New Orleans, Louisiana, USA, 12–14 December 2007; pp. 5979–5984.
21. Halton, J.H. On the efficiency of certain quasi-random sequences of points in evaluating multi-dimensional integrals. *Numer. Math.* **1960**, *2*, 84–90.
22. Frieze, A.; Galbiati, G.; Maffioli, F. On the worst-case performance of some algorithms for the asymmetric traveling salesman problem. *Networks* **1982**, *12*, 23–39.
23. Applegate, D.; Bixby, R.; Chvátal, V.; Cook, W. Concorde TSP Solver. Available online: http//www.tsp.gatech.edu/concorde (accessed on 9 July 2010).
24. Applegate, D.; Cook, W.; Rohe, A. Chained lin-kernighan for large traveling salesman problems. *INFORMS J. Comput.* **2003**, *15*, 82–92.
25. Bergamaschi, F.; Conway-Jones, D. ITA/CWP and ICB Technology Demonstrator: A Practical Integration of Disparate ISR/ISTAR Assets and Technologies. In *Proceedings of SPIE*, Baltimore, Maryland, USA, 23–26 April 2012; Volume 8389, p. 83890G.

Algorithms **2013**, *6*, 100-118; doi:10.3390/a6010100

OPEN ACCESS

algorithms

ISSN 1999-4893

www.mdpi.com/journal/algorithms

Article

Computing the Eccentricity Distribution of Large Graphs

Frank W. Takes * and Walter A. Kosters

Leiden Institute of Advanced Computer Science, Leiden University, P.O. Box 9512, 2300 RA Leiden, The Netherlands

* Author to whom correspondence should be addressed; E-Mail: ftakes@liacs.nl; Tel.: +31-0-71-5277143; Fax: +31-0-71-5276985.

Received: 1 November 2012; in revised form: 24 January 2013 / Accepted: 31 January 2013 / Published: 18 February 2013

Abstract: The eccentricity of a node in a graph is defined as the length of a longest shortest path starting at that node. The eccentricity distribution over all nodes is a relevant descriptive property of the graph, and its extreme values allow the derivation of measures such as the radius, diameter, center and periphery of the graph. This paper describes two new methods for computing the eccentricity distribution of large graphs such as social networks, web graphs, biological networks and routing networks. We first propose an exact algorithm based on eccentricity lower and upper bounds, which achieves significant speedups compared to the straightforward algorithm when computing both the extreme values of the distribution as well as the eccentricity distribution as a whole. The second algorithm that we describe is a hybrid strategy that combines the exact approach with an efficient sampling technique in order to obtain an even larger speedup on the computation of the entire eccentricity distribution. We perform an extensive set of experiments on a number of large graphs in order to measure and compare the performance of our algorithms, and demonstrate how we can efficiently compute the eccentricity distribution of various large real-world graphs.

Keywords: graphs; eccentricity; diameter; radius; periphery; center

Classification: MSC 05C85, 05C12

---

1. Introduction

Within the field of graph mining, researchers are often interested in deriving properties that describe the structure of their graphs. One of these properties is the *eccentricity distribution*, which describes the distribution of the eccentricity over all nodes, where the *eccentricity* of a node refers to the length of a longest shortest path starting at that node. This distribution differs from properties such as the distance distribution in the sense that eccentricity can be seen as a more "extreme" measure of distance. It also differs from indicators such as the degree distribution in the sense that determining the eccentricity of every node in the graph is computationally expensive: the traditional method computes the eccentricity of each node by running an All Pairs Shortest Path (APSP) algorithm, requiring $O(mn)$ time for a graph with n nodes and m edges. Unfortunately, this approach is too time-consuming if we consider large graphs with possibly millions of nodes.

The aforementioned complexity issues are frequently solved by determining the eccentricity of a random subset of the nodes in the original graph, and then deriving the eccentricity distribution from the obtained values [1]. While such an estimate may seem reasonable when the goal is to determine the overall average eccentricity value, we will show that this technique does not perform well when the actual *extreme values* of the distribution are of relevance. The nodes with the highest eccentricity values realize the diameter of the graph and form the so-called graph periphery, whereas the nodes with the lowest values realize the radius and form the center of the graph, and finding exactly these nodes can be useful within various application areas.

In routing networks, for example, it is interesting to know exactly which nodes form the periphery of the network and thus have the highest worst-case response time to any other device [2]. Also, when (routing) networks are modeled, for example for research purposes, it is important to measure the exact eccentricity distribution so that the model can be evaluated by comparing it with the distribution of real routing networks [3]. The eccentricity also plays a role in networks that model some biological system. There, proteins (nodes in the network) that have a low eccentricity value are easily functionally reachable by other components of the network [4]. The diameter, defined as the length of a longest shortest path, is the most frequently studied eccentricity-based measure, and efficient algorithms for its computation have been suggested in [5–7].

Generally speaking, the eccentricity can be seen as an extreme measure of centrality, *i.e.*, the relative importance of a node in a graph. Centroid centrality [8] and graph centrality [9] have been suggested as centrality measures based on the eccentricity of a node. Compared to other measures such as closeness centrality, the main difference is that a node with a very low eccentricity value is relatively close to *every* other node, whereas a node with a low closeness centrality value is close to all the other nodes *on average*.

In this paper we first discuss an algorithm based on eccentricity lower and upper bounds for determining the exact eccentricity of every node of a graph. We also present a useful pruning strategy, and show how our method significantly improves upon the traditional algorithm. To realize an even larger speedup, we propose to incorporate a sampling technique on a specific set of nodes in the graph which allows us to obtain the eccentricity distribution much faster, while still ensuring a high accuracy on the eccentricity distribution, and an exact result for the eccentricity-based graph properties such as the radius and diameter.

The rest of this paper is organized as follows. We consider some notation and formulate the main problems addressed in this paper in Section 2, after which we cover related work in Section 3. Section 4 describes an exact algorithm for determining the eccentricity distribution. In Section 5, we explain how sampling can be incorporated. Results of applying our methods to various large datasets are presented in Section 6, and finally Section 7 summarizes the paper and offers suggestions for future work.

2. Preliminaries

We consider graphs $G(V, E)$, where V is the set of $|V| = n$ vertices (nodes) and $E \subseteq V \times V$ is the set of $|E| = m$ edges (also called arcs or links). The distance $d(v, w)$ between two nodes $v, w \in V$ is defined as the length of a shortest path from v to w, *i.e.*, the minimum number of edges that have to be traversed to get from v to w. We assume that our graphs are *undirected*, meaning that $(v, w) \in E$ iff $(w, v) \in E$ and thus $d(v, w) = d(w, v)$ for all $v, w \in V$. Note that each edge (v, w) is thus included twice in E: once as a link from v to w and once as a link from w to v. We will also assume that G is connected, meaning that $d(v, w)$ is always finite. Furthermore it is assumed that there are no parallel edges and no loops linking a node to itself. The neighborhood $N(v)$ of a node v is defined as the set of all nodes connected to v via an edge: $N(v) = \{w \in V \mid (v, w) \in E\}$. The degree $deg(v)$ of a node v can then be defined as the number of nodes connected to that node, *i.e.*, its neighborhood size: $deg(v) = |N(v)|$.

The *eccentricity* $\varepsilon(v)$ of a node $v \in V$ is defined as the length of a longest shortest path from v to any other node: $\varepsilon(v) = \max_{w \in V} d(v, w)$. The *eccentricity distribution* counts the frequency $f(x)$ of each eccentricity value x, and can easily be derived when the eccentricity of each node in the graph is known. The *relative eccentricity distribution* lists for each eccentricity value x its relative frequency $F(x) = f(x)/n$, normalizing for the number of nodes in the graph. Figure 1 shows the relative eccentricity distributions of a number of large graphs (for a detailed description of these datasets, see Section 6.1).

Figure 1. Relative eccentricity distributions of various large graphs.

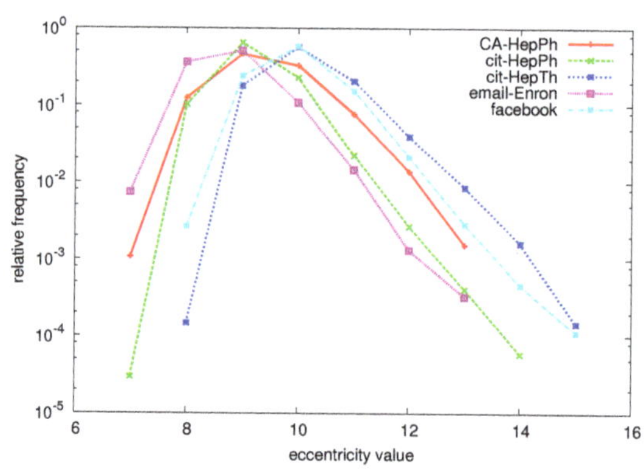

Various other measures can be derived using the notion of eccentricity, such as the *average eccentricity* $\bar{\varepsilon}(G)$ of a graph G, defined as $\bar{\varepsilon}(G) = \frac{1}{n}\sum_{v\in V}\varepsilon(v)$. Another related measure is the *diameter* $\Delta(G)$ of a graph G, which is is defined as the maximum eccentricity over all nodes in the graph: $\Delta(G) = \max_{v\in V}\varepsilon(v)$. Similarly, we define the *radius* $\Gamma(G)$ of a graph G as the minimum eccentricity over all nodes in the graph: $\Gamma(G) = \min_{v\in V}\varepsilon(v)$. The graph center $C(G)$ refers to the set of nodes with an eccentricity equal to the radius, $C(G) = \{v \in V \mid \varepsilon(v) = \Gamma(G)\}$. Similarly, the graph periphery $D(G)$ is defined as the set of nodes with an eccentricity value equal to the diameter of the graph: $D(G) = \{v \in V \mid \varepsilon(v) = \Delta(G)\}$. Each of the measures explained above can be derived when the eccentricity of all nodes is known. Figure 2 shows an example of a graph that explains the different measures covered in this section.

Figure 2. Toy graph showing the eccentricity of its 12 nodes, with average eccentricity 4.67, radius 3 realized by center node G, and diameter 6 realized by periphery nodes D, E and L.

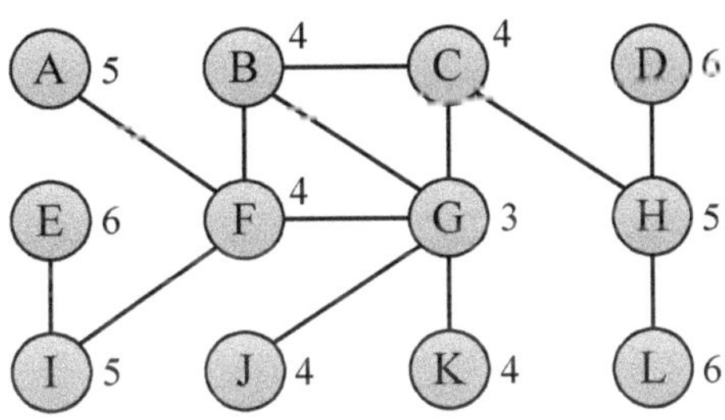

Computing the eccentricity of one node can be done by running Dijkstra's algorithm, and returning the largest distance found (*i.e.*, the distance to a node furthest away from the starting node). Because we only consider unweighted graphs and thus, starting from the current node, can simply explore the neighboring nodes in level-order, computing the eccentricity of one node can be done in $O(m)$ time. The process of determining the eccentricity of one node v is denoted by ECCENTRICITY(v) in Algorithm 1.

Algorithm 1 NAIVEECCENTRICITIES

```
Input: Graph G(V, E)
Output: Vector ε, containing ε(v) for all v ∈ V

for v ∈ V do
    ε[v] ← ECCENTRICITY(v)    // O(m)
end for

return ε
```

This algorithm simply computes the eccentricity for each of the n nodes, resulting in an overall complexity of $O(mn)$ to determine the eccentricity of every node in the graph. Clearly, in graphs with millions of nodes and possibly hundreds of millions of edges, this approach is too time-consuming. The rest of this paper describes more efficient approaches for determining the eccentricity distribution, where we are interested in two things:

- The (relative) eccentricity distribution as a whole.
- Finding the extreme values of the eccentricity distribution, *i.e.*, the radius and diameter, as well as derived measures such as the center and periphery of the graph.

We will address these issues by answering the following two questions:

- How can we obtain the *exact* eccentricity distribution by efficiently computing the exact value of $\varepsilon(v)$ for all nodes $v \in V$? (Section 4)
- How can we obtain an *accurate approximation* of the eccentricity distribution by using a sampling technique? (Section 5)

3. Related Work

Substantial work on the eccentricity distribution dates back to 1975, when the term "eccentric sequence" was introduced to denote the sequence that counts the frequency of each eccentricity value [10]. The facility location problem is an example of the usefulness of eccentricity as a measure of centrality. When considering the placement of emergency facilities such as a hospital or fire station, assuming the map is modelled as a graph, the node with the lowest eccentricity value might be a good location for such a facility. In other situations, for example for the placement of a shopping center, a related measure called closeness centrality, defined as a node's *average* distance to every other node ($c(v) = \frac{1}{n}\sum_{w \in V} d(v, w)$), is more suitable. Generally speaking, the eccentricity is a relevant measure when some strict criterion (the firetruck has to be able to reach *every* location within 10 minutes) has to be met [11]. An application of eccentricity as a measure on a larger scale is the network routing graph, where the eccentricity of a node says something about the worst-case response time between one machine and *all* other machines.

The most well-known eccentricity-based measure is the diameter, which has been extensively investigated in [5–7]. Several measures related to the eccentricity and diameter have also been considered. Kang *et al.* [12] study the effective radius, which they define as the 90th-percentile of all the shortest distances from a node. In a similar way, the effective diameter can be defined, which is shown to be decreasing over time for many large real-world graphs [13]. Each of these measures is computed by using an approximation algorithm [14] to determine the neighborhood of a node, a technique on which we will elaborate in Section 5.3.

To the best of our knowledge, there are no efficient techniques that have been specifically designed to determine the exact eccentricity distribution of a graph. Obviously, the naive approach, for example as suggested in [15], is too time-consuming. Efficient approaches for solving the APSP problem (which then makes determining the eccentricity distribution a trivial task) have been developed, for example using matrix multiplication [16]. Unfortunately, such approaches are still too complex in terms of time and memory requirements.

4. Exact Algorithm

In order to derive an algorithm that can compute the eccentricity of all n nodes in a graph faster than simply recomputing the eccentricity n times (once for each node in the graph), we have two options:

1. Reduce the size of the graph as a whole to speed up one eccentricity computation.
2. Reduce the number of eccentricity computations.

In this section we propose lower and upper bounds on the eccentricity, a strategy that accommodates the second type of speedup. We will also outline a pruning strategy that helps to reduce both the number of nodes that have to be investigated, as well as the size of the graph, realizing both of the two speedups listed above.

4.1. Eccentricity Bounds

We propose to use the following bounds on the eccentricity of all nodes $w \in V$, when the eccentricity of one node $v \in V$ has been computed:

Observation 1 *For nodes* $v, w \in V$ *we have* $\max(\varepsilon(v) - d(v,w), d(v,w)) \leq \varepsilon(w) \leq \varepsilon(v) + d(v,w)$.

The upper bound can be understood as follows: if node w is at distance $d(v,w)$ from node v, it can always employ v to get to every other node in $\varepsilon(v)$ steps. To get to node v, exactly $d(v,w)$ steps are needed, totalling $\varepsilon(v) + d(v,w)$ steps to get to any other node. The first part of the lower bound ($\varepsilon(v) - d(v,w)$) can be derived in the same way, by interchanging v and w in the previous statement. The second part of the lower bound, $d(v,w)$ itself, simply states that the eccentricity of w is at least equal to some found distance to w.

The bounds from Observation 1 were suggested in [6] as a way to determine which nodes could contribute to a graph's diameter. We extend the method proposed in that paper by using these bounds to compute the full eccentricity distribution of the graph. The approach is outlined in Algorithm 2.

First, the candidate set W and the lower and upper eccentricity bounds are initialized (lines 3–8). In the main loop of the algorithm, a node v is repeatedly selected (line 10) from W, its eccentricity is determined (line 11), and finally all candidate nodes are updated (line 12–19) according to Observation 1. Note that the value of $d(v,w)$ which is used in the updating process does not have to be computed, as it is already known because it was calculated for all w during the computation of the eccentricity of v. If the lower and upper eccentricity bounds for a node have become equal, then the eccentricity of that node has been derived and it is removed from W (lines 15–18). Algorithm 2 returns a vector containing the exact eccentricity value of each node. Counting the number of occurrences of each eccentricity value results in the eccentricity distribution.

An overview of possible selection strategies for the function SELECTFROM can be found in [6]. In line with results presented in that work, we found that when determining the eccentricity distribution, interchanging the selection of a node with a small lower bound and a node with a large upper bound, breaking ties by taking a node with the highest degree, yielded by far the best results. As described in [6], examples of graphs in which this algorithm would definitely not work are complete graphs and circle-shaped graphs. However, most real-world graphs adhere to the small world property [17], and in these graphs the eccentricity distribution is sufficiently diverse so that the eccentricity lower and upper bounds can effectively be utilized.

Algorithm 2 BOUNDINGECCENTRICITIES

Input: Graph $G(V, E)$
Output: Vector ε, containing $\varepsilon(v)$ for all $v \in V$

$W \leftarrow V$
for $w \in W$ **do**
    $\varepsilon[w] \leftarrow 0 \quad \varepsilon_L[w] \leftarrow -\infty \quad \varepsilon_U[w] \leftarrow +\infty$
end for

while $W \neq \emptyset$ **do**
    $v \leftarrow$ SELECTFROM(W)
    $\varepsilon[v] \leftarrow$ ECCENTRICITY(v)
    for $w \in W$ **do**
        $\varepsilon_L[w] \leftarrow \max(\varepsilon_L[w], \max(\varepsilon[v] - d(v,w), d(v,w)))$
        $\varepsilon_U[w] \leftarrow \min(\varepsilon_U[w], \varepsilon[v] + d(v,w))$
        if $(\varepsilon_L[w] = \varepsilon_U[w])$ **then**
            $\varepsilon[w] \leftarrow \varepsilon_L[w]$
            $W \leftarrow W - \{w\}$
        end if
    end for
end while

return ε

Figure 3. Eccentricity bounds of the toy graph in Figure 2 after subsequently computing the eccentricity of node G (left) and node E (right).

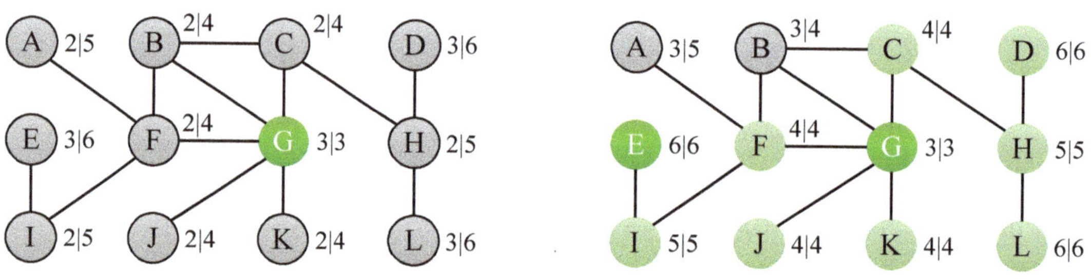

As an example of the usefulness of the bounds suggested in this section, consider the problem of determining the eccentricities of the nodes of the toy graph from Figure 2. If we compute the eccentricity of node G, which is 3, then we can derive bounds $2|4$ for the nodes at distance 1 (B, C, F, J and K), $2|5$ for the nodes at distance 2 (A, H and I) and $3|6$ for the nodes at distance 3 (D, E and L), as depicted by the left graph in Figure 3. If we then compute the eccentricity of node E, which is 6, we derive bounds $5|7$ for node I, $4|8$ for node F, $3|9$ for nodes A, B and G, $4|10$ for nodes C, J and K, $5|11$ for node K, and $6|12$ for nodes D and L. If we combine these bounds for each of the nodes, then we find that lower and upper bounds for a large number of nodes have become equal: $4|4$ for C, F, J and K, $5|5$ for H and

I, and 6|6 for D and L, as shown by the right graph in Figure 3. Finally, computing the eccentricity of nodes A and B results in a total of 4 real eccentricity calculations to compute the complete eccentricity distribution, which is a speedup of 3 compared to the naive algorithm, which would simply compute the eccentricity for all 12 nodes in the graph.

To give a first idea of the performance of the algorithm on large graphs, Figure 4 shows the number of iterations (vertical axis) that are needed to compute the eccentricity of all nodes with given eccentricity value (horizontal axis) for a number of large graphs (for a description of the datasets, see Section 6.1). We can clearly see that especially for the extreme values of the eccentricity distribution, very few iterations are needed to compute all of these eccentricity values, whereas many more iterations are needed to derive the values in between the extreme values.

Figure 4. Eccentricity values (horizontal axis) *vs.* number of iterations to compute the eccentricity of all nodes with this eccentricity value (vertical axis).

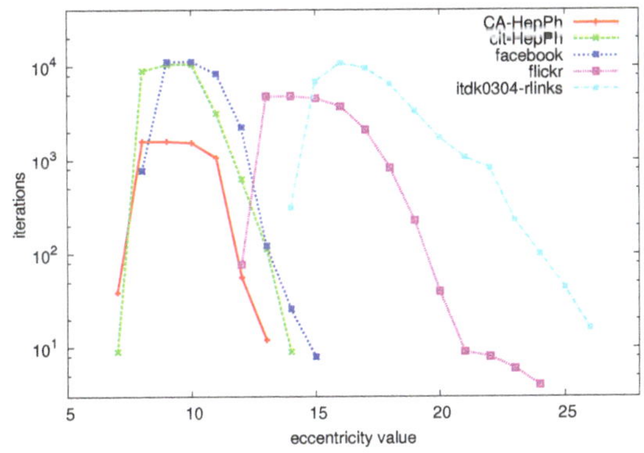

4.2. Pruning

In this subsection we introduce a pruning strategy, which is based on the following observation:

Observation 2 *Assume that* $n > 2$. *For a given* $v \in V$, *all nodes* $w \in N(v)$ *with* $deg(w) = 1$ *have* $\varepsilon(w) = \varepsilon(v) + 1$.

Node w is only connected to node v, and will thus need node v to reach every other node in the graph. If node v can do this in $\varepsilon(v)$ steps, then node w can do this is in exactly $\varepsilon(v) + 1$ steps. The restriction $n > 2$ on the graph size excludes the case in which the graph consists of v and w only.

All interesting real-world graphs have more than two nodes, making Observation 2 applicable in our algorithm, as suggested in [6]. For every node $v \in V$ we can determine if v has neighbors w with $deg(w) = 1$. If so, we can prune all but one of these neighbors, as their eccentricity will be equal, because they all employ v to get to any other node. In Figure 2, node G has two neighbors with degree one, namely J and K. According to Observation 2, the eccentricity values of these two nodes are equal to $\varepsilon(\text{J}) = \varepsilon(\text{K}) = \varepsilon(\text{G}) + 1 = 4$. The same argument holds for nodes D and L with respect to node H. We expect that Observation 2 can be applied quite often, as many of the graphs that are nowadays studied have a power law degree distribution [18], meaning that there are many nodes with a very low degree (such as a degree of 1).

Observation 2 can be beneficial to our algorithm in two ways. First, when computing the eccentricity of a single node, the pruned nodes can be ignored in the shortest path algorithm. Second, when the eccentricity of a node v has been computed (line 11 of Algorithm 2), and this node has adjacent nodes w with $deg(w) = 1$, then the eccentricity of these nodes w can be set to $\varepsilon(w) = \varepsilon(v) + 1$.

5. Sampling

Sampling is a technique in which a subset of the original dataset is evaluated in order to estimate (the distribution of) characteristics of the (elements in the) complete dataset, with faster computation as one of the main advantages. In this section we first discuss the use of sampling to determine the eccentricity distribution in Section 5.1. We focus on situations where we not only want to estimate the distribution of the eccentricity values, but also want to assess some parts of it (the extreme values) with higher reliability. For that purpose we propose a hybrid technique to determine the eccentricity distribution by that combines the exact approach from Section 4 with non-random sampling in Section 5.2. Finally in Section 5.3 we consider an adaptation of an existing approximation approach from literature.

5.1. Random Node Selection

If we want to apply sampling to the naive algorithm for obtaining the eccentricity distribution, we could choose to evaluate only a subset of size n' of the original n nodes, and multiply the values of the sampled eccentricity distribution by a factor n/n' to get an idea of the real eccentricity distribution, a process referred to as *random node selection*. Indeed, taking only a subset of the nodes would clearly speed up the computation of the eccentricity distribution and realize the second type of speedup discussed in Section 4. The trade-off here is that we no longer obtain the exact eccentricity distribution, but only get an approximation. The main question is then whether or not this approximation is representative of the original distribution. The effectiveness of sampling by random node selection with respect to various graph properties has been demonstrated in [19]. Using similar arguments as presented in [20,21], the absolute error can be assessed; indeed, when the chosen sampling subset is sufficiently large, the error is effectively bounded.

However, there are situations where we are not interested in minimizing the absolute error, but in minimizing the relative standard deviation (*i.e.*, the absolute standard deviation divided by the mean) of the distribution of a particular eccentricity value. This especially makes sense when each eccentricity value is of equal importance, which might be the case when the extreme values of the distribution that are realizing the radius and diameter are of relevance. Let us consider an example. The real exact eccentricity distribution over all nodes in the ENRON dataset [22] is as follows:

$\varepsilon(v)$	7	8	9	10	11	12	13
$f(\varepsilon(v))$	24	12210	17051	3647	485	44	11

Figure 5 shows the relative standard deviation for each eccentricity value for different sample sizes (1%, 2%, 5%, 10%, and 20%). For each sample size, we took 100 random samples to average the result. We note that low relative standard deviations can be observed for the more common eccentricity values (in this case, 8, 9 and 10). However, the standard deviation is quite large for the extreme values, meaning that on many occasions, the sample did not correctly reflect the frequency of that particular eccentricity value. Indeed, if only 11 out of 33,696 nodes (0.03%) have a particular eccentricity value (in this case, a value of 13), we need a sample size of at least $100\%/11 = 9\%$ if we want to expect just one node with that particular eccentricity value. Even with a large sample size of 20%, the standard deviation for the extreme value of 13 is very high (0.63). For sample sizes of 1% or 2%, the eccentricity value of 13, that exists in the real distribution, was never even found. Similar events were observed for our other datasets, which is not surprising: the eccentricity distributions are tailed on the extremes, and these tails are likely to be left out in a sample. So clearly sampling does not suffice when extreme values of the eccentricity distribution have to be found, because such extreme values are simply too rare. However, for the more common eccentricity values, errors are very low, even for small sample sizes.

Figure 5. Relative standard deviation (vertical axis) *vs.* eccentricity value (horizontal axis) for different random sample sizes of the ENRON dataset.

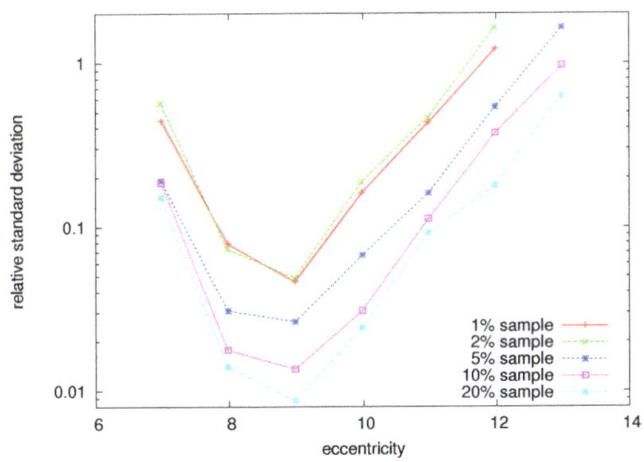

5.2. Hybrid Algorithm

From Figures 4,5 we can conclude that the exact approach is able to quickly derive the more extreme values of the eccentricity distribution, whereas a sampling technique is able to approximate the values in between the extremes with a very low error. Therefore we propose to combine the two approaches in order to quickly converge to an accurate estimation of the eccentricity distribution using a *hybrid* approach. This technique assumes that the eccentricity distribution has a somewhat unimodal shape, which is the case for all real-world graphs that we have investigated.

The *sampling window* consists of bounding variables ℓ and r that denote between which eccentricity values the algorithm is going to use the sampling technique. This window obviously depends on the distribution itself, which is not known until the exact algorithm has finished. Therefore we propose to set the value of ℓ and r dynamically, *i.e.*, $\ell = \min_{v \in V} \varepsilon_L[v]$ and $r = \max_{v \in V} \varepsilon_U[v]$. We furthermore change the stopping criterion in line 9 of Algorithm 2 to "**while** $|\{w \in W \mid \varepsilon_L[w] = \ell \text{ or } \varepsilon_U[w] = r\}| > 0$ **do**".

This means that the algorithm should stop when there are no more candidates that are potentially part of the center or the periphery of the graph. Note that these bounds apply to the candidate set W, but use information about all nodes V, ensuring that at least the center and periphery are known before the exact phase is terminated. When the exact algorithm has done its job, it can tighten ℓ and r even further, based on the eccentricity of the remaining candidate nodes: $\ell = \min_{v \in W} \varepsilon_L[v] - 1$ and $r = \max_{v \in W} \varepsilon_U[v] + 1$. After this, ℓ and r become static, and the rest of the eccentricity distribution will be derived by using the sampling approach outlined in Algorithm 3. We will refer to the adjusted version of Algorithm 2 as BOUNDINGECCENTRICITIESLR.

Algorithm 3 HYBRIDECCENTRICITIES

1: **Input:** Graph $G(V, E)$ and sampling rate q
2: **Output:** Vector f, containing the eccentricity distribution of G, initialized to 0

3: $\varepsilon' \leftarrow$ BOUNDINGECCENTRICITIESLR(G, ℓ, r)
4: $Z \leftarrow \emptyset$

5: **for** $v \in V$ **do**
6:     **if** $\varepsilon'[v] \neq 0$ **and** $(\varepsilon'[v] \leq \ell$ **or** $\varepsilon'[v] \geq r)$ **then**
7:         $f[\varepsilon'[v]] \leftarrow f[\varepsilon'[v]] + 1$
8:     **else**
9:         $Z \leftarrow Z \cup \{v\}$
10:     **end if**
11: **end for**

12: **for** $i \leftarrow 1$ **to** $n \cdot q$ **do**
13:     $v \leftarrow$ RANDOMFROM(Z)
14:     $\varepsilon[v] \leftarrow$ ECCENTRICITY(v)
15:     $f[\varepsilon[v]] \leftarrow f[\varepsilon[v]] + (1/q)$
16:     $Z \leftarrow Z - \{v\}$
17: **end for**

18: **return** f

Compared to Algorithm 2, the difference in terms of input is that the hybrid algorithm given in Algorithm 3 takes as input both the original graph and a sampling rate q between 0 and 1, where $q = 0.10$ means that 10% of the nodes have to be sampled. In Section 6 we will perform experiments to determine how q should be set. The result vector f holds the eccentricity distribution and is initialized based on the exact eccentricity values ε' for values outside the sampling window (line 7). Nodes for which the exact eccentricity is not yet known are added to the candidate set Z (line 9). In lines 12–17, the eccentricity of a total of $n \cdot q$ random nodes are calculated, and if this value lies within the specified window, the frequency of this eccentricity value is increased proportionally to the sample size. Finally, the eccentricity distribution f is returned.

5.3. Neighborhood Approximation

State of the art algorithms for computing the neighborhood function have been introduced in [12,14,23]. These algorithms can be adjusted as follows to also approximate the eccentricities. For an integer $h > 0$, the normalized size of the neighborhood $N_h(u)$ of a node u can be defined as:

$$N_h(u) = \frac{1}{n-1} \mid \{v \in V \mid 0 < d(u,v) \leq h\} \mid$$

If we determine the value of $N_h(u)$ for increasing values of h, then the eccentricity $\varepsilon(u)$ is the smallest h such that the approximated value of $N_h(u)$ is sufficiently close to 1 or does not change in successive iterations.

We have used the Approximate Neighborhood Function (ANF) [14] algorithm by Palmer *et al.* in order to approximate $N_h(u)$ (by using the C source code available at the author's website). Figure 6 shows the actual relative eccentricity distribution of the ENRON dataset, as well as the distribution that was approximated using the ANF-based approach. As ANF gives an approximate result, we averaged the result of 100 runs. We note that although the distribution shapes are very similar, ANF clearly underestimates the eccentricity values. We furthermore mention that the obtained distribution is clearly an approximation: a real eccentricity distribution would never have eccentricity values for which the smallest and largest value differ more than a factor of 2. Similar results were observed for other datasets, which leads us to believe that these approximation algorithms are not suitable for determining the eccentricity distribution, especially because they fail at assessing the extreme values of the distribution.

Figure 6. Exact and approximated relative eccentricity distribution of the ENRON dataset.

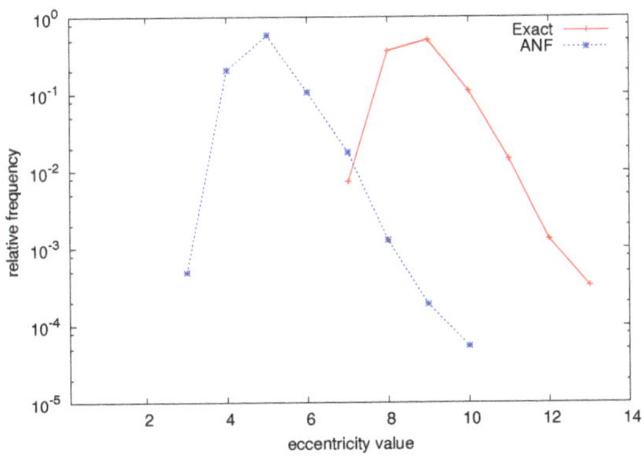

6. Experiments

In this section we will use a number of large real-world datasets to assess the performance of both the exact algorithm from Section 4 and the hybrid algorithm from Section 5. The performance of our algorithms is measured by comparing the number of iterations and thus is independent of the hardware and software that were used for the implementation.

6.1. Datasets

We use a variety of network datasets, of which the name, type and source are listed in the first three columns of Table 1. The set of graphs covers a broad range of network types, including citation networks, collaboration networks, communication networks, peer-to-peer networks, protein-protein interaction networks, router topology networks, social networks and webgraphs. We will only consider the largest connected component of each graph, which is always the vast majority of the original graph. We also mention that some directed graphs have been interpreted as if they were undirected, and that self-edges and parallel edges are ignored. These factors may cause minor differences between the number of nodes and edges that we present here, and the numbers presented in the source papers. In Table 1 we also present for each dataset the exact average eccentricity $\overline{\varepsilon}(G)$, radius $\Gamma(G)$, diameter $\Delta(G)$ and center and periphery sizes $|C(G)|$ and $|D(G)|$. For a more detailed description of these graphs, we refer the reader to the source papers in which the datasets were introduced.

Looking at the exact eccentricity distributions that we were able to compute, we can conclude that the distribution is not perfectly Gaussian as [32] suggests, but does appear to be unimodal. The distribution appears to be somewhat "tailed"; a positive skew is noticeable in Figure 1, which shows the relative eccentricity distribution of a number of graphs. The tail also becomes clear when comparing the average eccentricity value $\overline{\varepsilon}(G)$ with the radius and diameter of the graph: for every dataset, the average eccentricity is closer to the radius. For example, for the CIT-HEPTH dataset with radius 8 and diameter 15, the average eccentricity is equal to 10.14.

Table 1. Number of nodes, edges, average eccentricity, radius, diameter, center size and periphery size of our datasets.

Dataset	Type	Source	Nodes	Edges	$\overline{\varepsilon}(G)$	$\Gamma(G)$	$\Delta(G)$	$\lvert C(G)\rvert$	$\lvert D(G)\rvert$
YEAST	protein	[24]	1 846	4 406	13.28	11	19	48	4
CA-HEPTH	collab.	[25]	8 638	49 612	12.53	10	18	74	4
CA-HEPPH	collab.	[25]	11 204	235 238	9.40	7	13	12	17
DIP20090126	protein	[26]	19 928	82 406	22.01	15	30	1	2
CA-CONDMAT	collab.	[13]	21 363	182 572	10.58	8	15	6	11
CIT-HEPTH	citation	[13]	27 400	704 042	10.14	8	15	4	4
ENRON	commun.	[22]	33 696	361 622	8.77	7	13	248	11
CIT-HEPPH	citation	[13]	34 401	841 568	9.18	7	14	1	2
SLASHDOT	commun.	[27]	51 083	243 780	11.66	9	17	7	3
P2P-GNUTELLA	peer-to-peer	[25]	62 561	295 756	8.94	7	11	55	118
FACEBOOK	social	[28]	63 392	1 633 772	9.96	8	15	168	7
EPINIONS	social	[29]	75 877	811 478	9.74	8	15	614	6
SOC-SLASHDOT	social	[30]	82 168	1 008 460	8.91	7	13	484	3
ITDK0304-RLINKS	router	[26]	190 914	1 215 220	17.09	14	26	155	7
WEB-STANFORD	webgraph	[30]	255 265	3 883 852	106.49	82	164	1	3
WEB-NOTREDAME	webgraph	[31]	325 729	2 180 216	27.76	23	46	12	172
DBLP20080824	collab.	[26]	511 163	3 742 140	14.79	12	22	72	9
EU-2005	webgraph	[26]	862 664	37 467 426	14.03	11	21	3	4
FLICKR	social	[28]	1 624 992	30 953 670	15.03	12	24	17	3
AS-SKITTER	router	[13]	1 694 616	22 188 418	21.22	16	31	5	2

6.2. Exact Algorithm

In order to determine the performance of the exact algorithm (Algorithm 2), we can count the number of shortest path computations that are needed to obtain the full distribution, and compare this value to n, the number of iterations performed by the naive algorithm (Algorithm 1). The number of iterations performed by our exact algorithm is displayed in the fourth column of Table 2, followed by the speedup factor compared to the naive algorithm. We note that significant speedups can be observed in terms of the number of iterations, especially for datasets for which the eccentricity distribution is wide, *i.e.*, the difference between the radius and diameter is very large. We believe that this is due to the fact that the nodes that form the periphery of the network are sufficiently eccentric to have a large influence on the more central nodes, so that their lower and upper eccentricity bounds can very quickly be fixed by the bounding technique. We mention that the performance of our exact algorithm does not appear to be directly related to the number of nodes. The reduction in terms of the number of nodes as a result of our pruning strategy (see Section 4.2) is displayed in the column labeled "Pruned", and is diverse, yet sometimes very significant (anywhere between 1% and 34%).

To get a better idea of the performance of the algorithm, we propose to look at the quality of both the lower and upper bounds as the exact algorithm iterates over the candidate nodes. For this we define the measure of *bound accuracy* as the percentage of bound values that are correct at that iteration:

$$\textit{bound accuracy} = \frac{1}{n} \; |\{v \in V \mid \varepsilon_{real}(v) = \varepsilon_{bound}(v)\}|$$

Here, $\varepsilon_{real}(v)$ is the actual eccentricity value, and $\varepsilon_{bound}(v)$ is the (lower or upper) bound that we investigate. Figure 7 shows the lower and upper bound accuracy for a number of datasets. We can observe that for each of the datasets, after just a few iterations, the lower bound gives a very accurate indication of the actual eccentricity values. Apparently, the majority of the iterations are spent lowering the upper bound, whereas the lower bound quickly reflects the actual eccentricity distribution. Thus, in order to get an online estimate of the distribution, we could choose to consider only the lower bound, and obtain an accuracy of around 90% after only a handful of iterations.

Figure 7. Bound accuracy *vs*. number of iterations for Algorithm 2.

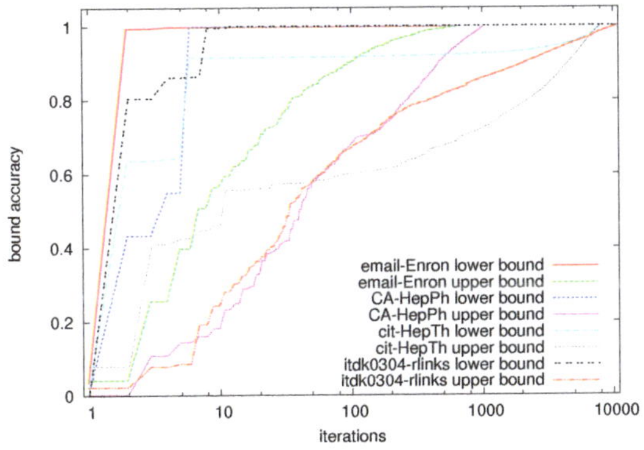

Table 2. Performance (number of pruned nodes, number of iterations and speedup) of the exact algorithm (Algorithm 2) and the hybrid algorithm (Algorithm 3).

Dataset	Nodes	Exact algorithm			Hybrid algorithm			
		Pruned	Iterations	Speedup	Exact	Sampling	Total	Speedup
YEAST	1 846	399	213	**8.7**	104	483	587	3.1
CA-HEPTH	8 638	351	1 055	8.2	150	350	500	**17.3**
CA-HEPPH	11 204	282	1 588	7.1	57	264	321	**34.9**
DIP20090126	19 928	3 032	224	**89.0**	8	1321	1 329	15.0
CA-CONDMAT	21 363	353	3 339	6.4	73	388	461	**46.3**
CIT-HEPTH	27 400	140	8 104	3.4	57	444	501	**54.7**
ENRON	33 696	8 715	678	**49.7**	536	145	681	49.5
CIT-HEPPH	34 401	150	10 498	3.3	37	271	308	**112**
SLASHDOT	51 083	19,255	31	**1648**	24	180	204	250
P2P-GNUTELLA	62 561	16 413	21 109	3.0	8 575	177	8 752	**7.1**
FACEBOOK	63 392	1 075	11 185	5.7	780	168	948	**66.9**
EPINIONS	75 877	20 779	4302	17.6	1 308	75	1 383	**54.9**
SOC-SLASHDOT	82 168	14 848	1460	56.3	990	156	1 146	**71.7**
ITDK0304-RLINKS	190 914	16 434	10 830	17.6	312	960	1 272	**150**
WEB-STANFORD	255 265	10 350	9	**28 363**	8	1 198	1 206	212
WEB-NOTREDAME	325 729	141,178	143	2277	94	1 381	1 475	**4528**
DBLP20080824	511 163	22 579	42 273	12.1	150	355	505	**1012**
EU-2005	862 664	26 507	59 751	14.4	71	1 630	1 701	**507**
FLICKR	1 624 992	553 242	4 810	338	200	1 618	1 818	**932**
AS-SKITTER	1 694 616	114 803	42 996	39.4	14	308	322	**5502**

6.3. Hybrid Algorithm

In our second set of experiments, we have evaluated the performance of the hybrid approach that incorporates sampling for the non-extreme values of the distribution (Algorithm 3). We will verify the quality of the obtained distribution by using the measure of *distribution accuracy*, defined as one minus the sum of the absolute difference between the eccentricity counts of real relative eccentricity distribution $F(x)$ and the estimated distribution $\hat{F}(x)$:

$$\textit{distribution accuracy} = 1 - \sum_{x=\Gamma(G)}^{\Delta(G)} |F(x) - \hat{F}(x)|$$

A distribution accuracy value of 1 indicates a perfect match between the actual and estimated relative eccentricity distributions. We note that for our hybrid approach, the error outside the sampling window is always equal to 0. As a result of the exact approach, we have access to the real eccentricity distribution. Therefore we can investigate the number of iterations that are needed to obtain an accuracy of 0.95 in order to determine how we should set the sampling rate q. The sixth column of Table 2 shows the number of iterations needed to (exactly) compute the extreme values (center and periphery), which together with the column titled "Sampling" (averaged over 10 runs) results in the value denoted in column "Total", which shows the total number of iterations needed to obtain an accuracy of 0.95. Apparently, for large graphs (over 100,000 nodes), a sampling rate of $q = 0.10$ is more than sufficient to accurately derive the eccentricity distribution. An alternative would be to change the number of samples to a constant number, which would ensure that the number of eccentricity calculations does not exceed some fixed maximum.

An advantage of the exact approach is obviously that the nodes that have a certain eccentricity value can be pointed out exactly, whereas this is only possible for the extreme values in case of the hybrid approach. The hybrid approach does however improve upon the exact algorithm in terms of computation time (number of iterations) in many cases, especially for the larger graphs (over 100,000 nodes) with relatively tight eccentricity distributions, as can be seen in the rightmost column of Table 2. A bold value indicates the largest of the two speedups when comparing the hybrid approach and the exact approach. The exact approach performs better than the hybrid approach in a few cases, which we believe is due to the fact that the sampling phase should not have a too large window when the number of nodes is very small, because then a large number of iterations would be needed to obtain a representative sample of the distribution. This is especially the case for WEB-STANFORD, which has a very long tail. For this dataset, the exact algorithm performs really well, whereas the hybrid approach needs quite a few more iterations. We mention that, analogously to the performance of the exact algorithm, the performance of our hybrid algorithm does not appear to be correlated with the number of nodes.

From the experiments in this section we can generally conclude that we have developed a flexible approach for determining the eccentricity distribution of a large graph with high accuracy, while guaranteeing an exact result on the extreme values of the distribution (center and periphery of the graph).

7. Conclusions

In this paper we have studied means of computing the eccentricity of all nodes in a graph, resulting in the (relative) eccentricity distribution of the graph. It turns out that the eccentricity distribution of real-world graphs has an unimodal shape and tends to have a positive tail. We have shown how large speedups compared to the traditional method can be achieved by considering lower and upper bounds on the eccentricity, and by applying a pruning strategy. Even when the exact algorithm does not immediately give a satisfying result, the lower bounds proposed in this paper can serve as a reliable online estimate of the distribution as a whole.

We have also investigated the use of sampling as a means of computing the eccentricity distribution. The resulting hybrid algorithm uses the exact approach to derive the extreme values of the distribution and a sampling technique within a specific sampling window to accurately assess the values in between the extreme values. This results in an overall approach that is able to accurately determine the eccentricity distribution with only a fraction of the number of computations required by the naive approach.

In future work we would like to investigate the extent to which eccentricity and other centrality measures are related, and when the eccentricity can be used as a meaningful centrality measure. We are also interested in how the eccentricity distribution of a graph changes over time as the graph is evolving through the addition and deletion of nodes and edges.

Acknowledgments

We kindly thank the anonymous reviewers for providing useful and constructive comments on our paper. This research is part of the COMPASS project, financed by NWO under grant number 612.065.926.

References

1. Sala, A.; Cao, L.; Wilson, C.; Zablit, R.; Zheng, H.; Zhao, B. Measurement-Calibrated Graph Models for Social Network Experiments. In *Proceedings of the 19th ACM International Conference on the World Wide Web (WWW)*, Raleigh, NC, USA, 26–30 April 2010; pp. 861–870.
2. Magoni, D.; Pansiot, J. Analysis of the autonomous system network topology. *ACM SIGCOMM Comput. Commun. Rev.* **2001**, *31*, 26–37.
3. Magoni, D.; Pansiot, J. Analysis and Comparison of Internet Topology Generators. In *Proceedings of the 2nd International Conference on Networking Technologies, Services, and Protocols; Performance of Computer and Communication Networks; and Mobile and Wireless Communications*, Pisa, Italy, 19–24 May 2002; pp. 364–375.
4. Pavlopoulos, G.; Secrier, M.; Moschopoulos, C.; Soldatos, T.; Kossida, S.; Aerts, J.; Schneider, R.; Bagos, P. Using graph theory to analyze biological networks. *BioData Min.* **2011**, *4*, article 10.
5. Magnien, C.; Latapy, M.; Habib, M. Fast computation of empirically tight bounds for the diameter of massive graphs. *J. Exp. Algorithm.* **2009**, *13*, article 10.
6. Takes, F.W.; Kosters, W.A. Determining the Diameter of Small World Networks. In *Proceedings of the 20th ACM International Conference on Information and Knowledge Management (CIKM)*, Glasgow, UK, 24–28 October 2011; pp. 1191–1196.
7. Crescenzi, P.; Grossi, R.; Habib, M.; Lanzi, L.; Marino, A. On computing the diameter of real-world undirected graphs. *Theor. Comput. Sci.* **2012**, in press.
8. Borgatti, S.P.; Everett, M.G. A graph-theoretic perspective on centrality. *Soc. Netw.* **2006**, *28*, 466–484.
9. Brandes, U. A faster algorithm for betweenness centrality. *J. Math. Sociol.* **2001**, *25*, 163–177.
10. Lesniak, L. Eccentric sequences in graphs. *Period. Math. Hung.* **1975**, *6*, 287–293.
11. Hage, P.; Harary, F. Eccentricity and centrality in networks. *Soc. Netw.* **1995**, *17*, 57–63.
12. Kang, U.; Tsourakakis, C.; Appel, A.; Faloutsos, C.; Leskovec, J. Hadi: Mining radii of large graphs. *ACM Trans. Knowl. Discov. Data (TKDD)* **2011**, *5*, article 8.
13. Leskovec, J.; Kleinberg, J.; Faloutsos, C. Graph evolution: Densification and shrinking diameters. *ACM Trans. Knowl. Discov. Data (TKDD)* **2007**, *1*, article 2.
14. Palmer, C.; Gibbons, P.; Faloutsos, C. ANF: A Fast and Scalable Tool for Data Mining in Massive Graphs. In *Proceedings of the 8th ACM International Conference on Knowledge Discovery and Data Mining (KDD)*, Edmonton, Canada, 23–26 July 2002; pp. 81–90.
15. Buckley, F.; Harary, F. *Distance in Graphs*; Addison-Wesley: Boston, MA, USA, 1990.
16. Yuster, R.; Zwick, U. Answering Distance Queries in Directed Graphs Using Fast Matrix Multiplication. In *Proceedings of the 46th IEEE Symposium on Foundations of Computer Science (FOCS)*, Pittsburgh, PA, USA, 23–25 October 2005; pp. 389–396.

17. Kleinberg, J. The Small-World Phenomenon: An Algorithm Perspective. In *Proceedings of the 32nd ACM symposium on Theory of Computing*, Portland, OR, USA, 21–23 May 2000; pp. 163–170.
18. Faloutsos, M.; Faloutsos, P.; Faloutsos, C. On power-law relationships of the internet topology. *ACM SIGCOMM Comput. Commun. Rev.* **1999**, *29*, 251–262.
19. Leskovec, J.; Faloutsos, C. Sampling from Large Graphs. In *Proceedings of the 12th ACM International Conference on Knowledge Discovery and Data Mining (KDD)*, Philadelphia, PA, USA, 20–23 August 2006; pp. 631–636.
20. Eppstein, D.; Wang, J. Fast Approximation of Centrality. In *Proceedings of the 12th ACM-SIAM Symposium on Discrete Algorithms (SODA)*, Washington, DC, USA, 7–9 January 2001; pp. 228–229.
21. Crescenzi, P.; Grossi, R.; Lanzi, L.; Marino, A. A Comparison of Three Algorithms for Approximating the Distance Distribution in Real-World Graphs. In *Proceedings of the Theory and Practice of Algorithms in (Computer) Systems (TAPAS), LNCS 6595*, Rome, Italy, 18–20 April 2011; pp. 92–103.
22. Klimt, B.; Yang, Y. The Enron Corpus: A New Dataset for Email Classification Research. In *Proceedings of the 15th European Conference on Machine Learning (ECML), LNCS 3201*, Pisa, Italy, 20–24 September 2004; pp. 217–226.
23. Boldi, P.; Rosa, M.; Vigna, S. HyperANF: Approximating the Neighbourhood Function of very Large Graphs on a Budget. In *Proceedings of the 20th ACM International Conference on the World Wide Web (WWW)*, Hyderabad, India, 16–20 April 2011; pp. 625–634.
24. Jeong, H.; Mason, S.; Barabási, A.; Oltvai, Z. Lethality and centrality in protein networks. *Nature* **2001**, *411*, 41–42.
25. Leskovec, J.; Kleinberg, J.; Faloutsos, C. Graph evolution: Densification and shrinking diameters. *ACM Trans. Knowl. Discov. Data* **2007**, *1*, article 2.
26. Sommer, C. *Graphs*; Available online: http://www.sommer.jp/graphs (accessed on 1 September 2012).
27. Gómez, V.; Kaltenbrunner, A.; López, V. Statistical Analysis of the Social Network and Discussion Threads in Slashdot. In *Proceedings of the 17th International Conference on the World Wide Web (WWW)*, Beijng, China, 21–25 April 2008; pp. 645–654.
28. Mislove, A.; Marcon, M.; Gummadi, K.; Druschel, P.; Bhattacharjee, B. Measurement and Analysis of Online Social Networks. In *Proceedings of the 7th ACM Conference on Internet Measurement*, San Diego, CA, USA, 24–26 October 2007; pp. 29–42.
29. Richardson, M.; Agrawal, R.; Domingos, P. Trust Management for the Semantic Web. In *Proceedings of the 2nd International Semantic Web Conference (ISWC), LNCS 2870*, Sanibel Island, FL, USA, 20–23 October 2003; pp. 351–368.
30. Leskovec, J.; Lang, K.; Dasgupta, A.; Mahoney, M. Community structure in large networks: Natural cluster sizes and the absence of large well-defined clusters. *Int. Math.* **2009**, *6*, 29–123.
31. Barabási, A.; Albert, R.; Jeong, H. Scale-free characteristics of random networks: The topology of the world-wide web. *Phys. Stat. Mech. Appl.* **2000**, *281*, 69–77.

32. Magoni, D.; Pansiot, J. Internet Topology Modeler Based on Map Sampling. In *Proceedings of the 7th International Symposium on Computers and Communications (ISCC)*, Taormina, Italy, 1–4 July 2002; pp. 1021–1027.

Algorithms **2013**, *6*, 119-135; doi:10.3390/a6010119

OPEN ACCESS

algorithms

ISSN 1999-4893

www.mdpi.com/journal/algorithms

Article

A Polynomial-Time Algorithm for Computing the Maximum Common Connected Edge Subgraph of Outerplanar Graphs of Bounded Degree

Tatsuya Akutsu * and Takeyuki Tamura

Bioinformatics Center, Institute for Chemical Research, Kyoto University, Gokasho, Uji, Kyoto 611-0011, Japan; E-Mail: tamura@kuicr.kyoto-u.ac.jp

* Author to whom correspondence should be addressed; E-Mail: takutsu@kuicr.kyoto-u.ac.jp; Tel.: +81-774-38-3015; Fax: +81-774-38-3022.

Received: 30 October 2012; in revised form: 27 January 2013 / Accepted: 7 February 2013 / Published: 18 February 2013

Abstract: The maximum common connected edge subgraph problem is to find a connected graph with the maximum number of edges that is isomorphic to a subgraph of each of the two input graphs, where it has applications in pattern recognition and chemistry. This paper presents a dynamic programming algorithm for the problem when the two input graphs are outerplanar graphs of a bounded vertex degree, where it is known that the problem is NP-hard, even for outerplanar graphs of an unbounded degree. Although the algorithm repeatedly modifies input graphs, it is shown that the number of relevant subproblems is polynomially bounded, and thus, the algorithm works in polynomial time.

Keywords: maximum common subgraph; outerplanar graph; dynamic programming

1. Introduction

Finding common parts of graph-structured data is an important and fundamental task in computer science. Among many such problems, the *maximum common subgraph problem* has applications in various areas, which include pattern recognition [1,2] and chemistry [3,4]. Although there are several variants, the maximum common subgraph problem (MCS) usually means the problem of finding a connected graph with the maximum number of edges that is isomorphic to a subgraph of each of the two input undirected graphs (*i.e.*, the maximum common connected edge subgraph problem).

Because of its importance in pattern recognition and chemistry, many practical algorithms have been developed for MCS and its variants [1–4]. Some exponential-time algorithms that are better than naive ones have also been developed [5,6]. Kann studied the approximability of MCS and related problems [7].

It is also important for MCS to study a polynomially solvable subclasses of graphs, because graph structures are restricted in many application areas. It is well-known that if input graphs are trees, MCS can be solved in polynomial time using maximum weight bipartite matching [8]. Akutsu showed that MCS can be solved in polynomial time if input graphs are almost trees of bounded degree, whereas MCS remains NP-hard for almost trees of unbounded degree [9], where a graph is called an almost tree if it is connected and the number of edges in each biconnected component is bounded by the number of vertices plus some constant. Yamaguchi *et al.* developed a polynomial-time algorithm for MCS and the maximum common induced connected subgraph problem for a degree bounded partial k-tree and a graph with a polynomially bounded number of spanning trees, where k is a constant [10]. However, the latter condition seems rather artificial. Schietgat *et al.* developed a polynomial-time algorithm for outerplanar graphs under the block-and-bridge preserving subgraph isomorphism [11]. However, they modified the definition of MCS by this restriction. Although it was announced that MCS can be solved in polynomial time if input graphs are partial k-trees and MCS must be k-connected (for example, see [12]), the restriction that subgraphs are k-connected is too strict from a practical viewpoint. As for the subgraph isomorphism problem, which is closely related to MCS, polynomial-time algorithms have been developed for biconnected outerplanar graphs [13,14] and for partial k-trees with some constraints, as well as their extensions [15,16].

In this paper, we present a polynomial-time algorithm for outerplanar graphs of a bounded degree (a preliminary version has appeared in [17]). Although this graph class is not a superset of the classes in previous studies [9,10], it covers a wide range of chemical compounds (it was reported that 94.4% of chemical compounds in the NCI database have outerplanar graph structures [18]). Furthermore, the algorithm and its analysis in this paper are not simple extensions or variants of those for the subgraph isomorphism problem for outerplanar graphs [13,14] or partial k-trees [15,16]. These algorithms heavily depend on the property that each connected component in a subgraph is not decomposed. However, to be discussed in Section 4, connected components from both input graphs can be decomposed in MCS, and considering all decompositions easily leads to exponential-time algorithms. In order to cope with this difficulty, we introduce the concept of a *blade*. The blade and its analysis play a key role in this paper.

It is to be noted that the number of MCS can be exponential even for trees [19]. Therefore, our proposed algorithm and all polynomial-time algorithms mentioned above are focusing on finding the one of MCS's. It should also be noted that the proposed algorithm is not practical, because the polynomial degree is very high, although it gives a non-trivial theoretical result on the computation of MCS.

2. Preliminaries

A graph is called *outerplanar* if it can be drawn on a plane such that all vertices lie on the outer face (*i.e.*, the unbounded exterior region) without crossing of edges. Although there exist many embeddings (*i.e.*, drawings on a plane) of an outerplanar graph, it is known that one embedding can be computed in linear time. Therefore, in this paper, we assume that each graph is given with its planar embedding. A path is called *simple* if it does not pass the same vertex multiple times. In this paper, a path always means a simple path that is not a cycle.

A *cut vertex* of a connected graph is a vertex whose removal disconnects the graph. A graph is *biconnected* if it is connected and does not have a cut vertex. A maximal biconnected subgraph is called a *biconnected component*. A biconnected component is called a *block* if it consists of at least three vertices; otherwise, it is an edge and called a *bridge*. An edge in a block is called an *outer* edge if it lies on the boundary of the outer face; otherwise, it is called an *inner* edge. It is well-known that any block of an outerplanar graph has a unique Hamiltonian cycle, which consists of outer edges only [20]. For the details of the terminology used in graphs and outerplanar graphs, refer to an appropriate textbook on graph theory (e.g., [21]).

If we fix an arbitrary vertex of a graph G as the root r, we can define the parent-child relationship on biconnected components. For two vertices, u and v, u is called *further* than v if every simple path from u to r contains v. A biconnected component, C, is called a *parent* of a biconnected component C' if C and C' share a vertex v, where v is uniquely determined, and every path from any vertex in C' to the root contains v. In such a case, C' is called a *child* of C. A cut vertex v is also called a *parent* of C if v is contained in both C and its parent component (both of a cut vertex and a biconnected component can be parents of the same component). Furthermore, the root, r, is a parent of C if r is contained in C.

For each cut vertex v, $G(v)$ denotes the subgraph of G induced by v and the vertices further than v. For a pair of a cut vertex v and a biconnected component, C, containing v, $G(v, C)$ denotes the subgraph of G induced by vertices in C and its descendant components. For a biconnected component, B, with its parent cut vertex, w, a pair of vertices, v and v', in B is called a *cut pair* if $v \neq v'$, $v \neq w$ and $v' \neq w$ hold. For a cut pair (v, v') in B, $VB(v, v')$ denotes the set of the vertices lying on the one of the two paths connecting v and v' in the Hamiltonian cycle that does not contain the parent cut vertex, except its endpoints. $B(v, v')$ is the subgraph of B induced by $VB(v, v')$ and is called a *half block*. It is to be noted that $B(v, v')$ contains both v and v'. Then, $G(v, v')$ denotes the subgraph of G induced by $VB(v, v')$ and the vertices in the biconnected components, each of which is a descendant of some vertex in $VB(v, v') - \{v, v'\}$, and $\overline{G}(v, v')$ denotes the subgraph of G induced by the vertices in $G(v, v')$ and descendant components of v and v', where descendants are defined via the parent-child relationship.

Example Figure 1 shows an example of an outerplanar graph $G(V, E)$. Blocks and bridges are shown by gray regions and bold lines, respectively. B_1, B_3 and e_2 are the children of the root r. B_4, B_6 and B_7 are the children of B_3, whereas B_4 and B_6 are the children of w. Both w and B_3 are the parents of B_4 and B_6. $G(w)$ consists of B_4, B_5 and B_6, whereas $G(w, B_4)$ consists of B_4 and B_5. (v, v') is a cut pair of B_7, and $B_7(v, v')$ is a region surrounded by a dashed bold curve. $\overline{G}(v, v')$ consists of $B_7(v, v')$, B_8, B_9, B_{10}, e_4, e_5 and e_6, whereas $G(v, v')$ consists of $B_7(v, v')$, B_{10}, e_4 and e_5.

If a connected graph, $G_c(V_c, E_c)$, is isomorphic to a subgraph of G_1 and a subgraph of G_2, we call G_c a *common subgraph* of G_1 and G_2. A common subgraph G_c is called a *maximum common connected edge subgraph* of G_1 and G_2 if its *size* is the maximum among all common subgraphs (we use MCS to denote both the problem and the maximum common subgraph), where the size means the number of edges. In what follows, for the sake of simplicity, a *maximum common subgraph* (MCS) always means a maximum common connected edge subgraph. In this paper, we consider the following problem.

Figure 1. Example of an outerplanar graph.

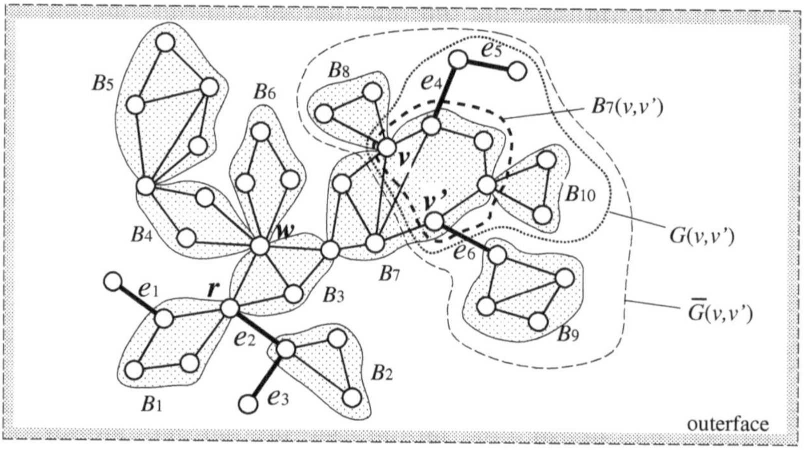

Maximum Common Subgraph of Outerplanar Graphs of Bounded Degree (OUTER-MCS)
Given two undirected connected outerplanar graphs, G_1 and G_2, whose maximum vertex degree is bounded by a constant, D, find a maximum common subgraph of G_1 and G_2.

Note that the degree bound is essential, because MCS is NP-hard for outerplanar graphs of unbounded degree, even if each biconnected component consists of at most three vertices [9]. Although we do not consider labels on vertices or edges, our results can be extended to vertex-labeled and/or edge-labeled cases in which label information must be preserved in isomorphic mapping. In the following, n denotes the maximum number of vertices of two input graphs (it should be noted that the number of vertices and the number of edges are in the same order, since we only consider connected outerplanar graphs).

In this paper, we implicitly make extensive use of the following well-known fact [13], along with outerplanarity of the input graphs.

Fact 1 *Let G_1 and G_2 be biconnected outerplanar graphs. Let $(u_1, u_2, \ldots, u_m)$ (resp. $(v_1, v_2, \ldots, v_n)$) be the vertices of G_1 (resp. G_2) arranged in clockwise order in a planar embedding of G_1 (resp. G_2). If there is an isomorphic mapping $\{(u_1, v_{i_1}), (u_2, v_{i_2}), \ldots, (u_m, v_{i_m})\}$ from G_1 to a subgraph of G_2, then $v_{i_1}, v_{i_2}, \ldots, v_{i_m}$ appear in G_2 in either clockwise or counterclockwise order.*

3. Algorithm for a Restricted Case

In this section, we consider the following restricted variant of OUTER-MCS, which is called SIMPLE-OUTER-MCS, and present a polynomial-time algorithm for it: (i) any two vertices in different biconnected components in a maximum common subgraph, G_c, must not be mapped to vertices in the same biconnected component in G_1 (resp. G_2); (ii) each bridge in G_c must be mapped to a bridge in G_1 (resp. G_2); (iii) the maximum degree need not be bounded.

It is to be noted from the definition of a common subgraph (regardless of the above restrictions) that no two vertices in different biconnected components in G_1 (resp. G_2) are mapped to vertices in the same biconnected component in any common subgraph, and no bridge in G_1 (resp. G_2) is mapped to an edge in a block in any common subgraph (otherwise there would exist a cycle containing the edge in a common subgraph, which would mean that the edge in G_1 (resp., G_2) is not a bridge).

SIMPLE-OUTER-MCS is intrinsically the same as the one studied by Schietgat *et al.* [11]. Although our algorithm is more complex and less efficient than their algorithm, we present it here, because the algorithm for a general (but bounded degree) case is rather involved and is based on our algorithm for SIMPLE-OUTER-MCS.

Here, we present a recursive algorithm to compute the size of MCS in SIMPLE-OUTER-MCS, which can be easily transformed into a dynamic programming algorithm to compute an MCS, as is true for many other dynamic programming algorithms. The following is the main procedure of the recursive algorithm.

Procedure $SimpleOuterMCS(G_1, G_2)$
$s_{\max} \leftarrow 0$;
for all pairs of vertices $(u, v) \in V_1 \times V_2$ **do**
Let (u, v) be the root pair (r_1, r_2) of (G_1, G_2);
$s_{\max} \leftarrow \max(s_{\max}, MCS_c(G_1(r_1), G_2(r_2)))$;
return $s_{\max}$.

The algorithm consists of a recursive computation of the following three scores:

$MCS_c(G_1(u), G_2(v))$: the size of an MCS G_c between $G_1(u)$ and $G_2(v)$, where (u, v) is a pair of the roots or a pair of cut vertices, and G_c must contain a vertex corresponding to both u and v.

$MCS_b(G_1(u, C), G_2(v, D))$: the size of an MCS G_c between $G_1(u, C)$ and $G_2(v, D)$, where (C, D) is either a pair of blocks or a pair of bridges, u (resp. v) is the cut vertex belonging to both C (resp. D) and its parent, G_c must contain a vertex corresponding to both u and v and G_c must contain a biconnected component (which can be empty) corresponding to a subgraph of C and a subgraph D.

$MCS_p(G_1(u, u'), G_2(v, v'))$: the size of an MCS G_c between $G_1(u, u')$ and $G_2(v, v')$, where (u, u') (resp. (v, v')) is a cut pair, and G_c must contain a cut pair (w, w') corresponding to both (u, u') and (v, v'). If there does not exist such G_c (which must be connected), its score is $-\infty$.

In the following, we describe how to compute these scores.

Computation of $MCS_c(G_1(u), G_2(v))$

As in the dynamic programming algorithm for MCS for trees or almost trees [9], we construct a bipartite graph and compute a maximum weight matching.

Let $C_1, \ldots, C_{h_1}, e_1, \ldots, e_{h_2}$ and $D_1, \ldots, D_{k_1}, f_1, \ldots, f_{k_2}$ be children of u and v respectively, where C_i's and D_j's are blocks and e_i's and f_j's are bridges (see Figure 2). We construct an edge-weighted bipartite graph $BG(X, Y; E)$ by

$$\begin{aligned} X &= \{C_1, \ldots, C_{h_1}, e_1, \ldots, e_{h2}\} \\ Y &= \{D_1, \ldots, D_{k_1}, f_1, \ldots, f_{k2}\} \\ E &= \{(x, y) \mid x \in X, y \in Y\} \\ w(C_i, f_j) &= 0 \end{aligned}$$

$$w(C_i, D_j) = MCS_b(G_1(u, C_i), G_2(v, D_j))$$
$$w(e_i, D_j) = 0$$
$$w(e_i, f_j) = MCS_b(G_1(u, e_i), G_2(v, f_j))$$

Then, we let $MCS_c(G_1(u), G_2(v))$ be the weight of the maximum weight bipartite matching of $BG(X, Y; E)$. It is to be noted that $w(C_i, f_j) = 0$ (resp., $w(e_i, D_j) = 0$) comes from the fact that f_j must be mapped to a bridge in G_c, but a bridge in G_c must not be mapped to an edge in any block (e.g., C_i), because of the condition (ii) of SIMPLE-OUTER-MCS.

Figure 2. Computation of $MCS_c(G_1(u), G_2(v))$.

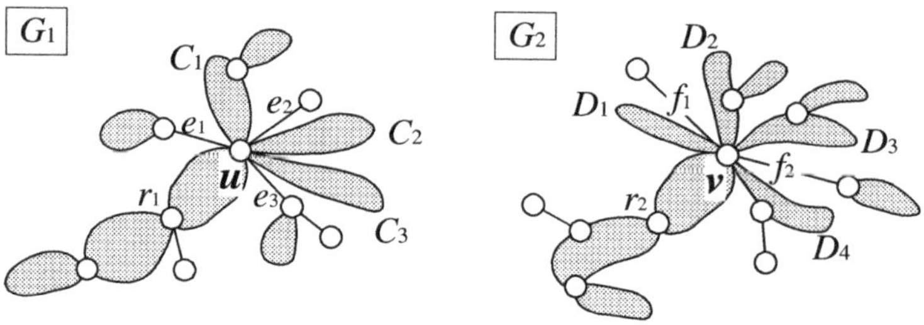

Computation of $MCS_b(G_1(u, C), G_2(v, D))$

Let $(u_1, u_2, \ldots, u_h)$ be the sequence of vertices in $G_1(u, C)$, such that there exists an edge, $\{u_i, u\}$, for each u_i, where $u_1, u_2, \ldots, u_h$ are arranged in clockwise order. $(v_1, v_2, \ldots, v_k)$ is defined for $G_2(v, D)$ in the same way. It is to be noted that (C, D) is either a pair of blocks or a pair of bridges. A pair of subsequences $((u_{i_1}, u_{i_2}, \ldots, u_{i_g}), (v_{j_1}, v_{j_2}, \ldots, v_{j_g}))$ is called an *alignment* if $i_1 < i_2 < \cdots < i_g$ and $j_1 < j_2 < \cdots < j_g$ or $j_g < j_{g-1} < \cdots < j_1$ hold (the latter ordering is required for handling mirror images.), where $g = 0$ is allowed. We compute $MCS_b(G_1(u, C), G_2(v, D))$ by the following (see Figure 3):

Procedure $SimpleOuterMCS_b(G_1(u, C), G_2(v, D))$
  $s_{\max} \leftarrow 0$;
  for all alignments $((u_{i_1}, u_{i_2}, \ldots, u_{i_g}), (v_{j_1}, v_{j_2}, \ldots, v_{j_g}))$ **do**;
    if C is a block and $g = 1$ **then continue**; /* blocks must be preserved */
    $s \leftarrow 0$;
    for $t = 1$ **to** g **do** $s \leftarrow s + 1 + MCS_c(G_1(u_{i_t}), G_2(v_{j_t}))$;
    for $t = 2$ **to** g **do** $s \leftarrow s + MCS_p(G_1(u_{i_{t-1}}, u_{i_t}), G_2(v_{j_{t-1}}, v_{j_t}))$;
    $s_{\max} \leftarrow \max(s, s_{\max})$;
  return $s_{\max}$.

In the above procedure, the first inner **for** loop takes care of blocks, such as C_1, C_4, D_1 and D_4 in Figure 3, whereas the second inner **for** loop takes care of half blocks, such as C_2, C_3, D_2, D_3 and D_5 in Figure 3.

For example, consider an alignment, $((u_1, u_2, u_3), (v_1, v_2, v_4))$, in Figure 3, where all alignments are to be examined in the algorithm. Then, the score of this alignment is given by

$3+MCS_b(G_1(u_1,C_1),G_2(v_1,D_1))+MCS_p(G_1(u_1,u_2),G_2(v_1,v_2))+MCS_p(G_1(u_2,u_3),G_2(v_2,v_4))$. $MCS_b(G_1(u_1,C_1),G_2(v_1,D_1))$ comes via the computation of $MCS_c(G_1(u_1),G_2(v_1))$, in which $BG(X,Y;E)$ is given by $X = \{C_1\}$, $Y = \{D_1\}$, $E = \{(C_1,D_1)\}$, and thus, the maximum weight matching is given by $w(C_1,D_1) = MCS_b(G_1(u_1,C_1),G_2(v_1,D_1))$. In this case, an edge, $\{v,v_3\}$, is removed and then v_3 is treated as a vertex on the path connecting v_2 and v_4 in the outer face. For another example, consider an alignment $((u_1),(v_1))$ in the same figure. Then, this alignment is ignored by the "**if** ... **then** ..." line of the procedure, because a bridge in G_c, which would correspond to $\{u,u_1\}$ in G_1 and $\{v,v_1\}$ in G_2, must not be mapped to an edge in C or D. However, if both $\{u,u_1\}$ and $\{v,v_1\}$ are bridges, the resulting score would be $1 + MCS_c(G_1(u_1),G_2(v_1))$.

Figure 3. Computation of $MCS_b(G_1(u,C),G_2(v,D))$.

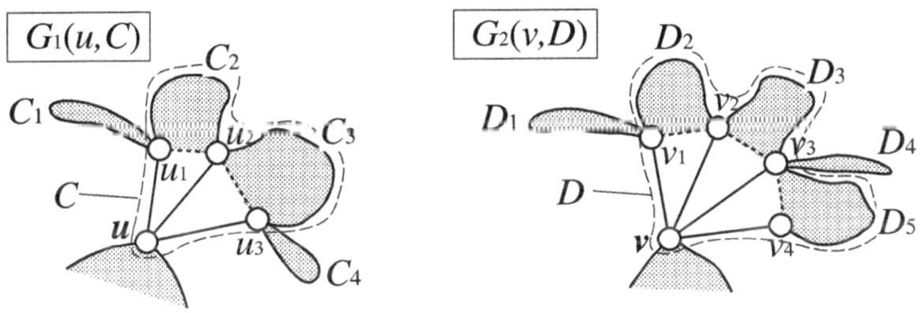

Since the above procedure examines all possible alignments, it may take exponential time. However, we can modify it into a dynamic programming procedure, as shown below, where we omit a subprocedure for handling mirror images, because it is trivial. In this procedure, $u_1,u_2,\ldots,u_h$ and $v_1,v_2,\ldots,v_k$ are processed from left to right. In the first **for** loop, $M[s,t]$ stores the size of MCS between $G_1(u_s)$ and $G_2(v_t)$ plus one (corresponding to a common edge between $\{u,u_s\}$ and $\{v,v_t\}$). The double **for** loop computes an optimal alignment. $M[s,t]$ stores the size of MCS between $G_1(u,C)$ and $G_2(v,D)$ up to u_s and v_t, respectively. $flag$ is introduced to ensure the connectedness of a common subgraph. For example, $flag = 0$ if $G_1(u)$ is a triangle, but $G_2(v)$ is a rectangle. If C (and also D) is an edge, $flag = 0$, but the procedure returns $M[1,1]$.

```
for all (s,t) ∈ {1,...,h} × {1,...,k} do
   M[s,t] ← 1 + MCS_c(G_1(u_s), G_2(v_t));
flag ← 0;
for s = 2 to h do
   for t = 2 to k do
      M[s,t] ← M[s,t] + max_{s'<s,t'<t}{M[s',t'] + MCS_p(G_1(u_{s'},u_s), G_2(u_{t'},u_t))};
      if M[s,t] > −∞ then flag ← 1;
if C is a block and flag = 0 then return 0 else return max_{s,t} M[s,t].
```

Computation of $MCS_p(G_1(u,u'),G_2(v,v'))$

Let $(u_1,u_2,\ldots,u_h)$ be the sequence of vertices in $G_1(u,u')$, such that there exists an edge $\{u_i,u\}$ or $\{u_i,u'\}$ for each u_i, where $u_1,u_2,\ldots,u_h$ are arranged in clockwise order. $(v_1,v_2,\ldots,v_k)$ is defined for $G_2(v,v')$ in the same way. For a pair, (u_i,v_j), $l(u_i,v_j) = 1$ if $\{u_i,u\} \in E_1$ and $\{v_j,v\} \in E_2$ hold, otherwise, $l(u_i, v_j) = 0$. Similarly, for a pair, (u_i, v_j), $r(u_i, v_j) = 1$ if $\{u_i, u'\} \in E_1$ and $\{v_j, v'\} \in E_2$ hold, otherwise, $r(u_i, v_j) = 0$. We compute $MCS_p(G_1(u, u'), G_2(v, v'))$ by the following procedure, where it does not examine alignments with $j_g < j_{g-1} < \cdots < j_1$:

Procedure $SimpleOuterMCS_p(G_1(u, u'), G_2(v, v'))$
  if $\{u, u'\} \in E_1$ and $\{v, v'\} \in E_2$ **then** $s_{\max} \leftarrow 1$ **else** $s_{\max} \leftarrow -\infty$;
  for all alignments $((u_{i_1}, u_{i_2}, \ldots, u_{i_g}), (v_{j_1}, v_{j_2}, \ldots, v_{j_g}))$ **do**
    if $l(u_{i_t}, v_{j_t}) = 0$ and $r(u_{i_t}, v_{j_t}) = 0$ hold for some t **then continue**;
    if $l(u_{i_1}, v_{j_1}) = 0$ or $r(u_{i_g}, v_{j_g}) = 0$ holds **then continue**;
    if $\{u, u'\} \in E_1$ and $\{v, v'\} \in E_2$ **then** $s \leftarrow 1$ **else** $s \leftarrow 0$;
    for $t = 1$ **to** g **do** $s \leftarrow s + l(u_{i_t}, v_{j_t}) + r(u_{i_t}, v_{j_t}) + MCS_c(G_1(u_{i_t}), G_2(v_{j_t}))$;
    for $t = 2$ **to** g **do** $s \leftarrow s + MCS_p(G_1(u_{i_{t-1}}, u_{i_t}), G_2(v_{j_{t-1}}, v_{j_t}))$;
    $s_{\max} \leftarrow \max(s, s_{\max})$;
  return $s_{\max}$.

This procedure returns $-\infty$ if there is no connected common subgraph between $G_1(u, u')$ and $G_2(v, v')$ that contains (w, w') corresponding to both (u, u') and (v, v'). It should be noted that the first line in the body of the main loop puts the constraint that all corresponding pairs, (u_{i_t}, v_{j_t}), in an alignment must be connected to either (u, v) or (u', v'), and the second line puts the constraint that (u_{i_1}, v_{j_1}) must be connected to (u, v) and (u_{i_g}, v_{j_g}) must be connected to (u', v').

As an example, consider an alignment, $((u_1, u_2, u_3, u_4), (v_1, v_2, v_3, v_5))$, in Figure 4. Then, the score is given by $4 + MCS_p(G_1(u_1, u_2), G_2(v_1, v_2)) + MCS_p(G_1(u_2, u_3), G_2(v_2, v_3)) + MCS_b(G_1(u_3, C_3), G_2(v_3, D_4)) + MCS_p(G_1(u_3, u_4), G_2(v_3.v_5))$, where $MCS_b(G_1(u_3, C_3), G_2(v_3, D_4))$ is given via the computation of $MCS_c(G_1(u_3), G_2(v_3))$.

Figure 4. Computation of $MCS_p(G_1(u, u'), G_2(v, v'))$.

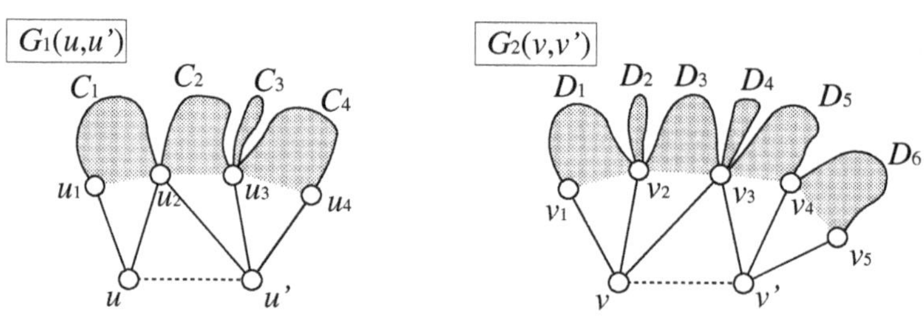

For another example, the score is $-\infty$ for each of alignments, $((u_1, u_3), (v_4, v_5))$, $((u_1, u_2), (v_1, v_2))$ and $((u_3), (v_3))$, whereas the score of $((u_2), (v_3))$ is 2, since $\{u, u'\} \notin E$, $\{v, v'\} \notin E$, $l(u_2, v_3) = 1$, $r(u_2, v_3) = 1$ and $MCS_c(G_1(u_2), G_2(v_3)) = 0$. It is to be noted that vertices not appearing in an alignment can match in a later dynamic programming process; for example, u_2 can match with v_2 under an alignment of $((u_1, u_3), (v_1, v_4))$, although edges $\{u, u_2\}$ and $\{v, v_2\}$ are ignored.

As in the case of $SimpleOuterMCS_b(G_1(u, C), G_2(v, D))$, $SimpleOuterMCS_p(G_1(u, u'), G_2(v, v'))$ can be modified into a dynamic programming version.

Then, we have the following theorem:

Theorem 1 *SIMPLE-OUTER-MCS can be solved in polynomial time.*

Proof. First we consider the correctness of the algorithm $SimpleOuterMCS(G_1, G_2)$. The crucial points of the algorithm are that it examines all possible combinations of the neighbors via alignments examined in $SimpleOuterMCS_b(G_1(u, C), G_2(v, D))$ for each pair of cut vertices (u, v) and via alignments examined in $SimpleOuterMCS_p(G_1(u, u'), G_2(v, v'))$ for each pair of cut pairs $((u, u'), (v, v'))$, where the connectedness in the latter case is taken care of by the use of $l(u_i, v_j)$ and $r(u_i, v_j)$. It should be noted that non-neighbors of u cannot be neighbors of a node corresponding to u in MCS, and the ordering of neighbors must be preserved by Fact 1. Therefore, examination of all alignments covers all valid combinations of neighbors. Based on these facts, it is straightforward to see that $SimpleOuterMCS(G_1, G_2)$ correctly computes the size of MCS.

Next, we consider the time complexity. Since we examine $O(n^2)$ possible root pairs, we focus on the case where the roots are fixed, where n is the maximum number of vertices in G_1 and G_2.

Although $SimpleOuterMCS(G_1, G_2)$ is described as a recursive algorithm, the numbers of required scores of $MCS(G_1(u), G_2(v))$, $MCS(G_1(u, C), G_2(v, D))$ and $MCS(G_1(u, u'), G_2(v, v'))$ are $O(n^2)$, $O(n^2)$ and $O(n^4)$, respectively. Therefore, by storing these values in some tables, we can transform $SimpleOuterMCS\ (G_1, G_2)$ into a dynamic programming algorithm.

Computation of $MCS(G_1(u), G_2(v))$ can be done in $O(n^3)$ time per call, because a maximum weight bipartite matching can be computed in $O(n^3)$ time [22]. Using the dynamic programming version, the computation of each of $MCS(G_1(u, C), G_2(v, D))$ and $MCS(G_1(u, u'), G_2(v, v'))$ can be done in $O(h^2k^2) \leq O(n^4)$ time per call.

Therefore, the total time complexity is $O(n^2) \times (O(n^2) \times O(n^3) + O(n^2) \times O(n^4) + O(n^4) \times O(n^4)) = O(n^{10})$. □

Though it might be possible to substantially reduce the degree of polynomial by some simplification, as done in [11], we do not go further, because our main purpose is to present a polynomial-time algorithm for the non-restricted (but bounded degree) case.

4. Algorithm for Outerplanar Graphs of Bounded Degree

In order to extend the algorithm in Section 3 for a general (but bounded degree) case, we need to consider the decomposition of biconnected components. For example, consider graphs G_1 and G_2 in Figure 5. We can see that in order to obtain a maximum common subgraph, biconnected components in G_1 and G_2 should be decomposed, as shown in Figure 5, where there can be multiple ways of optimal decompositions in general. This is the crucial point, because considering all possible decompositions easily leads to exponential-time algorithms. In order to characterize decomposed components, we introduce the concept of a *blade*, as shown below (see also Figure 6).

Suppose that $v_{i_1}, \ldots, v_{i_k}$ are the vertices of a half block arranged in this order, and v_{i_1} and v_{i_k} are respectively connected to v and v', where v and v' can be the same vertex. If we cut one edge, $\{v_{i_h}, v_{i_{h+1}}\}$ for $i_h \in \{2, 3, ..., k-2\}$, we obtain two half blocks, one induced by $v_{i_1}, v_{i_2}, \ldots, v_{i_h}$ and the other induced by $v_{i_k}, v_{i_{k-1}}, \ldots, v_{i_{h+1}}$. However, only one half block is obtained in the case of $i_1 = i_h$ or $i_k = i_{h+1}$, and no half block is obtained in the case of $k = 2$ (see Figure 7). Each of these half blocks is a chain of biconnected components called a *blade body*, and a subgraph consisting of a blade body and its descendants is called a *blade*. Vertices v_{i_1} and v_{i_k}, an edge $\{v_{i_h}, v_{i_{h+1}}\}$ and vertices $v_{i_h}, v_{i_{h+1}}$ are called *base vertices*, a *tip edge* and *tip vertices*, respectively. The sequence of edges in the shortest path from v_{i_1} to v_{i_h} (resp. from v_{i_k} to $v_{i_{h+1}}$) is called the *backbone* of a blade. As a result, the edges between two blades are deleted (it does not cause a problem, because all possible configurations are examined, as discussed later). In addition, there exists three subcases, depending on the existence of edges $\{v_{i_1}, v_{i_k}\}$ and $\{v', v_{i_1}\}$ (cases with $\{v, v_{i_k}\}$ can be handled in an analogous way). We need not consider the case where $\{v', v_{i_1}\}$ is deleted, but $\{v_{i_1}, v_{i_k}\}$ remains, because deletion of $\{v', v_{i_1}\}$ can be handled in the computation of $MCS_p(G_1(u, u'), G_2(v, v')))$:

- both $\{v_{i_1}, v_{i_k}\}$ and $\{v', v_{i_1}\}$ are deleted
- $\{v_{i_1}, v_{i_k}\}$ is deleted, but $\{v', v_{i_1}\}$ remains
- both $\{v_{i_1}, v_{i_k}\}$ and $\{v', v_{i_1}\}$ remain

where these three cases are respectively denoted by "deletion of e", "deletion of $\overline{e}$" and "deletion of $\hat{e}$" (see Figure 7). It is to be noted that, in any case, we cannot have multiple tip edges simultaneously for the same pair, (v, v'), because disconnected component(s) would appear if multiple tip edges exist.

Figure 5. Example of a difficult case.

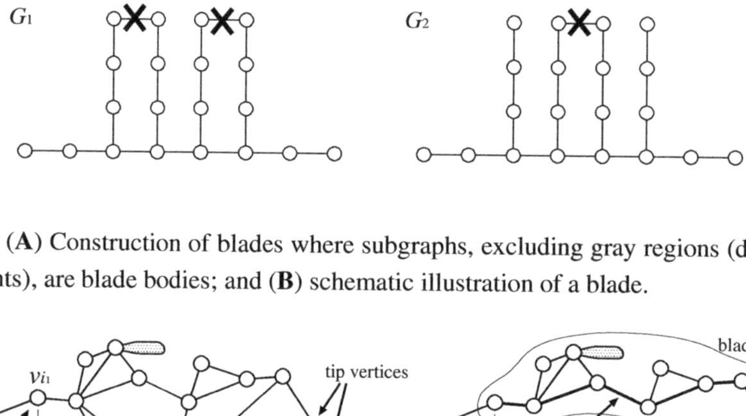

Figure 6. (**A**) Construction of blades where subgraphs, excluding gray regions (descendant components), are blade bodies; and (**B**) schematic illustration of a blade.

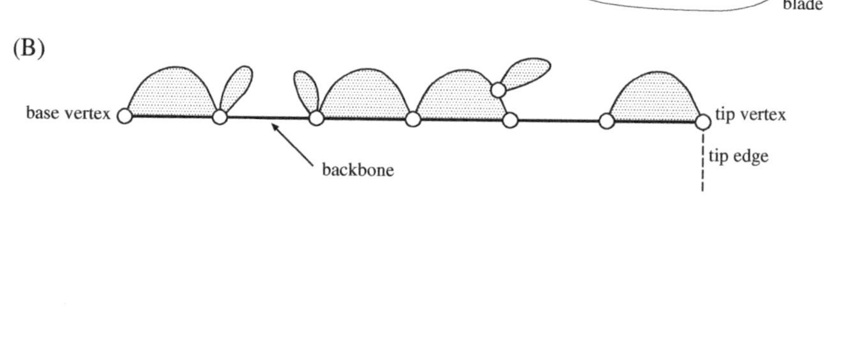

Figure 7. Types and subcases of blades, where two other subcases for (ii) and another subcase (*i.e.*, $\{v', v_{i_1}\}$ remains) for (iii) and (iv) are omitted.

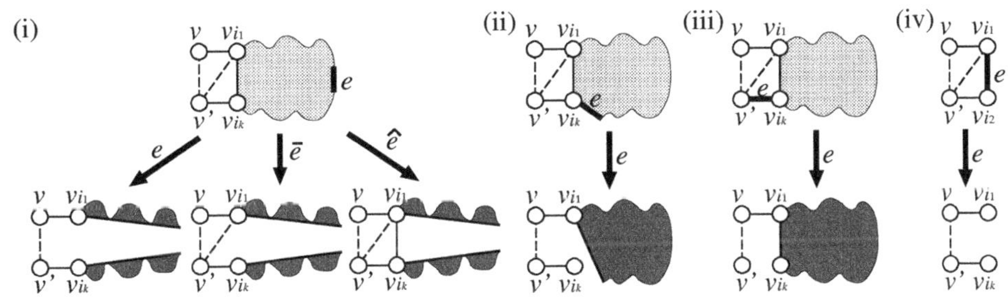

In addition, we allow $\{v, v_{i_1}\}$ (resp. $\{v', v_{i_k}\}$) to be a tip edge. In this case, after removing this tip edge, the resulting half block induced by $v_{i_k}, \ldots, v_{i_2}, v_{i_1}$ (resp. $(v_{i_1}, v_{i_2}, \ldots, v_{i_k})$) is a blade body, where v_{i_k} (resp. v_{i_1}) becomes the base vertex. For example, the rightmost blade in Figure 8 is created by removing a tip edge $\{u, u_5\}$ and u_4 becomes the base vertex.

Figure 8. Example of configuration and its resulting subgraph of $G_1(u)$. Black circles, dark gray regions and thin dotted lines denote selected vertices, blades and removed edges, respectively. Block C_1 and edges e_1, e_2 are the children of u in $G_1(u)$, where block H_1 is a child of e_1, blocks H_2, H_3 are children of C_1 and block H_4 is a child of e_2. Edges, e_a, e_b, are tip edges, where $\{u, u_5\}$ is also regarded as a tip edge. Then, edge e_1 is deleted along with block H_1, whereas edge e_2 remains as it is. Block C_1 is divided into block C_1', blades $B_1, \ldots, B_5$ and edge e_1', where blocks, H_2, H_3, and blades, B_1, B_2, B_3, are children of C_1' and blades, B_4, B_5, are children of e_1'. In the resulting subgraph, block, C_1', and edges, e_1', e_2', are the children of u.

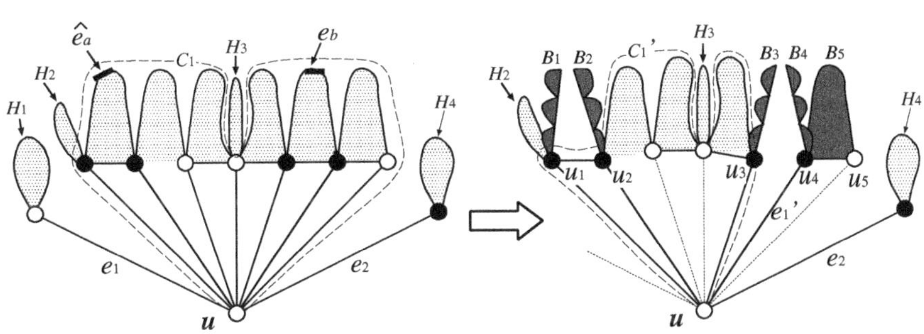

Since a blade can be specified by a pair of base and tip vertices and an orientation (clockwise or counterclockwise), there exist $O(n^2)$ blades in G_1 and G_2. Of course, we need to consider the possibility that during the execution of the algorithm, other subgraphs may appear from which new blades are created. However, we will show later that blades appearing in the algorithm are restricted to be those in G_1 and G_2.

4.1. Description of Algorithm

In this subsection, we describe the algorithm as a recursive procedure, which can be transformed into a dynamic programming one, as stated in Section 3.

The main procedure, $OuterMCS(G_1, G_2)$ is the same as that mentioned in Section 3, and we recursively compute three kinds of scores: $MCS_c(G_1(u), G_2(v))$, $MCS_b(G_1(u, C), G_2(v, D))$ and $MCS_p(G_1(u, u'), G_2(v, v'))$, where cut vertices, cut pairs, blocks and bridges do not necessarily mean those in the original graphs, but may mean those in subgraphs generated by the algorithm.

Computation of $MCS_c(G_1(u), G_2(v))$

Let $C_1, \ldots, C_{h_1}$ and $e_1, \ldots, e_{h_2}$ be children of u, where C_i's and e_j's are blocks and bridges, respectively. Let $u_{i_1}, \ldots, u_{i_h}$ be the neighboring vertices of u that are contained in the children of u. We define a *configuration* as a tuple of the following (see Figure 8).

$s(u_{i_j}) \in \{0, 1\}$ for $j = 1, \ldots, k$: $s(u_{i_j}) = 1$ means that u_{i_j} is selected as a neighbor of u in a common subgraph, otherwise $s(u_{i_j}) = 0$. u_{i_j} is called a *selected vertex* if $s(u_{i_j}) = 1$.

$tip(u_{i_j}, u_{i_k})$: $e = tip(u_{i_j}, u_{i_k})$ is an edge in $B(u_{i_j}, u_{i_k})$, where B is the block containing u_{i_j}, u_{i_k} and u. This edge is defined only for a consecutive selected vertex pair, u_{i_j} and u_{i_k}, in the same block (*i.e.*, $B(u_{i_j}, u_{i_k})$ does not contain any other selected vertex). e is used as a tip edge, where e can be empty, which means that we do not cut any edge in $B(u_{i_j}, u_{i_k})$. It is to be noted that, at most, one edge in $B(u_{i_j}, u_{i_k})$ can be a tip edge, and thus, each $B(u_{i_j}, u_{i_k})$ is divided into, at most, two blade bodies; further decomposition will be done in later steps. We also consider $\overline{e}$ and $\hat{e}$ for $e = tip(u_{i_j}, u_{i_k})$ whenever available.

Each configuration defines a subgraph of $G_1(u)$ as follows:

- $e_i = \{u_{i_j}, u\}$ ($i \in \{1, \ldots, h_2\}$) remains if $s(u_{i_j}) = 1$. Otherwise, e_i is removed along with its descendants.
- If no vertex in C_i is selected, it is removed along with its descendants. Otherwise, C_i is divided into blocks, blade bodies (according to $s(\ldots)$'s and $tip(\ldots)$'s) and bridges, where edges, $\{u_{i_j}, u\}$ with $s(u_{i_j}) = 0$, are removed.

Let $C'_1, \ldots, C'_{p_1}$ and $e'_1, \ldots, e'_{p_2}$ be the resulting blocks and bridges containing u, which are new 'children' of u, for a configuration, F_1. Configurations are defined for $G_2(v)$ in an analogous way. Let $D'_1, \ldots, D'_{q_1}$ and $f'_1, \ldots, f'_{q_2}$ be the resulting new children of v for a configuration F_2 of G_2. As stated in Section 3, we construct a bipartite graph BG_{F_1,F_2} by

$$\begin{aligned} w(C'_i, f'_j) &= 0 \\ w(C'_i, D'_j) &= MCS_b(G_1(u, C'_i), G_2(v, D'_j)) \\ w(e'_i, D'_j) &= 0 \\ w(e'_i, f'_j) &= MCS_b(G_1(u, e'_i), G_2(v, f'_j)) \end{aligned}$$

and we compute the weight of the maximum weight matching for each configuration pair (F_1, F_2) (although a bridge cannot be mapped on a block here, a bridge can be mapped to an edge in a block of an input graph by converting the block into smaller blocks and bridges using tip edge(s)). The following is a procedure for computing $MCS_c(G_1(u), G_2(v))$:

Procedure $OuterMCS_c(G_1(u), G_2(v))$
  $s_{\max} \leftarrow 0$;
  for all configurations F_1 for $G_1(u)$ **do**
    for all configurations F_2 for $G_2(v)$ **do**
      $s \leftarrow$ weight of the maximum weight matching of BG_{F_1,F_2};
      if $s > s_{\max}$ **then** $s_{\max} \leftarrow s$;
  return $s_{\max}$.

Computation of $MCS_b(G_1(u, C'), G_2(v, D'))$

This score can be computed, as stated in Section 3, although we should take blades into account. In this case, we can directly examine all possible alignments, because the number of neighbors of u or v is bounded by a constant, and we need to examine a constant number of alignments.

Computation of $MCS_p(G_1(u, u'), G_2(v, v'))$

As in $OuterMCS_c(G_1(u), G_2(v))$, we examine all possible configurations by specifying selected vertices and tip edges (see Figure 9). Each configuration defines a subgraph of $G_1(u, u')$ (resp. $G_2(v, v')$). This subgraph contains three kinds of biconnected components:

(i) components connecting only to u (resp. v)
(ii) components connecting only to u' (resp. v') and
(iii) component connecting to both u and u' (resp. v and v'), where this type (iii) component is uniquely determined.

Figure 9. Example of configuration and its resulting subgraph for $G_1(u, u')$. Black circles, dark gray regions and thin dotted lines denote selected vertices, blade, and removed edges, respectively. Edges, e_a, e_b, are tip edges, where $\{u', u''\}$ is also regarded as a tip edge. In the resulting subgraph, C'_1 is a type (i) component, e'_1 and e'_2 are type (ii) components and $C_0(u, u')$ is a type (iii) component.

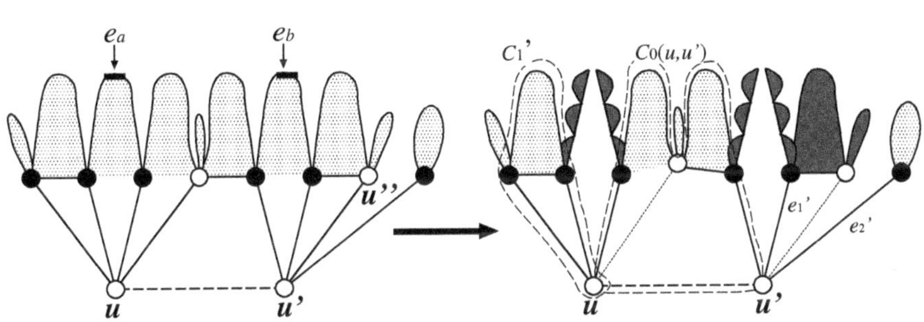

For each of type (i) and type (ii) components, we construct a bipartite graph, as in $OuterMCS(G_1(u), G_2(v))$, although blades might appear in the recursive process. Let the resulting bipartite graphs be $BG^l_{F_1,F_2}$ and $BG^r_{F_1,F_2}$, respectively. Let $C_0(u, u')$ and $D_0(v, v')$ be type (iii)

components (*i.e.*, half blocks) for $G_1(u, u')$ and $G_2(v, v')$, respectively. For this pair of components, we compute a maximum common subgraph, as in $SimpleOuterMCS(G_1(u, u'), G_2(v, v'))$. The following is a pseudocode of $OuterMCS(G_1(u, u'), G_2(v, v'))$:

```
Procedure OuterMCS(G1(u,u'), G2(v,v'))
  s_max ← 0;
  for all configurations F1 for G1(u,u') do
    for all configurations F2 for G2(v,v') do
      s ← score of the maximum common subgraph between C0(u,u') and D0(v,v');
      s ← s + weight of the maximum weight matching of BG^l_{F1,F2};
      s ← s + weight of the maximum weight matching of BG^r_{F1,F2};
      if s > s_max then s_max ← s;
  return s_max.
```

4.2. Analysis

As mentioned before, each blade is specified by base and tip vertices in G_1 or G_2 and an orientation. Each half block is also specified by two vertices in a block in G_1 or G_2. We show that this property is maintained throughout the execution of the algorithm and bound to the number of half blocks and blades, as below.

Lemma 1 *The number of different half blocks and blades appearing in* $OuterMCS(G_1, G_2)$ *is* $O(n^2)$.

Proof. We prove it by mathematical induction on the number of steps in the execution of the algorithm. At the beginning of the algorithm, this property is trivially maintained, because we only have G_1 and G_2. A new half block (along with its descendants) or a new blade is created only when graphs are modified according to a configuration or alignment. In the alignment case, it is straightforward to see that new half blocks are half blocks of the current block or current half block. It can also be seen that whenever a blade is newly created, it is a half block (along with descendants) of the current block or current half block. The crucial cases lie when an existing blade is modified according to a configuration. Let u and $\{u, w\}$ be the base vertex and a backbone edge in a blade BD, respectively. Let C_0 be the block in G_1 (resp. G_2) from which BD was created. Then, we need to consider the following three cases (Figure 10) (new blades may also be created by a tip edge in a half block specified by a pair of selected vertices):

(a) w is not selected.
The base vertex of a new blade is the selected vertex nearest to w in the first block (*i.e.*, block containing u) of BD. Since the original blade body was a half block of a block C_0, the resulting blade body is also a half block of C_0.

(b) w is selected, and there is no tip edge between w and its nearest selected vertex.
The resulting blade body begins from w (in the next step), which is a half block of C_0.

(c) w is selected, and there is a tip edge between w and its nearest selected vertex.
The resulting blade body begins from w, which is a half block of C_0. Furthermore, two (or less) new blade bodies are created, both of which are half blocks of C_0.

Therefore, we can see that every half block or blade appearing in the algorithm is specified by two vertices in a block of G_1 or G_2, from which the lemma follows. □

Figure 10. Three cases considered in the proof of Lemma 1. Bold lines and dark gray regions denote backbone edges and new blade bodies, respectively.

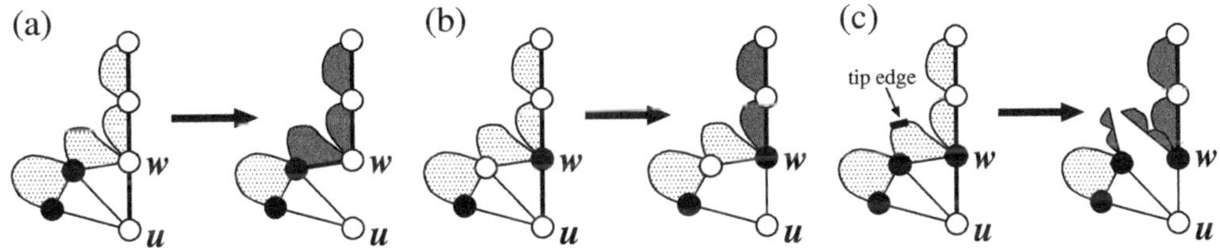

Finally, we obtain the following theorem.

Theorem 2 *A maximum common connected edge subgraph of two outerplanar graphs of bounded degree can be computed in polynomial-time.*

Proof. It is straightforward to check the correctness of the algorithm, because it implicitly examines all possible common subgraphs via alignment, decomposition by configurations and bipartite matching, where Fact 1 enables us to use alignment and dynamic programming. Therefore, we focus on the time complexity.

Since the number of half blocks and blades is $O(n^2)$ and the maximum degree is bounded, the number of different $G_1(u)$'s and $G_1(u, u')$'s (resp. $G_2(v)$'s and $G_2(v, v')$'s) appearing in the algorithm, some of which can be obtained from subgraphs of G_1 (resp. G_2), is $O(n^3)$, where an additional $O(n)$ factor comes from the fact that $O(n)$ new blocks and bridges may be created per blade. Therefore, we can transform the recursive algorithm into a dynamic programming algorithm using $O(n^3) \times O(n^3) = O(n^6)$ size tables.

For each subgraph appearing in $OuterMCS(G_1(u), G_2(v))$ or $OuterMCS(G_1(u, u'), G_2(v, v'))$ as an argument, the number of configurations is $O(n^{2D-3})$, because there exists at most $2D-2$ neighboring vertices (excluding those nearer to the root) of u and u' (resp. v and v') for a constant, D, ($D > 2$) and a tip edge lies between a path connecting two neighboring vertices. For some block pair, we need to examine all possible alignments. Since the maximum degree is bounded by constant, D, we need to examine a constant number of alignments, and thus, this calculation can be done in constant time. By the same reason, a maximum matching can be computed in constant time. All other miscellaneous operations, which include modification of edges and summation of scores, can be performed in $O(n^2)$ time per pair of configurations, pair of biconnected components and pair of half blocks. Since we need to examine $O(n^2)$ pairs of the roots, the total computation time is:

$$O(n^2) \times O(n^6) \times O(n^{2D-3}) \times O(n^{2D-3}) \times O(n^2) = O(n^{4D+4})$$

for a constant, D (a constant factor depending only on D is ignored here, because we assume that D is a constant). □

5. Concluding Remarks

We have presented a polynomial-time algorithm for the maximum common connected edge subgraph problem for outerplanar graphs of bounded degree. However, it is not practically efficient. Therefore, development of a much faster algorithm is left as an open problem. Although the proposed algorithm might be modified for outputting all maximum common subgraphs, it would not be an output-polynomial-time algorithm. Therefore, such an algorithm should also be developed.

Recently, it has been shown that the maximum common connected edge subgraph problem is NP-hard, even for partial k-trees of a bounded degree, where $k = 11$ [23]. Since outerplanar graphs have treewidth 2 and most chemical compounds have a treewidth of at most 3 [10,18], to decide whether the problem for partial k-trees is NP-hard for $k = 3$ is left as an interesting open problem.

Acknowledgments

Tatsuya Akutsu was partly supported by JSPS, Japan (Grants-in-Aid 22240009 and 22650045). Takeyuki Tamura was partly supported by JSPS, Japan (Grant-in-Aid for Young Scientists (B) 23700017).

References

1. Conte, D.; Foggia, P.; Sansone, C.; Vento, M. Thirty years of graph matching in pattern recognition. *Int. J. Pattern Recognit. Artif. Intell.* **2004**, *18*, 265–298.
2. Shearer, K.; Bunke, H.; Venkatesh, S. Video indexing and similarity retrieval by largest common subgraph detection using decision trees. *Pattern Recognit.* **2001**, *34*, 1075–1091.
3. Raymond, J.W.; Willett, P. Maximum common subgraph isomorphism algorithms for the matching of chemical structures. *J. Comput. Aided Mol. Des.* **2002**, *16*, 521–533.
4. Hans-Christian Ehrlich, H-C.; Rarey, M. Maximum common subgraph isomorphism algorithms and their applications in molecular science: A review. *WIREs Comput. Mol. Sci.* **2011**, *1*, 68–79.
5. Abu-Khzam, F.N.; Samatova, N.F.; Rizk, M.A.; Langston, M.A. The Maximum Common Subgraph Problem: Faster Solutions via Vertex Cover. In *Proceedings of the 2007 IEEE/ACS International Conference Computer Systems and Applications, IEEE*, Piscataway, NJ, USA, 2007; pp. 367–373.
6. Huang, X.; Lai, J.; Jennings, S.F. Maximum common subgraph: Some upper bound and lower bound results. *BMC Bioinforma.* **2006**, *7 (Suppl. 4)*, S6:1–S6:9.
7. Kann, V. On the Approximability of the Maximum Common Subgraph Problem. In *Proceedings of the 9th Symposium Theoretical Aspects of Computer Science*; Springer: Heidelberg, Germany, 1992; Volume 577, pp. 377–388.
8. Garey, M.R.; Johnson, D.S. *Computers and Intractability*; Freeman: New York, NY, USA, 1979.
9. Akutsu, T. A polynomial time algorithm for finding a largest common subgraph of almost trees of bounded degree. *IEICE Trans. Fundam.* **1993**, *E76-A*, 1488–1493.
10. Yamaguchi, A.; Aoki, K.F.; Mamitsuka, H. Finding the maximum common subgraph of a partial k-tree and a graph with a polynomially bounded number of spanning trees. *Inf. Proc. Lett.* **2004**, *92*, 57–63.

11. Schietgat, L.; Ramon, J.; Bruynooghe, M. A Polynomial-Time Metric for Outerplanar Graphs. In *Proceedings of the Workshop on Mining and Learning with Graphs*, Firenze, Italy, 1 August 2007.
12. Bachl, S.; Brandenburg, F-J.; Gmach, D. Computing and drawing isomorphic subgraphs. *J. Graph Algorithms Appl.* **2004**, *8*, 215–238.
13. Lingas, A. Subgraph isomorphism for biconnected outerplanar graphs in cubic time. *Theoret. Comput. Sci.* **1989**, *63*, 295–302.
14. Syslo, M.M. The subgraph isomorphism problem for outerplanar graphs. *Theoret. Comput. Sci.* **1982**, *17*, 91–97.
15. Dessmark, A.; Lingas, A.; Proskurowski, A. Faster algorithms for subgraph isomorphism of k-connected partial k-trees. *Algorithmica* **2000**, *27*, 337–347.
16. Hajiaghayi, M.; Nishimura, N. Subgraph isomorphism, log-bounded fragmentation, and graphs of (locally) bounded treewidth. *J. Comput. Syst. Sci.* **2007**, *73*, 755–768.
17. Akutsu, T.; Tamura, T. A Polynomial-Time Algorithm for Computing the Maximum Common Subgraph of Outerplanar Graphs of Bounded Degree. In *Proceedings of the 37th International Symposium on Mathematical Foundations of Computer Science*; Springer: Heidelberg, Germany, 2012; Volume 7464, pp. 76–87.
18. Horváth, T.; Ramon, J.; Wrobel, S. Frequent Subgraph Mining in Outerplanar Graphs. In *Proceedings of the 12th ACM SIGKDD Int. Conf. Knowledge Discovery and Data Mining*; ACM: New York, NY, USA, 2006; pp. 197–206.
19. Akutsu, T. An RNC algorithm for finding a largest common subtree of two trees. *IEICE Trans. Inf. Syst.* **1992**, *E75-D*, 95–101.
20. Syslo, M.M. Characterizations of outerplanar graphs. *Disc. Math.* **1979**, *26*, 47–53.
21. Chartrand, G.; Lesniak, L.; Zhang, P. *Graphs and Digraphs, Fifth Edition*; Chapman and Hall/CRC: Boca Raton, FL, USA, 2010.
22. Cormen, T.H.; Leiserson, C.E.; Rivest, R.L.; Stein, C. *Introduction to Algorithms, Third Edition*; The MIT Press: Cambridge, MA, USA, 2009.
23. Akutsu, T.; Tamura, T. On the Complexity of the Maximum Common Subgraph Problem for Partial k-trees of Bounded Degree. In *Proceedings of the 23rd International Symposium Algorithms and Computation*; Springer: Heidelberg, Germany, 2012; Volume 7676, pp. 146–155.

Algorithms **2013**, *6*, 396-406; doi:10.3390/a6030396

OPEN ACCESS

algorithms

ISSN 1999-4893

www.mdpi.com/journal/algorithms

Article

New Heuristics for Rooted Triplet Consistency †

Soheil Jahangiri Tazehkand [1,2,*], Seyed Naser Hashemi [1] and Hadi Poormohammadi [3]

[1] Amirkabir University of Technology (Tehran Polytechnic), 424 Hafez Ave, Tehran, Iran; E-Mail: nhashemi@aut.ac.ir

[2] Bioinformatics Group, School of Computer Science, Institute for Research in Fundamental Sciences (IPM), Niavaran, Tehran, Iran

[3] Shahid Beheshti University, Evin, Tehran 19839-63113, Iran; E-Mail: poormohammadi@ipm.ir

† An extended abstract of this article has appeared in the proceedings of the Annual International Conference on Bioinformatics and Computational Biology (BICB 2011) in Singapore.

* Author to whom correspondence should be addressed; E-Mail: s.jahangiri@aut.ac.ir; Tel.: +98-936-9220139.

Received: 14 April 2013; in revised form: 26 June 2013 / Accepted: 26 June 2013 / Published: 11 July 2013

Abstract: Rooted triplets are becoming one of the most important types of input for reconstructing rooted phylogenies. A rooted triplet is a phylogenetic tree on three leaves and shows the evolutionary relationship of the corresponding three species. In this paper, we investigate the problem of inferring the maximum consensus evolutionary tree from a set of rooted triplets. This problem is known to be APX-hard. We present two new heuristic algorithms. For a given set of m triplets on n species, the *FastTree* algorithm runs in $O(m + \alpha(n)n^2)$ time, where $\alpha(n)$ is the functional inverse of Ackermann's function. This is faster than any other previously known algorithms, although the outcome is less satisfactory. The Best Pair Merge with Total Reconstruction (BPMTR) algorithm runs in $O(mn^3)$ time and, on average, performs better than any other previously known algorithms for this problem.

Keywords: phylogenetic tree; rooted triplet; consensus tree; approximation algorithm

---

1. Introduction

After the publication of Charles Darwin's book *On the Origin of Species by Means of Natural Selection*, the theory of evolution was widely accepted. Since then, remarkable developments in evolutionary studies brought scientists to phylogenetics, a field that studies the biological or morphological data of species to output a mathematical model, such as a tree or a network, representing the evolutionary interrelationship of species and the process of their evolution. Interestingly, phylogenetics is not only limited to biology, but may also arise anywhere that the concept of evolution appears. For example, a recent study in evolutionary linguistics employs a phylogeny inference to clarify the origin of the Indo-European language family [1]. Several approaches have been introduced to infer evolutionary relationships [2]. Among those, well-known approaches are character-based methods (e.g., maximum parsimony), distance-based methods (e.g., neighbor joining and UPGMA) and quartet-based methods (e.g., QNet). Recently, rather new approaches, namely, triplet-based methods, have been introduced. Triplet-based methods output rooted trees and networks, due to the rooted nature of triplets. A rooted triplet is a rooted unordered leaf-labeled binary tree on three leaves and shows the evolutionary relationship of the corresponding three species. Triplets can be obtained accurately using a maximum likelihood method, such as the one introduced by Chor *et al.* [3], or the Sibley-Ahlquist-style DNA-DNA hybridization experiments [4]. Indeed, we expect highly accurate results from triplet-based methods. However, sometimes, due to experimental errors or some biological events, such as hybridization (recombination) or horizontal gene transfer, it is not possible to reconstruct a tree that satisfies all of the input constraints (triplets). There are two ways to overcome this problem. The first approach is to employ a more complex model, such as a network, which is the proper approach when the mentioned biological events have actually happened. The second approach tries to reconstruct a tree satisfying as many input triplets as possible. This approach is more useful when the input data contains errors. The latter approach forms the subject of this paper. In the next section, we will provide necessary definitions and notations. Section 3 contains an overview of previous results. We will present our algorithms and experimental results in Section 4. Finally, in Section 5, open problems and ideas for further improvements are discussed.

2. Preliminaries

An *evolutionary tree (phylogenetic tree)* on a set, S, of n species, $|S| = n$, is a rooted binary (More precisely, an evolutionary tree can also be unrooted; however, triplet-based methods output rooted phylogenies)unordered tree in which leaves are distinctly labeled by members of S (see Figure 1(a)). A *rooted triplet* is a phylogenetic tree with three leaves. The unique triplet of leaves, x, y, z, is denoted by $((x, y), z)$ or $xy|z$, if the lowest common ancestor of x and y is a proper descendant of the lowest common ancestor of x and z or, equivalently, if the lowest common ancestor of x and y is a proper descendant of the lowest common ancestor of y and z (see Figure 1(b)). A triplet, t (e.g., $xy|z$) is *consistent* with a tree, T, or, equivalently, T is consistent with t) if t is an embedded subtree of T. This means that t can be obtained from T by a series of edge contractions (*i.e.*, if in T, the lowest common ancestor of x and y is a proper descendant of the lowest common ancestor of x and z). We also say T *satisfies* t, if T is consistent with t.

The tree in Figure 1(a) is consistent with the triplet in Figure 1(b). A phylogenetic tree, *T*, is consistent with a set of rooted triplets if it is consistent with every triplet in the set. We call two leaves *siblings* or a *cherry* if they share the same parent. For example, $\{x, y\}$ in Figure 1(a) form a cherry.

Figure 1. Example of a phylogenetic tree and a consistent triplet. (**a**) A phylogenetic tree; (**b**) the triplet $xy|z$.

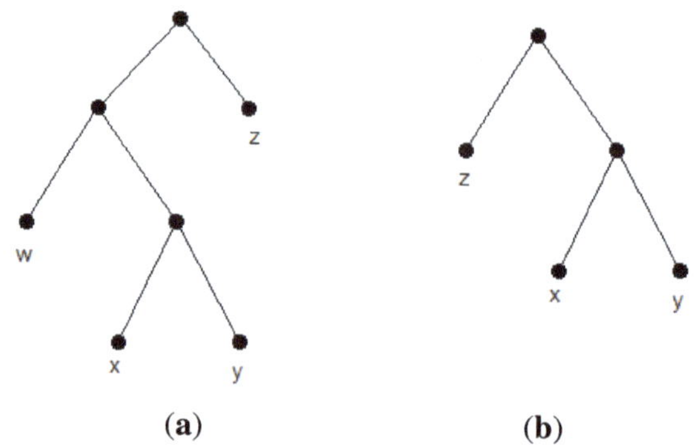

A set of triplets, *R*, is called *dense* if for each set of three species, $\{x, y, z\}$, *R*, contains at least one of three possible triplets, $xy|z$, $xz|y$ or $yz|x$. If *R* contains exactly one triplet for each set of three species, it is called *minimally dense*, and if it contains every possible triplet, it is called *maximally dense*. Now, we can define the problem of reconstructing an evolutionary tree from a set of rooted triplets. Suppose *S* is a finite set of species of cardinality, *n*, and *R* is a finite set of rooted triplets of cardinality, *m*, on *S*. The problem is to find an evolutionary tree leaf-labeled by members of *S*, which is consistent with the maximum number of rooted triplets in *R*. This problem is called the *Maximum Rooted Triplets Consistency (MaxRTC)* problem [5] or the *Maximum Inferred Local Consensus Tree (MILCT)* problem [6]. This problem is NP-hard (see Section 3), which means no polynomial-time algorithm can be found to solve the problem optimally unless P= NP. For this and similar problems, one might search for polynomial-time algorithms that produce approximate solutions. We call an algorithm an *approximation algorithm* if its solution is guaranteed to be within some factor of optimum solution. In contrast, *heuristics* may produce good solutions, but do not come with a guarantee on their quality of solution. An algorithm for a maximization problem is called an $\alpha - approximation$ algorithm, for some $\alpha > 1$, if for any input, the output of the algorithm is at most α-times worse than the optimum solution. The factor, α, is called the *approximation factor* or *approximation ratio*.

3. Related Works

Aho *et al.* [7] investigated the problem of constructing a tree consistent with a set of rooted triplets for the first time. They designed a simple recursive algorithm, which runs in $O(mn)$ time and returns a tree consistent with all of the given triplets, if at least one tree exists. Otherwise, it returns null. Later, Henzinger *et al.* [8] improved Aho *et al.*'s algorithm to run in $min\{O(n+mn^{1/2}), O(m+n^2logn)\}$ time. The time complexity of this algorithm was further improved to $min\{O(n + mlog^2n), O(m + n^2logn)\}$ by Jansson *et al.* [9] using more recent data structures introduced by Holm *et al.* [10]. MaxRTC is proven to be NP-hard [6,11,12]. Byrka *et al.* [13] reported that this proof is an L-reduction from an APX-hard problem, meaning that the problem is APX-hard, in general (non-dense case). Later, Van Iersel *et al.* [14] proved that MaxRTC is NP-hard, even if the input triplet set is dense.

Several heuristics and approximation algorithms have been presented for the so-called MaxRTC problem, each performing better in practice on different input triplet sets. Gasieniec *et al.* [15] proposed two algorithms by modifying Aho *et al.*'s algorithm. Their first algorithm, which is referred to as `One-Leaf-Split` [5] runs in $O((m + n)logn)$ time, and the second one, which is referred to as `Min-Cut-Split` [5], runs in $min\{O(mn^2 + n^3logn), O(n^4)\}$ time. The tree generated by the first algorithm is guaranteed to be consistent with at least one third of the input triplet set. This gives a lower bound for the problem. In another study, Wu [11] introduced a bottom-up heuristic approach called BPMF (Best Pair Merge First), which runs in $O(mn^3)$ time. In the same study, he proposed an exact exponential algorithm for the problem, which runs in $O((m + n^2)3^n)$ time and $O(2^n)$ space. According to the results of Wu [11], BPMF seems to perform well on average on randomly generated data. Later, Maemura *et al.* [16] presented a modified version of BPMF, called BPMR (Best Pair Merge with Reconstruction), which employs the same approach, but with a little bit different of a reconstruction routine. BPMR runs in $O(mn^3)$ time and, according to Maemura *et al.*'s experiments, outperforms BPMF. Byrka *et al.* [13] designed a modified version of BPMF to achieve an approximation ratio of three. They also investigated how MinRTI (Minimum Rooted Triplet Inconsistency) can be used to approximate MaxRTC and proved that MaxRTC admits a polynomial-time, $(3 - \frac{2}{n-2})-$, approximation.

4. Algorithms and Experimental Results

In this Section, we present two new heuristic algorithms for the MaxRTC problem.

4.1. FastTree

The first heuristic algorithm has a bottom-up greedy approach, which is faster than the other previously known algorithms employing a simple data structure.

Let *R(T)* denote the set of all triplets consistent with a given tree, *T*. *R(T)* is called the *reflective triplet set* of *T*. It forms a minimally dense triplet set and represents *T* uniquely [17]. Now, we define the *closeness* of the pair, $\{i,j\}$. The closeness of the pair, $\{i,j\}$, $C_{i,j}$, is defined as the number of triplets of the form, $ij|k$, in a triplet set. Clearly, for any arbitrary tree, *T*, the closeness of a cherry species equals $n - 2$, which is maximum in *R(T)*. The reason is that every cherry species has a triplet with every other species. Now, suppose we contract every cherry species of the form, $\{i,j\}$, to their parents, p_{ij}, and then update *R(T)* as follows. For each contracted cherry species, $\{i,j\}$, we remove triplets of the form, $ij|k$, from *R(T)* and replace *i* and *j* with p_{ij} within the remaining triplets. The updated set, $R'(T')$, would be the reflective triplet set for the new tree, T'. Observe that, for cherries of the form, $\{p_{ij}, k\}$, in T', $C_{i,k}$ and $C_{j,k}$ would equal n-3 in *R(T)*. Similarly, for cherries of the form, $\{p_{ij}, p_{kl}\}$, in T', $C_{i,k}$, $C_{j,k}$, $C_{i,l}$ and $C_{j,l}$ would equal n-4 in *R(T)*. This forms the main idea of the first heuristic algorithm. We first compute the closeness of pairs of species by visiting triplets. Furthermore, sorting the pairs according to their closeness gives us the reconstruction order of the tree. This routine outputs the unique tree, *T*, for any given reflective triplet set, *R(T)*. Yet, we have to consider that the input triplet set is not always a reflective triplet set. Consequently, the reconstruction order produced by sorting may not be the right order. However, if the loss of triplets admits a uniform distribution, it will not affect the reconstruction order. An approximate solution for this problem is refining the closeness. This can be done by reducing the closeness of the pairs, $\{i,k\}$ and $\{j,k\}$, for any visited triplet of the form, $ij|k$. Thus, if the pair, $\{i,j\}$, is actually cherries, then the probability of choosing the pairs, $\{i,k\}$ or $\{j,k\}$, before choosing the pair, $\{i,j\}$, due to triplet loss, will be reduced. We call this algorithm FastTree. See Algorithm 1 for the whole algorithm.

Algorithm 1 FastTree

```
1: Initialize a forest, F, consisting of n one-node trees labeled by species.
2: for each triplet of the form ij|k do
3:     C_{i,j}: = C_{i,j}+1
4:     C_{i,k}: = C_{i,k}−1
5:     C_{j,k}: = C_{j,k}−1
6: end for
7: Create a list, L, of pairs of species.
8: Sort L according to the refined closeness of pairs with a linear-time sorting algorithm.
9: while |L|>0 do
10:    Remove the pair, {i,j}, with maximum, C_{i,j}.
11:    if i and j are not in the same tree then
12:        Add a new node and connect it to roots of trees containing i and j.
13:    end if
14: end while
15: if F has more than one tree then
16:    Merge trees in any order, until there would be only one tree.
17: end if
18: return the tree in F
```

Theorem 1. *FastTree runs in* $O(m + \alpha(n)n^2)$ *time.*

Proof. Initializing a forest in Step 1 takes $O(n)$ time. Steps 2–6 take $O(m)$ time. We know that the closeness is an integer value between 0 and $n - 2$. Thus, we can employ a linear-time sorting algorithm [18]. There are $O(n^2)$ possible pairs; therefore, Step 8 takes $O(n^2)$ time. Similarly, the while loop in Step 9 takes $O(n^2)$ time. Each removal in Step 10 can be done in $O(1)$ time. By employing optimal data structures, which are used for disjoint-set unions [18], the amortized time complexity of Steps 11 and 12 will be $O(\alpha(n))$, where $\alpha(n)$ is the inverse of the function, $f(x) = A(n,n)$, and A is the well-known fast-growing *Ackermann* function. Furthermore, Step 16 takes $O(n\alpha(n))$ time. Hence, the running time of FastTree would be $O(m + \alpha(n)n^2)$. □

Since $A(4,4) = 2^{2^{2^{65536}}}$, $\alpha(n)$ is less than four for any practical input size, *n*. In comparison to the fast version of Aho *et al.*'s algorithm, FastTree employs a simpler data structure and, in comparison to Aho *et al.*'s original algorithm, it has lower time complexity. Yet, the most important advantage of FastTree to Aho *et al.*'s algorithm is that it will not stick if there is not a consistent tree with the input triplets, and it will output a proper tree in such a way that the clusters are very similar to that of the real network. The tree in Figure 2 is the output of FastTree on a dense set of triplets based on the yeast, *Cryptococcus gattii*, data. There is no consistent tree with the whole triplet set; however, Van Iersel *et al.* [19] presented a level-2 network consistent with the set (see Figure 3). This set is available online [20]. In comparison to BPMR and BPMF, FastTree runs much faster for large sets of triplets and species. However, for highly sparse triplet sets, the output of FastTree may satisfy considerably less triplets than the tree constructed by BPMF or BPMR.

Figure 2. Output of FastTree for a dense triplet set of the yeast, *Cryptococcus gattii*, data.

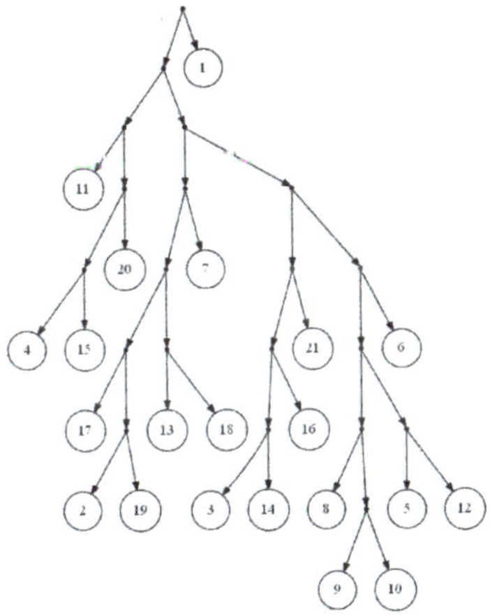

4.2. BPMTR

Before explaining the second heuristic algorithm, we need to review BPMF [11] and BPMR [16]. BPMF utilizes a bottom-up approach similar to hierarchical clustering. Initially, there are *n* trees, each containing a single node representing one of *n* given species. In each iteration, the algorithm computes a function, called e_score, for each combination of two trees. Furthermore, two trees with the maximum e_score are merged into a single tree by adding a new node as the common parent of the selected trees. Wu [11] introduced six alternatives for computing the e_score using combinations of *w*, *p* and *t*. (see Table 1). However, in each run, one of the six alternatives must be used. In the function, $e\_score(C_1, C_2)$, *w* is the number of triplets satisfied by merging C_1 and C_2, which is the number of triplets of the form $ij|k$, in which *i* is in C_1, *j* is in C_2 and *k* is neither in C_1 nor in C_2. The value of *p* is the number of triplets that are in conflict with merging C_1 and C_2. It is the number of triplets of the form, $ij|k$, in which *i* is in C_1, *k* is in C_2 and *j* is neither in C_1 nor in C_2. The value of *t* is the total number of triplets of the form, $ij|k$, in which *i* is in $C_1$and *j* is C_2. Wu compared the BPMF with `One-Leaf-Split` and `Min-Cut-Split` and showed that BPMF works better on randomly generated triplet sets. He also pointed out that none of the six alternatives of e_score is significantly better than the other.

Figure 3. A Level-2 network for a dense triplet set of the yeast, *Cryptococcus gattii*, data.

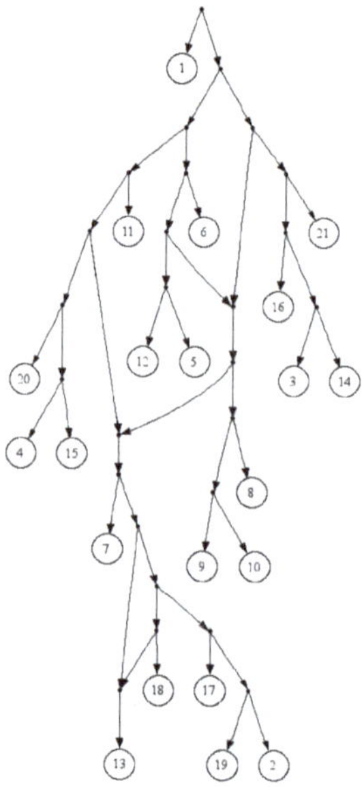

Table 1. The six alternatives of *e_score*.

If-Penalty	Ratio Type		
False	w	w/(w + p)	w/t
True	w − p	(w − p)/(w + p)	(w − p)/t

Maemura *et al.* [16] introduced a modified version of BPMF, called BPMR, that outperforms the results of BPMF. BPMR works very similarly in comparison to BPMF, except for a reconstruction step used in BPMR. Suppose T_x and T_y are two trees having the maximum, e_score, at some iteration and are selected to merge into a new tree. By merging T_x and T_y, some triplets will be satisfied, but some other triplets will be in conflict. Without loss of generality, suppose T_x has two subtrees, namely the left subtree and the right subtree. In addition, suppose a triplet, $ij|k$, in which i is in the left subtree of T_x, k is in the right subtree of T_x and j is in T_y. Observe that by merging T_x and T_y, the mentioned triplet becomes inconsistent. However, swapping T_y with the right subtree of the T_x satisfies this triplet, while some other triplets become inconsistent. It is possible that the resulting tree of this swap satisfies more triplets than the primary tree. This is the main idea behind the BPMR. In BPMR, in addition to the regular merging of T_x and T_y, T_y is swapped with the left and the right subtree of T_x, and also, T_x is swapped with the left and the right tree of T_y. Finally, among these five topologies, we choose the one that satisfies the most triplets.

Suppose the left subtree of the T_x also has two subtrees. Swapping T_y with one of these subtrees would probably satisfy new triplets, while some old ones would become inconsistent. There are examples in which this swap results in a tree that satisfies more triplets. This forms our second heuristic idea that swapping of T_y with every subtree of T_x should be checked. T_x should also be swapped with every subtree of T_y. At every iteration of BPMF after choosing two trees maximizing the , the algorithm tests every possible swapping of these two trees with subtrees of each other and, then, chooses the tree with the maximum consistency of the triplets. We call this algorithm BPMTR (Best Pair Merge with Total Reconstruction). See Algorithm 2 for details of the BPMTR.

Algorithm 2 BPMTR

1: Initialize a set, T, consisting of n one-node trees labeled by species.
2: **while** $|T|>1$ **do**
3:    Find and remove two trees, T_x, T_y, with maximum e_score.
4:    Create a new tree, T_{merge}, by adding a common parent to T_x and T_y
5:    $T_{best} := T_{merge}$
6:    **for each** subtree T_{sub} of T_x **do**
7:       Let $T_{swapped}$ be the tree constructed by swapping T_{sub} with T_y
8:       **if** the number of consistent triplets with $T_{swapped}$ was larger than the number of triplets consistent with T_{best} **then**
9:          $T_{best} := T_{swapped}$
10:       **end if**
11:    **end for**
12:    **for each** subtree T_{sub} of T_y **do**
13:       Let $T_{swapped}$ be the tree constructed by swapping T_{sub} with T_x
14:       **if** the number of consistent triplets with $T_{swapped}$ was larger than the number of triplets consistent with T_{best} **then**
15:          $T_{best} := T_{swapped}$
16:       **end if**
17:    **end for**
18:    Add T_{best} to T.
19: **end while**
20: **return** the tree in T

Theorem 2. *BPMTR runs in $O(mn^3)$ time.*

Proof. Step 1 takes $O(n)$ time. In Step 2, initially, T contains n clusters, but in each iteration, two clusters merge into a cluster. Hence, the while loop in Step 2 takes $O(n)$ time. In Step 3, e_score is computed for every subset of T of size two. By applying Bender and Farach-Colton's preprocessing algorithm [21], which runs in $O(n)$ time for a tree with n nodes, every LCAquery can be answered in $O(1)$ time. Therefore, the consistency of a triplet with a cluster can be checked in $O(1)$ time. Since there are m triplets, Step 3 takes $\binom{|T|}{2}O(m)$ time. In Steps 5, 9 and 15, T_{best} is a pointer that stores the best topology found so far during each iteration of the while loop in $O(1)$ time. The complexity analysis of the loops in Steps 6–11 and 12–17 are similar, and it is enough to consider one. Every rooted binary tree with n leaves has $O(n)$ internal nodes, so the total number of swaps in Step 7 for any two clusters will be at most $O(n - |T|)$. In Step 8, computing the number of consistent triplets with $T_{swapped}$ takes no more than $O(m)$ time. Steps 4, 7 and 18 are implementable in $O(1)$ time. Accordingly, the running time of Steps 2–19 would be:

$$\sum_{|T|=2}^{n}\left[m\binom{|T|}{2} + O(n-|T|)+m)\right] = O(mn^3) \tag{1}$$

Step 20 takes $O(1)$ time. Hence, the time complexity of BPMTR is $O(mn^3)$. □

We tested BPMTR over randomly generated triplet sets with n = 15, 20 species and m = 500, 1,000 triplets. We experimented hundreds of times for each combination of n and m. The results in Table 2 indicate that BPMTR outperforms BPMR. However, in these hundreds of tests, there were a few examples of BPMR performing better than BPMTR. For n = 30 and m = 1,000, in 62 triplet sets out of a hundred randomly generated triplet sets, BPMTR satisfied more triplets. In 34 triplet sets, BPMR and BPMTR had the same results, and in four triplet sets, BPMR satisfied more triplets.

Table 2. Performance results of Best Pair Merge with Total Reconstruction (BPMTR) in comparison to Best Pair Merge with Reconstruction (BPMR).

No. of species and triplets	% better results	% worse results
n = 20, m = 500	%29	%0.0
n = 20, m = 1000	%37	%1
n = 30, m = 500	%61	%3
n = 30, m = 1000	%62	%4

5. Conclusion and Unsolved Problems

In this paper, we presented two new algorithms for the so-called MaxRTC problem. For a given set of m triplets on n species, the FastTree algorithm runs in $O(m + \alpha(n)n^2)$ time, which is faster than any other previously known algorithm, although the outcome can be less satisfactory for highly sparse triplet sets. The BPMTR algorithm runs in $O(mn^3)$ time and, on average, performs better than any other previously known approximation algorithm for this problem. There is nonetheless still more room for improvement of the described algorithms.

1. In the FastTree algorithm, in order to compute the closeness of pairs of species, we check triplets, and for each triplet of the form, $ij|k$, we add a weight, w, to $C_{i,j}$ and subtract a penalty, p, from $C_{i,k}$ and $C_{j,k}$. In this paper, we set $w = p = 1$. If one assigns different values for w and p, the closeness of the pairs of species will be changed, and the reconstruction order will be affected. It would be interesting to check for which values of w and p FastTree performs better.

2. Wu [11] introduced six alternatives for e_score, each of which performs better for different input triplet sets. It would be interesting to find a new function that can outperform all the alternatives for any input triplet set.

3. The best-known approximation factor for the MaxRTC problem is three [13]. This is the approximation ratio of BPMF. Since MaxRTC is APX-hard, a PTASis unattainable, unless P = NP. However, [5] suggests that an approximation ratio in the region of 1.2 might be possible. Finding an $\alpha-$approximation algorithm for MaxRTC with $\alpha < 3$ is still open.

4. It would also be interesting to find the approximation ratio of FastTree, in general, and for reflective triplet sets.

Acknowledgments

The authors are grateful to Jesper Jansson and Fatemeh Zareh for reviewing this article, providing useful comments and answering our endless questions.

Conflict of Interest

The authors declare no conflict of interest.

References

1. Bouckaert, R.; Lemey, P.; Dunn, M.; Greenhill, S.J.; Alekseyenko, A.V.; Drummond, A.J.; Gray, R.D.; Suchard, M.A.; Atkinson, Q.D. Mapping the origins and expansion of the Indo-European language family. *Science* **2012**, *337*, 957–960.
2. Felsenstein, J. *Inferring Phylogenies*; Sinauer Associates: Sunderland, MA, USA, 2004.
3. Chor, B.; Hendy, M.; Penny, D. Analytic Solutions for Three-Taxon ML_{MC} Trees with Variable Rates Across Sites. In *Algorithms in Bioinformatics*; Gascuel, O., Moret, B., Eds.; Springer: Berlin, Germany, 2001; *Lecture Notes in Computer Science*, Volume 2149, pp. 204–213.
4. Kannan, S.K.; Lawler, E.L.; Warnow, T.J. Determining the evolutionary tree using experiments. *J. Algorithms* **1996**, *21*, 26–50.
5. Byrka, J.; Gawrychowski, P.; Huber, K.T.; Kelk, S. Worst-case optimal approximation algorithms for maximizing triplet consistency within phylogenetic networks. *J. Discret. Algorithms* **2010**, *8*, 65–75.
6. Jansson, J. On the complexity of inferring rooted evolutionary trees. *Electron. Notes Discret. Math.* **2001**, *7*, 50–53.
7. Aho, A.V.; Sagiv, Y.; Szymanski, T.G.; Ullman, J.D. Inferring a tree from lowest common ancestors with an application to the optimization of relational expressions. *SIAM J. Comput.* **1981**, *10*, 405–421.
8. Henzinger, M.R.; King, V.; Warnow, T. Constructing a tree from homeomorphic subtrees, with applications to computational evolutionary biology. *Algorithmica* **1999**, *24*, 1–13.
9. Jansson, J.; Ng, J.H.K.; Sadakane, K.; Sung, W.K. Rooted Maximum Agreement Supertrees. *Algorithmica* **2005**, *43*, 293–307.
10. Holm, J.; de Lichtenberg, K.; Thorup, M. Poly-logarithmic deterministic fully-dynamic algorithms for connectivity, minimum spanning tree, 2-edge, and biconnectivity. *J. ACM* **2001**, *48*, 723–760.
11. Wu, B.Y. Constructing the maximum consensus tree from rooted triples. *J. Comb. Optim.* **2004**, *8*, 29–39.
12. Bryant, D. Building Trees, Hunting for Trees, and Comparing Trees—Theory and Methods in Phylogenetic Analysis. PhD thesis, University of Canterbury, 1997.

13. Byrka, J.; Guillemot, S.; Jansson, J. New Results on Optimizing Rooted Triplets Consistency. In *Algorithms and Computation*; Hong, S.H., Nagamochi, H., Fukunaga, T., Eds.; Springer: Berlin, Germany, 2008; *Lecture Notes in Computer Science*, Volume 5369, pp. 484–495.
14. Van Iersel, L.; Kelk, S.; Mnich, M. Uniqueness, intractability and exact algorithms: Reflections on level-k phylogenetic networks. *J. Bioinform. Comput. Biol.* **2009**, *7*, 597–623.
15. Gasieniec, L.; Jansson, J.; Lingas, A.; Ostlin, A. On the complexity of constructing evolutionary trees. *J. Comb. Optim.* **1999**, *3*, 183–197.
16. Maemura, K.; Jansson, J. Ono, H.; Sadakane, K.; Yamashita, M. Approximation Algorithms for Constructing Evolutionary Trees from Rooted Triplets. In Proceedings of 10th Korea-Japan Joint Workshop on Algorithms and Computation, Gwangju, Korea, 9-10 August 2007.
17. Jansson, J.; Sung, W.K. Inferring a level-1 phylogenetic network from a dense set of rooted triplets. *Theor. Comput. Sci.* **2006**, *363*, 60–68.
18. Cormen, T.T.; Leiserson, C.E.; Rivest, R.L. *Introduction to Algorithms*; MIT Press: Cambridge, MA, USA, 1990.
19. Van Iersel, L.; Keijsper, J.; Kelk, S.; Stougie, L.; Hagen, F.; Boekhout, T. Constructing Level-2 Phylogenetic Networks from Triplets. In *Research in Computational Molecular Biology*; Vingron, M., Wong, L., Eds.; Springer: Berlin, Germany, 2008; *Lecture Notes in Computer Science*, Volume 4955, pp. 450–462.
20. Kelk, S. LEVEL2: A fast algorithm for constructing level-2 phylogenetic networks from dense sets of rooted triplets, 2008.
21. Bender, M.A.; Farach-Colton, M. The LCA Problem Revisited. In *LATIN 2000: Theoretical Informatics*; Gonnet, G.; Viola, A., Eds.; Springer: Berlin, Germany, 2000; *Lecture Notes in Computer Science*, Volume 1776, pp. 88–94.

MDPI AG
Grosspeteranlage 5
4052 Basel
Switzerland
Tel.: +41 61 683 77 34

Algorithms Editorial Office
E-mail: algorithms@mdpi.com
www.mdpi.com/journal/algorithms

www.ingramcontent.com/pod-product-compliance
Lightning Source LLC
Chambersburg PA
CBHW061607210926
51850CB00009B/2239
* 9 7 8 3 7 2 5 8 4 5 0 9 5 *